Conceptual Aspects of Human Factors

Conceptual Aspects of Human Factors

DAVID MEISTER

THE JOHNS HOPKINS UNIVERSITY PRESS

Baltimore and London

The Johns Hopkins University Press
701 West 40th Street
Baltimore, Maryland 21211
The Johns Hopkins Press Ltd., London

The paper used in this publication meets
the minimum requirements of American National
Standard for Information Sciences—Permanence
of Paper for Printed Library Materials,
ANSI Z39.48–1984.

Library of Congress Cataloging-in-Publication Data

Meister, David.
    Conceptual aspects of human factors.

    Bibliography: p.
    Includes index.
    1. Human engineering.   I. Title.
TA166.M395   1989   620.8′2   88-32055
ISBN 0-8018-3742-4 (alk. paper)

To the memory of my wife,
Shirley Davis Meister

Contents

Preface

A preface gives the author an opportunity to communicate with readers directly and intimately about such things as what motivated the author to write and what the author hopes to achieve. In my case, a number of ideas have been fermenting for more than twenty years, and at a certain point in the process I felt they should be presented as an integrated whole.

When the thought of writing this book first came to me, my conscious ambition was to describe (if not create) the conceptual foundation of the discipline known as human factors. That task, I quickly found out, is beyond me, although perhaps not beyond others. What I have produced is a description of the technical and nontechnical factors and variables and the conceptual and attitudinal factors and variables influencing the discipline, and suggestions for overcoming problems. In the process the reader will find more questions than answers.

This is a book about human factors as a unitary discipline, not about the special interest areas—for example, human-computer interaction, workload, and embedded training—of which human factors is comprised. My assumption is that this discipline is superordinate to any of the interest areas and has special characteristics not found in the interest areas, and therefore imposes requirements on how research in those areas should be conducted. I believe that, despite its strong applied orientation, human factors is a scholarly discipline.

This is also a book about concepts. Because the ideas it contains will stimulate thinking and discussion about human factors and how to enhance its progress, it is directed to senior undergraduates, graduate students, university faculty, industrial psychologists, and not least, human factors professionals—in fact, everyone who has an interest in the behavior and performance of men and women at work.

It is only fair to warn the reader that I carry a load of biases that may not match those of the reader. One bias is in favor of realism, and the reader will see this exemplified in Chapter 8, where I discuss government, industry, education, and even fellow professionals with a frankness that some may find disconcerting. Another bias is shown in my orientation to the concept of the *system* and a tendency to view human factors as a system-oriented discipline. I am told that this leads me to emphasize the human factors of large, complex systems as opposed to the human factors of smaller equipment units—for example, designing pushbuttons for telephones. This is related to another bias, which stems more from experience than from preference, a tendency to concentrate on military as opposed to civilian or consumer systems. I believe that military systems impose such extraordinary demands on the human that the behavioral problems encountered and the solutions found for such systems are much more innovative than those stemming from nonmilitary entities. The same principles should apply to both military and civilian systems and equipment, however, and what I have to say about one, therefore, should apply almost equally to the other.

Much of what I say in this book might be considered heresy against traditional attitudes by some, but this in itself is good because much of the thinking within human factors has been pedestrian and requires stirring up. Others may feel that the questions I raise are "old hat," that "everyone" knows about them. This belief among some professionals that once a point has been made it is no longer worth discussing, that its importance has been devalued because it is no longer "original," is an excellent device for avoiding consideration of serious problems and makes it difficult to develop a meaningful discussion about the problems of human factors.

I make no apology for the fact that this is a very personal book in the sense that it is based to a large extent on my nonreproducible observations, which, however, I have tried to verify by discussion with colleagues and by soliciting the opinions of distinguished members of the human factors profession. I am particularly indebted to the following colleagues, who graciously answered my questionnaire and inquiries: W. B. Askren, M. M. Ayoub, C. Bennett, G. Chaikin, A. Chapanis, J. M. Christensen, K. B. DeGreene, S. Deutsch, C. Drury, T. E., Enderwick, A. Fregly, H. Fururstig, I. L. Goldstein, L. Hanes, A. Harabedian, D. H. Harris, S. Hart, H. W. Hendrick, C. O. Hopkins, R. J. Hornick, R. D. Huchingson, B. H. Kantowitz, E. T. Klemmer, W. B. Knowles, K.H.E. Kroemer, K. R. Laughery, Sr., T. B. Malone, B. Morgan, F. A. Muckler, J. J. O'Hare, H. M. Parsons, S. O. Parsons, R. Pearson, R. Pew, M. Ritchie, T. H. Rockwell, G. Salvendy, M. Sanders, J. Seminara, T. Sheridan, A. D. Swain, D. Topmiller, J. Uhlaner, H. P. Van Cott, C. Wickens, E. Wiener, W. W. Wierwille, W. E. Woodson, and J. Zeidner.

I would also like to thank A. Adams, J. Adkins, I. Alderman, K. Allan, M. W. Altom, C. Baer, W. E. Baker, K. P. Banning, W. Barbee, R. P. Bateman, K. Boff, G. Calhoun, S. Caplan, S. Card, P. W. Caro, R. Carter, J. M. Childs, J. Kadlac, M. Kahn, W. J. Kaminski, J. Karat, M. Katz, R. Kaye, J. F. Kelly, and K. L. Kessel. A special note of thanks to the reviewer (unknown to me) who critiqued the first version of this book and stimulated me to think anew about the questions I have raised.

As usual, the staff of the Navy Personnel Research and Development Center Library, in particular, Marie McDowell, was invariably helpful, and Joanne Newton did the illustrations with her usual efficiency.

Conceptual Aspects of Human Factors

CHAPTER 1

Introduction to Human Factors

The purpose of this book is twofold: (1) to describe the infrastructure of the discipline of human factors—that is, its concepts and assumptions—and to examine the implications of this infrastructure, and (2) to examine the methodological and other problems that the discipline faces. This chapter introduces the varied concepts that are the basis of the discipline and provides a précis of what the reader will encounter in the remainder of the book.

Before we begin, a note about terms is in order. First, the term *human factors* includes other terms often used to designate the discipline—this is, *engineering psychology* and *ergonomics*. Second, in this book those who perform human factors work will be referred to as *specialists*. These "specialists" are further subdivided into *researchers*, who perform research, and *practitioners*, who apply human factors principles and data to system development and operation. But too much should not be made of the distinction between researchers and practitioners; many specialists are both. The difference is noted only to emphasize that the two may have different attitudes toward their work and differing needs for research products.

The concept structure of human factors is of more than purely theoretical interest. Because these concepts direct our activities, analysis of them could lead to modification and expansion of those activities, which in turn might make the discipline more effective. Moreover, the conceptual infrastructure of a discipline is the logical place to begin considering that discipline.

The discipline of human factors developed out of World War II (although it has more remote antecedents; see e.g., Taylor [1911] and Gilbreth [1911]). Wartime urgency hurried its development. When psychologists were co-opted to work on behavioral problems associated with the new and immensely more complex systems arising out of the war, including problems of personnel selection and training, no one deliberately set out to develop a new discipline. It is possible that the quantum jump in system complexity created the need for a new discipline and that if technological progress at that time had not been so great the distinctiveness of human factors might not have been recognized.

1

In any case, only afterward was thought given to what had been done. An analysis and measurement methodology had been created, but not much effort went into formal development of the concept structure (see, however, Chapanis, Garner, and Morgan 1949; Chapanis 1986; Smith 1987). What there is of such a structure has been developed informally and almost incidentally to the solution of other problems.

DEFINITIONS

It is necessary to introduce the author's concept of human factors, because when we examine later the results of a survey of specialist attitudes toward the discipline, there is a element of ambiguity about what it includes. Over time human factors has been defined in diverse ways according to the special interests of the people in the profession. For example, some specialists see human factors as essentially cognitive psychology and computer science, because many specialists are particularly interested in these topics. There has also been a progressive change in subject matter complexity, from a concentration on relatively molecular "knobs and dials" to much more molar topics, such as workload, stress, and even organizational dynamics (for example, note the increasing interest in something called "macro-ergonomics" [Hendrick 1987]).

The varying definitions of human factors differ primarily in wording and nuance (Meister 1976; Erickson 1983). In this text, human factors is the study of how humans accomplish work-related tasks in the context of human-machine system operation and how behavioral and nonbehavioral variables affect that accomplishment. Human factors is also the application of behavioral principles to the design, development, testing, and operation of equipment and systems.

The relationship between human factors and the individual research interest areas of which it is composed is of special concern because it has implications for the fragmentation of the discipline. Examples of these interest areas are human-computer interaction, vigilance, workload, and embedded training. There is a tendency among researchers—one does not find a parallel phenomenon among practitioners—to lose sight of the overall discipline in their preoccupation with their own special interests. A basic assumption I make is that human factors as an umbrella discipline for these individual interest areas makes certain demands on them, demands that will be considered later in more detail. In general it would appear that these demands have not been satisfied. At the moment it is sufficient to ask: What *should* the relationship between human factors and its component interest areas be? This question too will be discussed later.

The range of the discipline is quite broad. On the one hand, it is concerned with human-machine systems (henceforth referred to simply as "systems") of massive size—for example, aircraft carriers, factories, and army divisions. On the other hand, its interests encompass the individual component within a piece of equipment—for example, a switch. The size factor has significant implications for research and practice. Most effort in human factors research and development has been applied to the smaller end of the spectrum.

Human factors also encompasses both research and application, and the relationship between the two is significant. It emphasizes work or task performance—only behavior that is relevant to task performance is of interest. Thus the consciousness of the performer, except as it affects his or her performance, is of no interest to us. This is not to say that human factors ignores the subjective aspects of that performance (quite the contrary), but to the specialist consciousness is largely instrumental, a means of securing data about performance.

The performance that human factors is concerned with is work-related and by extension system-related, because I assume that work always takes place in some sort of system, whether the influence of that system context is great or small. For example, cooking in the household kitchen takes place in a "home system," which probably is viewed mostly as an environment and has only a minor effect on the housewife, while cooking in a restaurant occurs in the context of a "restaurant system" with more complex equipment and procedures that almost certainly have a much greater effect on human performance. I reserve the term *performance* for task-related (work-related) events and phenomena, and the term *behavior* for activity that is *not* task-related. Purely idiosyncratic behavior (e.g., daydreaming) is of no concern to the discipline because it is not instrumental in task accomplishment (although idiosyncratic behavior can have negative effects on task accomplishment—interfering with it or delaying it—and in that context only would the specialist be concerned with behavior).

Human factors also has multiple goals. In its research mode it endeavors to understand and explain how variables affect human performance in work, differing from other behavioral sciences only in its emphasis on work. In its application mode its goal is to optimize the system of which the human is an element; it attempts to improve both human and system efficiency by modifying the interface between the operator and his or her equipment. Human factors is concerned for the individual, of course, but also just as much or more for the entity of which the individual is a part. One must be concerned for the individual's well-being—it is self-defeating to drive operators excessively, to ignore their natural motivations, or to imperil their safety—but this concern is subordinate to the purposes and requirements of the system in which the worker functions. The "quality of working life" practitioners (e.g., Davis and Cherns 1975) may quarrel with this emphasis, but the assumption is that if the system that includes humans as an essential element performs well, the system personnel usually will be satisfied. The reverse is also true: if personnel are dissatisfied, the system cannot function with maximum effectiveness.

ELEMENTS OF THE CONCEPTUAL STRUCTURE

A conceptual structure is a complex of beliefs on the basis of which those who pursue a particular discipline conduct the operations of that discipline. The conceptual structure of human factors contains the following elements: *beliefs* held by specialists about science in general and about human factors in particular; *definitions* of human factors elements—for example, the number of personnel, their skill, characteristics of the human-machine interface; *assumptions* about how these elements function; *variables* that are presumed to influence these elements; *hypotheses* about how these variables exercise their influence; *conclusions* that result from empirical tests of these hypotheses. In our discussion we shall be concerned mainly with beliefs, definitions, and assumptions.

Outside the conclusions that result from testing, the conceptual structure is one all-encompassing belief because it does not represent "received knowledge" or empirically verified fact and could therefore be incorrect. The most important part of the structure consists of the individual beliefs held by specialists. Because these beliefs largely determine the direction in which the discipline proceeds, they warrant examination. Because human factors beliefs are both heterogeneous and modifiable, the course laid out for the discipline can be changed. If one is dissatisfied with the present status of human factors, it is at least theoretically possible to nudge the discipline in a somewhat different direction.

Belief Characteristics

Beliefs may be informal (without logical structure) and general, or formal and specific—as in mathematics, for example. Some of these beliefs (like variables and hypotheses) are relatively molecular, testable, and only moderately held until they are tested and verified; other beliefs (assumptions and definitions) are more fundamental and not testable, and therefore must be strongly held if held at all. As beliefs become more formal, they are transformed into definitions and assumptions and lead to empirical testing, data collection, and expansion of the discipline's knowledge base.

Exactly how such a conceptual structure is developed is somewhat unclear. To the extent that human factors is part of modern science, it derives certain beliefs—such as the need for experimentation—from general scientific thinking. Other beliefs, of a more specific behavioral nature, may have developed by observation and experience in applying the discipline. For example, the application of human factors to system development may have had the effect of presenting situations to practitioners that led to the development of such beliefs as the centrality of the human-machine interface in explaining personnel performance. Once developed, scientific beliefs are inculcated in new scientific generations by education and by the interaction of scientists with their colleagues.

The human factors structure is largely informal and only grossly differentiated. It is possible to identify only one relatively formal belief structure within human factors: the *system concept*, which is formal only because it is derived from General System Theory (Bertalanffy 1968). A serious deficiency of an informal conceptual structure is that it is difficult to derive testable hypotheses from it, which means that it is less likely to lead to empirical testing and therefore more likely to remain molar and undifferentiated.

It is necessary to distinguish between a conceptual structure and a theory. The six structure elements can be found in a theory also, but in that context they are much more specific. For example, it is the difference between the belief that experimentation is necessary to expand the bounds of a discipline, and a theory that the effect of workload on performance has an inverse U-shape (Streufert and Swezey 1987).

Beliefs and Concepts

The conceptual structure I have been discussing is that of the human factors discipline as a whole, rather than that of individual, specialized interest areas, such as workload, vigilance, or manual control. Specialized interest areas also possess a conceptual structure, but their structure is much more formal, molecular, specific, and overt (written about and discussed) than that of human factors. The rather gross concepts of human factors do not occur in the theoretical structures developed for the individual interest areas, although human factors beliefs serve as a *context* for the individual theoretical structures. For example, the belief in experimentation serves as the prerequisite and context for the empirical testing of interest-area theories.

One must ask what benefits a belief supplies, because without such benefits the belief would inevitably decay over time. The benefit lies in the belief's ability to organize for the believer certain phenomena that would otherwise be uninterpretable, or at least less meaningfully related. In this respect there is no difference between a belief and theory, except for the latter's testability. A belief cannot contradict an observable fact or the belief will decay, but because the belief structure of a discipline is largely nontestable, evidence contrary to it is not easily unearthed.

Fortunately for the development of a science, a concept structure may change over time as a result of experience and observation. For example, specialists have witnessed the expansion of human factors performance units from "knobs and dials" early in its history to much larger present-day units, such as "macrosystems," from hardware equipment to software and organizations.

Where the structure is not formally expressed, as it is in mathematics, it must be inferred from what scientists do and say. For example, the belief that human factors follows technology can be inferred from the fact that its research interests change rapidly when a new technology—for example, computerization—is introduced. Alternatively, one can ask scientists to describe what they believe. In examining the conceptual structure of human factors in this book, I utilize both methods.

Many of the beliefs of human factors specialists are common to all scientists because, despite the special characteristics of human factors that lead to beliefs peculiar to the discipline, human factors is part of the mainstream of science and this identity is reflected in common modes of thinking. To use a very simplistic example, human factors specialists would consider that research is essential to the pursuit of science. This belief would be held by all who consider themselves scientists. However, the special character of human factors will produce beliefs that reflect its special character and will be idiosyncratic to the discipline. This is true of other disciplines as well—for example, concern for beliefs and values in psychology has prompted much recent discussion (Scarr 1985; Howard 1985; Krasner and Houts 1984).

Most specialists pursue their work without consciously wondering about the concepts that underlie that work, but this does not mean that they are uninfluenced by the nature of these concepts. These beliefs produce a mind-set that directs what specialists do and do not do. This is particularly true of those who perform research or are in a position to decide what should be studied or how research should be applied. If one wants to know the past direction of human factors and to infer its future direction, one must examine the beliefs that specialists have had and presently have.

Because all scientists are not the same, dichotomous or antagonistic beliefs can exist in the same structure—and perhaps even in the same individual, although this may be less common. For example, it is possible for some specialists to believe in the critical importance of experimental laboratory studies and for others to feel that meaningful research can be performed only in the field environment. The antagonism of diametrically opposed beliefs creates an intellectual tension that can stimulate new ways of thinking about the discipline. This is important to anyone who wants to push the discipline along.

HUMAN FACTORS BELIEFS

Since the seminal work of philosophers of science like Kuhn (1970), it is accepted that scientific theory is strongly influenced by nontechnical factors, among which are beliefs. A belief is not testable when its subject matter is so abstract or so global that the operations needed to validate it do not exist or cannot practically be implemented.

For example, an almost universally accepted belief among human factors practitioners is that the application of behavioral principles and data to system development results in more effective systems. One could conceivably test this belief, but to do so would require that for each system to which one applied those principles a second, identical system for which there were no such inputs would have to be developed. It is almost inconceivable that the money would be found to perform such an experiment, an experiment that would have to be replicated at least several times before one had confidence in its conclusions. It is of course possible to adduce anecdotal evidence (Price et al. 1980a, 1980b) or to survey designers, practitioners, system personnel, and users to bolster the belief that human factors is effective in system development, but this is not adequate proof.

One dimension on which beliefs vary is that of strength. Beliefs that are more strongly held will exercise a greater influence over the discipline. There is rarely complete consensus on all beliefs. In any group of scientists there will be contradictory ("minority") beliefs. One can say, perhaps arbitrarily, that if 50 percent of a population espouse a point of view strongly or moderately, that point of view constitutes a belief. On the other hand, if 20 percent of the population maintain an opposed point of view, it is a minority belief. Viewed in this way, the human factors structure contains both majority and minority beliefs.

It is possible that the effect of opposing beliefs is to create a state of tension in the discipline, and the greater the percentage of the population who strongly hold opposing beliefs, the greater the tension. This tension may be either positive or negative. If it leads to research to resolve the tension, the effect is positive; if the tension is submerged or leads to polemic and controversy, it is negative.

There are many beliefs on which all or almost all specialists agree. Even for opposing beliefs, the average specialist will probably adopt a compromise position. He or she may accept a particular belief as being generally correct, except for certain precisely defined conditions. For example, a specialist may believe that all laboratory research is neither completely generalizable to system development problems nor completely without value for that development. It is possible to accept the utility of laboratory research results when the conditions for that utility are present.

Even if conscious of their beliefs, most specialists are not likely to make those beliefs the basis for a significant contribution to the discipline. There is, however, a small group of scientists—an elite whom one can call "influentials"—who, it is hypothesized, make a disproportionate impact on a discipline by asking questions and exploring new avenues intellectually. For them awareness of the tensions created by opposing beliefs can serve as a stimulus to changes in the discipline's concept structure.

Most specialists have so integrated their beliefs into their thinking that these beliefs are almost unconscious; only when beliefs are challenged or otherwise highlighted do they become aware of them. Nonetheless, it is assumed that these beliefs have a significant influence on specialist behavior, provided the specialists are in a position to exercise influence over the discipline.

Opposing Beliefs

Opposing beliefs in human factors have several foci, but I hypothesize that these center on the dichotomy of research and application, a dichotomy that often produces a visible tension. Human factors is unique in that it is the only behavioral science that is also, in its application mode, engineering-oriented. In that mode, research is considered by practitioners to be of little value unless it can be related to physicalistic parameters and can provide specific, quick, and quantitative answers to development problems. On the other hand, research is traditionally associated with beliefs that are representative of sophisticated science—for example, highly controlled laboratory studies, studies testing hypotheses derived from theory, and concern for fundamental knowledge.

Consequently, we can discern signs of tension, such as the continuing complaints of practitioners (Meister 1979) that human factors research is largely irrelevant to system design and to development variables. The tension between research and application may present a problem of identity for the specialist, as reflected in the attempt to make invidious distinctions between a more pragmatic human factors, in the United States, and a more research-oriented European ergonomics (Montmollin and Bainbridge 1985).

We can now identify certain critical points in the beliefs of the human factors specialist, points about which much debate is possible:

1. The dichotomy between research and application produces opposing beliefs about the utility of behavioral research for application purposes.

2. Even more fundamental are beliefs about the nature of human factors and its goals and functions. Is human factors primarily an application discipline, or is it molded in the framework of traditional science? Is it a scholarly pursuit? What does human factors exist to do? What should its relationships with other disciplines—primarily psychology and engineering—be?

3. The reference situation—what Hillner (1985) calls the prototypical situation, the one that epitomizes the mechanisms typically present in human factors—is the situation to which all other human factors situations are compared. The reference situation represents reality for human factors. In terms of beliefs, is the reality human performance in a controlled situation, such as a laboratory, or is reality a situation in which personnel function in operational systems routinely performing their missions in the operational environment (Meister 1988)?

4. Related to this is the adequacy of concepts for analyzing and measuring work-related human performance. If systems are large, complex, interdependent entities, can one break them down into more molecular subentities without losing something of the quality that emerges when systems are unified, or is it necessary to deal with such systems as total entities?

5. Another focal point in the belief structure is the criterion (or criteria) that should be used to evaluate worth—the worth of methods, data, principles, and

the discipline as a whole. Although human factors is a very pragmatic discipline, should utility be an applicable criterion? Scientific disciplines refer to the pursuit of knowledge as the justification for their existence. If human factors is viewed as a science, should not the same criterion apply? This question ties in with the research-application dimension: utility as a criterion of research (that only demonstrably useful or applicable research should be performed) brings research into the sphere of application, and many specialists reject this. The controversy over research utility is a vigorous one in human factors (Meister 1985a).

Alternative Viewpoints

It is possible to look at each of the preceding themes in alternative ways. For example, in considering the relationship between research and application we could say that there need not be any relationship between them and that therefore it is unnecessary to take application into account in planning research because some unknown process occurring over time will ultimately make all research products applicable, or, we could say, on the contrary, that research exists only to provide useful products (i.e., principles and data) for application. It is also possible to believe that research is absolutely indispensable for applying human factors to system development or, on the contrary, that research has provided little of value in solving system development problems. One might believe that human factors methods in system development are effective but that resistance from design engineers reduces their effectiveness, or we could say that these methods are crude, primitive, and not very effective, which is why they are not more often employed.

These beliefs, untested and functioning something like illogical prejudices, affect the way the entire discipline functions, although they are only one of a number of factors influencing what the individual specialist does, one major factor also being his or her job opportunities. All other things being equal, however, the specialist's belief structure may cause him or her to opt in favor of one type of work over another—for example, to concentrate on field studies instead of laboratory work, or vice versa.

Specialists are also likely to develop beliefs appropriate to the type of work they find themselves doing. In addition to guiding what the specialist does, these beliefs may support what the specialist does for other than scientific reasons. The belief structure may serve not only as a stimulus for actions the specialist takes, but also as reinforcers for those actions, once taken.

Belief Effects

We can hypothesize about what the effects of these beliefs—expressed below somewhat simplistically as dichotomous, either/or statements—might be:

1. *Human factors is only a special subarea of psychology, or conversely,*

human factors is a unique discipline related to but independent of other disciplines. If the specialist considers human factors to be a branch of psychology, he or she will be less likely to look for unique solutions to human factors problems, more likely to make use of traditional techniques used in psychology (e.g., the laboratory, experimental design) and in other disciplines, and less likely to be engaged in system development work. Those who think of human factors as a unique discipline are more likely to conduct research outside the laboratory environment, more likely to be involved in system development, and more likely to be concerned about application of behavioral principles.

2. *Human factors is primarily an application discipline, or conversely, it is more research-oriented.* The belief that human factors is primarily an application discipline is linked to the belief that human factors is merely a special branch of psychology. People who think of human factors as primarily application will probably engage less in research or, if they are researchers, their research topics will be more pragmatic, oriented more to the "real world." Specialists who think of human factors as primarily a research discipline are more likely to find themselves in a laboratory and to perform research without considering its use in practice.

3. *Human factors research has done very little to support the practitioner, or conversely, developmental application depends ultimately on research.* People who believe that research has little to offer human factors practice (e.g., system development work) are less likely to be researchers or to utilize research data; the reverse is more likely to be true if a person believes that practice depends on research.

4. *The laboratory is the only really effective means of studying behavioral phenomena, or conversely, the laboratory environment is so artificial that its research outputs are largely irrelevant to real-world problems.* Someone who adopts the viewpoint that behavioral phenomena can be adequately studied only in the laboratory is less likely to go outside the laboratory to perform research or to consider real-world applications of that research. The reverse is more likely if the specialist believes that the laboratory environment is too artificial to apply to real-world problems.

5. *Subjective data are as valid as objectively gathered data, or conversely, one can have confidence only in objective data.* A specialist who has confidence in subjective data is more likely to conduct research or gather data in situations in which subjective data are available. A specialist whose confidence is in objective data only is likely to restrict the research topics he or she will investigate only or largely to those that will permit the specialist to gather objective data; such an individual is more likely to be a laboratory researcher and less interested in application of research to real-world questions.

6. *All human factors research will ultimately be found to be applicable, or conversly, research cannot be useful unless it is designed to be useful.* Those who believe research is its own justification will probably not be concerned

about the immediate application of their work to real-world problems and may demand complete autonomy in the selection of the topics to be investigated. Those who feel that utility must be designed into research are more likely to perform immediately applicable research.

7. *Human performance is so complex and variable that it cannot be predicted, or conversely, it is possible to predict human performance quantitatively.* Those who reject the attempt to predict human performance because behavior is overly complex are more likely to confine themselves to research topics that are relatively discrete and concrete. Those who believe it is possible to predict human performance quantitatively are more likely to attempt to make such predictions and to work in less structured, less controlled situations.

8. *Validation of laboratory-derived conclusions should be accomplished in the operational environment with operational systems or in realistic simulations of these, or conversely, validation can be accomplished in the laboratory situation.* Specialists who believe that real-world validation is necessary are likely to be somewhat contemptuous of laboratory research, to look for real-world application uses of research, and to derive their research topics from questions arising from the operational environment. Those who do not consider real-world validation necessary are likely to be less critical of their research, to be exponents of laboratory studies, and to be unconcerned about the application of research.

The general belief structure of human factors, and the opposing viewpoints, are themes that we shall examine in subsequent chapters. They are important also because they are the primary sources of intellectual tension within the discipline.

A MAP OF THE HUMAN FACTORS BELIEF STRUCTURE

So far I have presented no data to verify the hypothesis that human factors professionals hold these beliefs. The simplest way to confirm or refute that hypothesis is to ask human factors professionals to report how they feel about various aspects of their belief structure. Investigation of such structures by means of a questionnaire is not novel, as witnessed by the study of psychological beliefs by Kimble (1984).

The Survey Instrument

The survey instrument consisted of statements oriented around nine topics or themes: what human factors consists of; the perceived effectiveness of human factors; the relationship of human factors to other disciplines; the relationship of human factors to the real world; the system concept and its implications for human factors; the purpose of human factors research, its application, and the environment in which such research can best be performed; the adequacy and availability of human factors data; human factors in relation to system development; and validation of human factors principles and data. Respondents were asked to indicate their agreement (strong, moderate, or slight) or disagreement (strong, moderate, slight) with each of forty statements presented randomly. An intermediate, "neutral" position (don't know, don't care) was also available. This provided the respondent with a seven-point scale. A belief was defined to exist if 50 percent or more of the respondents checked their agreement or disagreement with the statement as strong or moderate. A minority belief was defined as one in which 20 percent or more of the respondents approved a contrary position strongly or moderately. (Slight agreement or disagreement did not constitute a belief.)

The questionnaire was sent to sixty-two human factors specialists, whom I considered to be members of the "influentials"—intellectual pacesetters, writers of books and papers, heads of research organizations, past and present officers of the Human Factors Society, people who are well-known in the profession. The criteria for selection were solely my own; a more systematic means of selecting respondents would have been desirable but was not feasible. In any event, forty-five graciously responded (the names of those responding are included in the acknowledgments in the Preface).

Because forty-five respondents are only one percent of the total membership of the Human Factors Society, the sample cannot be considered representative of specialists in general. However, the survey was intended to tap the attitudes of influentials only, on the assumption that this elite drives the discipline as a whole. As it turned out, a small sample taken from the general population provided many of the same answers. The frequency of response on each item was transformed into a percentage because not everyone answered every item (although the smallest N for any item was forty-two). The weighted means of the responses and their standard deviations were also determined.

What Human Factors Is

I began by defining what human factors consists of because the nature of a discipline defines what one does with it. This topic was represented by three items in the questionnaire:

1. Human factors is an application discipline. (50 percent agreement, 23 percent disagreement)

2. Human factors is distinctive from other disciplines because it is the only behavioral discipline that integrates behavior (personnel performance) with physical (equipment) parameters. (61 percent agreement, 26 percent disagreement)

3. Human factors is a behavioral discipline in its research mode; in its application to system development it assumes many engineering characteristics. (57 percent agreement, 20 percent disagreement)

The most striking aspect of the data dealing with this theme is the existence of minority viewpoints, which, as it relates to the definition of the discipline, suggests that there is some ambiguity and indecisiveness in how specialists view their field.

The Effectiveness of Human Factors

The next theme was the effectiveness of human factors, on which there were seven items:

1. The usefulness of human factors in system development is undeniable. (100 percent agreement)

2. Human factors analytic and measurement techniques are ineffective. (93 percent disagreement)

3. Human factors research is of little use in applying behavioral principles to system development. (86 percent disagreement)

4. Human factors has had little real success in influencing the way systems are designed. (62 percent disagreement)

5. Human factors analytic and measurement techniques are effective. (86 percent agreement)

6. The application of human factors to system development has produced more effective systems. (89 percent agreement)

7. By any measures that can be applied, human factors is a productive, useful discipline. (86 percent agreement)

Human factors was viewed as effective by almost all respondents. There was little or no variability in responses, and no minority point of view. The absence of a minority viewpoint suggests that there is a degree of complacency that may or may not be warranted.

Human Factors and Other Disciplines

The next questions concerned the relationship between human factors and other disciplines. Is human factors distinctive? This is a critical question, because if it is distinctive, methods and approaches derived from other disciplines may not be adequate for it. Items in the survey dealing with this theme were:

1. Only in the application of human factors to system development is there a significant difference between psychology and human factors. (50 percent disagreement)

2. Most of what we know and do in human factors is taken over from psychology. (53 percent disagreement)

3. Human factors is distinctly different from psychology or engineering, although it makes use of contributions from both. (75 percent agreement)

4. Human factors does not overlap with psychology. (86 percent disagreement)

There were no minority beliefs. It appears, then, that most influentials view human factors as a distinctive discipline, even taking into account contributions from other disciplines, but the amount of consensus is not overwhelming. There is a special relationship with psychology.

Human Factors and the Real World

Next, respondents' feelings about the relationship between human factors and the real world—the real world being defined as the operational system performing its assigned tasks in the operational environment—were noted by examining responses to the following statements:

1. Only crude human factors principles seem to apply to human performance in the real world. (78 percent disagreement)

2. Behavioral principles and data are meaningful only if they relate to performance in the real world. (Did not satisfy 50 percent criterion)

Responses to these two statements are ambiguous. Most felt that human factors principles could be applied to the real world, but they would not use the "real world" as a criterion of the meaningfulness of those principles. This raises the question of what determines the meaningfulness of these principles.

The System Concept and Human Factors

An essential part of the human factors concept structure, according to most textbooks (e.g., Meister 1985b), is the *system concept*. The strength with which specialists believe in this concept was tested with the following items:

1. The system concept is fundamental to human factors research and practice. (80 percent agreement; no minority viewpoint)

2. The system concept has little influence over human factors research and practice. (73 percent disagreement; no minority viewpoint)

Influentials agree that the system concept is crucial to human factors, but to what extent do they draw the appropriate implications from that belief? The implications of the system concept are listed in Table 1.1 and were represented in the following survey statements:

1. Most systems are so complex that to analyze or measure them it is necessary to break them up into their component parts. (53 percent agreement; no minority viewpoint)

2. Some human performance results from purely chance factors. (Did not satisfy 50 percent criterion)

3. The ease and comfort of personnel is as important a goal of system design as performance efficiency. (Did not satisfy 50 percent criterion)

4. The performance of any man-machine unit changes as soon as it is divorced from the subsystem or system of which it is a part. (Did not satisfy 50 percent criterion)

5. Personnel performance in the system context must be controlled by overall system requirements. (76 percent agreement; no minority viewpoint)

6. The human-machine system is the natural object of study for human

Table 1.1 Implications of the System Concept for Human Factors

---

- The human-machine system is the natural object of human factors study.
- The reference situation for human factors is the operational system performing in the operational environment.
- Human performance cannot be studied in isolation from its system context.
- Human performance is meaningful only in relation to system performance.
- All variables affecting human-machine interaction must be considered in system design, testing, and operation.
- The human in the system is subordinate to system requirements.
- The system mission or goal is superordinate to and directs the performance of all system elements.
- All deficiencies in system performance result from inadequacies in one or more system elements.

---

factors. (75 percent agreement; no minority viewpoint)

7. Inadequacies in personnel performance are always the result of some system (e.g., design or training) factor. (54 percent disagreement; 21 percent agreement)

8. The system mission or goal is the one element that is more important than all other considerations in system operation. (Did not satisfy 50 percent criterion)

9. The operator and the system are two separate entities. (73 percent disagreement; no minority viewpoint)

10. Personnel performance in the context of system operation is meaningful only when it contributes to the performance of the total system. (Did not satisfy 50 percent criterion)

There is a certain ambivalence concerning the implications of the system concept. Although that concept was accepted by 80 percent of those responding, no strong feeling was manifested for five of the ten statements describing specific implications or corollaries of that concept. Although the system concept is generally accepted by specialists, for them it is a very gross, undifferentiated belief, which suggests that the concept is not ordinarily implemented in research.

Human Factors Research

Because research and its purpose, environment, and application are to a great extent derived from the conceptual structure, viewpoints about research should reveal concept characteristics. The items involved were:

1. The major purpose of human factors research is to understand and explain the factors affecting how personnel perform in the work environment. (61 percent agreement; 20 percent minority point of view)

2. The major purpose of human factors research is to develop guidelines for applying behavioral principles to the development of new systems. (Did not satisfy 50 percent criterion)

3. Sooner or later, whatever its immediate purpose, all human factors re-

search will be found to have useful applications. (Did not satisfy 50 percent criterion)

4. The only meaningful environment in which to perform human factors research is in the operational environment with operational systems or in realistic simulations of those systems. (59 percent disagreement)

5. The laboratory is the only completely effective means of studying behavioral phenomena. (84 percent disagreement)

Because all but one of the statements above did not produce a strong consensus, it was clear that there is some ambiguity or dissension about the purpose of human factors research and how it should be conducted. The results may also reflect an unwillingness to adopt extreme belief positions.

Data in Human Factors

Data is another central theme in any research-oriented conceptual structure. Three items in the questionnaire dealt with this topic:

1. The only scientifically acceptable data are objective data. (68 percent disagreement; no minority viewpoint)

2. The most serious deficiency in human factors is the lack of quantitative data. (Did not satisfy 50 percent criterion)

3. There is plenty of human factors data available in journals and papers. (Did not satisfy 50 percent criterion)

What can one say about the data component of the belief structure? Only that the influentials do not seem to have any strong feeling about data. Many people see the lack of data, if there is one, as a problem, but just as many do not. In any event, the feeling is not strong enough to be considered a belief. A majority are also willing to accept nonobjective data.

Human Factors and System Development

Attitudes toward system development as the major area of human factors application should also be strongly represented among beliefs. A bare majority (54 percent) disagreed with the proposition that the application of human factors to system development needs intuition and experience more than research principles or data. This could represent either ambivalence or indifference to the topic; more likely, it represents a lack of familiarity with system development. There is far more unanimity (84 percent agreement) with regard to the proposition that industry is reluctant to make use of human factors. There was no minority position here.

Validation in Human Factors

Finally, 73 percent of the respondents disagreed that validation of laboratory results in the real world is complex and expensive. There was no minority viewpoint. Validation in the real world appears to be an article of faith to most specialists but this appears to be at variance with actual validation efforts.

CHARACTERISTICS OF THE BELIEF STRUCTURE

What does all this mean? The human factors belief structure is by no means a monolithic one; there are many opposing viewpoints. Except for a few themes on which almost all specialists can agree—the effectiveness of human factors and its techniques, the reluctance of industry to make use of the discipline, the importance of the system concept, the utility of human factors in system development, the relationship of human factors to other disciplines—there is little unanimity.

The existence of many minority positions suggests that there is a certain ambiguity in the belief structure. One can see diverse viewpoints as indicating intellectual democracy in response to the varied problems the discipline encounters, or as potentially disruptive tension points, or as a reflection of the discipline's immaturity. Does this diversity reflect the multidimensionality of the situations with which human factors professionals have to deal? Or perhaps contrasting viewpoints can be held simultaneously because the beliefs were created to deal with the varying situations? Whatever this ambiguity means, it should be considered and discussed by specialists.

The belief structure is an optimistic one, or perhaps it is complacent, as manifested by unanimity in items concerning the effectiveness and utility of human factors and its techniques. It is a balanced structure, meaning that the most common attitude appears to be a compromise among extreme viewpoints because specialists may feel intuitively that contrasting viewpoints are equally valid. For example, the importance of the laboratory is recognized, but so is the importance of the operational environment. At the same time, the structure is superficial and rather shallow, as seen in the lack of interest in data and the weakness of the system concept. There is almost complete unanimity that the system concept does influence and is fundamental to human factors research and practice and that the human-machine system is the natural object of behavioral study. However, when one inquires about the implications of the system concept, the belief structure tends to dissipate.

THE SYSTEM CONCEPT

The beliefs discussed so far have largely been informal beliefs, very general attitudes about science and research and not associated with theory. The *system concept*,[1] which is a theoretical orientation toward science and research, is more formal.

The system concept is not an indigenous belief, having been applied to other disciplines before human factors picked it up. Its application to human factors

1. The term *system concept* has also been spelled as *systems concept* in other texts. I have used the singular to refer to the general notion of *the* system in much the same way that one refers to system development and system personnel (not systems development or systems personnel).

makes it possible to develop a formal concept structure for the discipline. As we shall see, it is possible to develop from this belief definitions, assumptions, variables, and hypotheses of a formal nature, something that is not possible with the other beliefs.

In the human factors context, the system concept is the belief that human performance in work can be conceptualized meaningfully only in terms of organized wholes and that for work performance that organized whole is the *human-machine system* (henceforth referred to simply as "the system"). More specifically, one can conceive of worker performance only in terms of an interaction between operators and the nonbehavioral elements of the workplace—their machines, their operating procedures, their environment, and the technical data they utilize.

In terms of the preceding definition it may seem that the system concept should make little difference in how the discipline is conducted, because human factors has traditionally been conceived of in interaction terms (e.g., the human-machine interface). At the end of this section, however, the reader will see that the system concept implies much more than interaction and that its adoption as a methodological orientation makes a great deal of difference to research and practice.

As with beliefs in general, the system concept is valuable because it helps organize human performance phenomena conceptually—which is eminently satisfying, particularly for people who are attuned to relationships among disparate objects or phenomena. There are people who see things in "wholes," as opposed to those who view things in terms of their differences. The former "see" things in terms of similarities, the latter see the same things in terms of their differences. There may be a personality-determined preference for the system approach.

The History of the System Concept

The system movement reflects a variety of aspects of system study, but first and foremost it is a philosophical point of view—a belief as defined in this book and a methodology arising out of that belief. Mattessich (1982) traced it back to concepts expressed in the philosophies of Lao-tzu, Heraclitus, Leibniz, Vico, Marx, and others. Van Gigch (1974) emphasized Hegel, to whom are attributed the ideas that the whole is more than the sum of its parts, that the whole determines the nature of its parts, that the parts cannot be understood if considered in isolation from the whole, and that the parts are dynamically interrelated or interdependent. The psychologically oriented reader will recognize the above as fundamental concepts in the Gestalt framework (Koffka 1935).

The interest in system thinking blossomed at the beginning of the twentieth century because systems were becoming extremely large and the reductionistic thinking of the time appeared to be inadequate to deal with such large entities; that was particularly so for the biologists of the 1920s. System thinking was further developed by control and communications engineers in the 1940s, and it found practical expression in the work done in World War II by operations researchers. Checkland (1981b) dated the system movement we are familiar with from the late 1940s. In the case of human factors, the impact was felt about the mid-1950s, working back from the paper by Christensen (1962).

The antithesis of the system concept is reductionism, an approach that has dominated science since Descartes (1596–1650). If the performance unit being examined is large and complex, it may be necessary to break it down into more manageable subunits. Reductionism assumes, among other things, that more molar entities are composed of less molar entities, and that the former can be decomposed into the latter without (and this point is critical) changing the original characteristics of the larger whole. If one can explain the actions of the whole in terms of the actions of its parts, then the classic scientific techniques, such as laboratory experimentation, are quite justifiable. Clearly, it is possible to break entities into their component parts, but system theory would say that the action of the parts, no matter how variables can be made to interact in an experiment, cannot adequately explain how those variables function when they are part of the whole.

There is nothing wrong with reductionism per se when it is required by the characteristics of the system, but if it is carried too far it will lose its value and become counterproductive. An example in psychology is the school of structuralism, which made reductionism so central to its philosophy that it attempted to decompose all stimuli into atomistic sensory elements. This effectively ensured the failure of the conceptual system. The problem with reductionism in human factors is that behavior and performance as one perceives them in action are molar rather than molecular; after one breaks a performance or behavioral unit into its elements for analysis or measurement, one must reconstitute them to explain the phenomena meaningfully—which is not easy. Nevertheless, there is no reason that reductionism and the system approach cannot coexist as long as we are pragmatic about both. The problem arises when one is over-emphasized at the expense of the other.

Key Concepts in the System Approach

A problem that people who are interested in the "system approach" have is how to define exactly what is meant by that framework. Checkland (1981a) divided theory into two types: substantive theory, which is concerned with subject matter (e.g., workload, visual performance), and methodological theory, which is concerned with how to go about investigating subject matter. The system concept is a methodological theory—also a belief, in my terms.

Mattessich (1982) broke the system approach into four areas—system philosophy, system analysis, empirical system research, and system engineering—all of which have actual or potential parallels in human factors. *System philosophy* deals with epistemology and methodology, and much of the discussion in this book involves these two. *System analysis* involves the development of mathematical system theories and models (the parallel in human factors is the development of mathematical models, such as those of Siegel and Wolf [1969]). *Empirical system research* considers the system itself a source of research for studies of system behavior, for development and testing of system laws, and for simulation studies of system models (very little in this line is being performed by human factors). Finally, *system engineering* involves the development of artificial systems (the parallel in human factors is perhaps system development).

When performed correctly, *system design* is akin to system engineering problem-solving. It begins with determination of the goals for design, specification of functions to be performed by the system, conceptualization of alternative ways of performing these functions (alternative problem solutions), analysis and comparison of these alternatives, and selection of the most effective alternative. In human factors, the equivalent of system analysis consists of the mission, function, and task analysis with which system development begins.

There is, then, considerable compatibility between the analyses and evaluations performed in human factors system development and the system analyses and engineering processes derived from the system concept. Although it is not clear whether these behavioral analyses and evaluations were directly influenced by the system approach—they may have been more directly influenced by the engineering framework in which they had to fit, and this context may have been previously affected by the system approach—the commonality suggests that it should be possible to apply the system concept effectively to all aspects of human factors.

Before concluding this discussion, we should ask whether the characteristics of the human-machine entity correspond to those of other biological or physical systems. Van Gigch (1974) summarized the elements in systems as follows: *elements* (in the human-machine entity these would be personnel, equipment, technical data, etc.); *conversion processes*, changes in system state, elements combining with one another to form new elements (in the human-machine entity these are represented by human-machine interactions); *inputs and/or resources* (e.g., visual stimuli, personnel skills, technical data); *outputs* (in an entity like an aircraft these would be distance traveled or speed achieved); *environment* (the human-machine entity has both an internal and an external environment); *purpose and functions* (the human-machine entity has both by definition); *attributes* (in the human-machine entity these would be complexity, determinacy, sensitivity, etc.); *goals and objectives* (derived from the purpose of the entity); *components, programs, and missions* (the human-machine entity has all these); *management, agents, and decision-makers* (in the human-machine entity the human assumes these roles); *structure* or relationships binding system elements together (in the human-machine complex this is its organization). It is clear that the human-machine entity has all the characteristics of a system.

The system approach is based on the insight that the interrelationships among elements may result in an entity—the system—that has its own special properties. The approach emphasizes relations among these elements and between the system and the surrounding environment. System thinking considers the function, purpose, and goals of the system and how the goals of the system can be reconciled with those of the "suprasystem" of which it is a part and with the subsystems that form part of it. The approach emphasizes input-output features and a purpose orientation, aspects that are particularly appropriate for sciences with a high degree of application.

Characteristic of the system approach is *the concept of emergent properties* that are meaningful only in terms of the whole, not in terms of its components. This presupposes some special qualities or attributes that characterize wholes, and the reader may feel that this smacks of witchcraft, of something being derived from nothing. But this represents a misunderstanding based on a tendency to think of emergent properties in biological terms. Clearly, a system is distinctly different from any of its parts and should therefore have attributes other than those of its parts. Checkland (1981b) used the bicycle as an example. A bicycle is composed of wheels, gears, sprockets, a frame, and so on. As dispersed parts, these have no power to move a human. Put together as a bicycle, the function of transportation or movement has "emerged." In large, complex systems the emergence of system functions may appear to be mysterious because the mind has difficulty apprehending the combinatorial process, which is much easier to understand in the bicycle.

The emergent-property question is linked to what Van Gigch (1974) termed "conversion" and what I have termed "transformation." In a general sense, design is a transformation from a set of verbal or numerical requirements to functioning hardware or software. Within human factors applications, this transformation occurs when behavioral principles are equated with physical mechanisms. Ideally, this equation should be a mathematical one, but in most cases such equations are qualitative only, because the relationships involved are incompletely understood. This transformation both relates and transcends the behavioral and physical domains. A further behavioral transformation with which one must be concerned is that performance at one system level (e.g., personnel performance) is transformed into and emerges at a higher level as a part of a subsystem or system output. How this occurs is a fundamental human factors research question. The concept of emergent properties forces one to discover the mechanisms that produce the emergence, and this is not easy.

Demands Imposed on Human Factors by the System Concept

The system concept is a very general one. Because it is a methodological belief or theory it may not lead to substantive changes in subject matter, so it is easy to agree with the concept in principle (as the survey respondents do), but difficult to see what the practical consequences are because these are not linked very directly to subject matter outputs. Failure to implement the system concept in one's work means that one simply ignores the interaction among system elements. This is particularly unfortunate if one is working with actual systems. It may have unfortunate consequences for research quality, but it is perfectly possible for a researcher to make his or her life work the study of effects of temperature on human performance, for example, without considering the relationship between temperature and other system elements.

The system concept presents us with certain demands:

1. It requires us to consider *all* factors that could possibly influence the phenomena one wants to measure or to explain. Comprehensiveness is a major element in the specialist's system concept belief. The result in experimentation is that we must either vary many more variables than we would otherwise, or control them. We cannot leave variables uncontrolled except at our peril.

2. It requires us not only to account for all interactive variables, but also to study the nature of these interactions, which are in fact dependency relationships.

3. In evaluating human performance we must also relate that performance to the system goal or output. We are thus required not only to note system output, but also to measure the relationship between the personnel subsystem and that output.

4. The notion of hierarchical levels of performance (individual, team, subsystem, system) means that we are now required to measure at all these levels and to relate the measures taken at one level to measures taken at another level.

5. Because the system cannot be understood outside the larger whole (the suprasystem) in which it is embedded, the system concept requires us to consider the effect of the environment in which the system functions. That environment can be considered the internal environment of the suprasystem in which our system is embedded. Failure to consider the environment in which the system functions produces incomplete research outputs.

Because it is content-free, the system concept unfortunately does not suggest a special experimental or data collection methodology that would mitigate its demands. It is still necessary to collect data using traditional designs and methods (e.g., observation, interviews, instrumentation). From that standpoint the system concept is a mixed blessing; presumably it expands our understanding of system phenomena, but it also increases our empirical difficulties tremendously.

The Relationship between the System and Human Factors

The relationship between the system and human factors is analyzed by examining the behavioral definitions, assumptions, variables, and hypotheses that can be derived from the system concept.

Objects and Systems. A human-machine system is an organization of physical and behavioral elements that function in concert to achieve a specified goal. Others (see Erickson 1983) have used slightly different words to express the same notion. Nevertheless, all systems have the same outstanding characteristics: interaction of elements, a hierarchy of levels, purpose(s) and goal(s), and inputs and outputs.

To define the limits of the system in relation to human factors, two questions must be answered: Is every physical entity with which humans interact a system? And are all human-machine systems essentially the same? Although a system and an object or device are both physical things with which humans interact, a system must be differentiated from an object because the behavioral implications of each are different. In most cases, a system is much larger than an object, but certain objects (e.g., automobiles or individual machines) are quite large. What differentiates a system from an object is that the system has a purpose given to it by its developers, a purpose that inheres in the system and includes the personnel who work in or as part of that system. With an object, the purpose inheres not in the object but in the user of that object. Objects have functions, the initiator of which is the user of the object, but the object has no purpose of its own because purpose implies volition or will and, while systems possess the will that is given them by their developers and that is energized by personnel, the same cannot be said of objects.

The purpose is inherent in the system, so there is an interaction between the requirement stemming from that purpose and the operator within the framework established by the system developer. Actions taken by equipment can cause the operator to modify his or her performance, but this is only partly true of objects. The system can and does control its personnel, but an object can never control its user.

An example of an object is a toaster. Its performance is initiated by a user, but the toaster has no influence on the user's performance (unless it malfunctions and the bread is burned). There is no interaction between user and object in the sense of the object fostering a change in user performance; the toaster has function but not purpose, and it lacks control over its user. The complex object or device, such as an automobile, appears to be an exception to this rule, but the automobile lacks certain system-derived characteristics—namely, control over its driver—and a superordinate purpose that controls both automobile and driver.

Perhaps the characteristic that most differentiates an object from a system is that the system is linked with a higher-order system context but an object is not. A pocket knife can be used in many contexts—in camping, in a garage, in a kitchen—without changing its basic function, but the system is linked to a mission-related context, its operational environment, and one has difficulty using it elsewhere. It is possible to use an object as part of a system, but then the object assumes system-like characteristics. A CRT terminal is an object, but if one requires its use as part of an air traffic control system, it assumes certain system-related requirements—for example, a required equipment reliability and a required resolution.

There are several consequences from the difference between systems and objects, beyond their obvious difference in complexity. In the system the interaction between the system and its operators demands much greater attention in the system than with the object. For example, the system partly controls what the operator does, so the need to design appropriate feedback information into the system becomes extremely important. The complexity of the system requires the developer to consider what special aptitudes and training will be required of the operator, but for the user of an object this is not usually as necessary.

These differences are on a continuum. A complex object like an automobile requires that the skills needed to use that object be considered. "Good" human engineering is needed in the design of an object, just as it is in system design. To a large extent, what we are talking about is a difference in scale, although true differences (e. g. , information flow and hierarchical relationships in systems) do exist between the system and the object.

Because much human factors design is performed on such objects as toasters or watch displays, it is possible to overemphasize the importance of the system concept. Human factors research on the design of those objects and on the objects themselves can be performed without considering system implications. For example, in designing the arrangement of pushbuttons on telephones (Conrad and Hull 1968) it is hardly likely that the researchers considered what they were studying in terms of the complexities of the telephone exchange as the suprasystem for the telephone. However, consideration of the overall system may assist object research and design, even if the system concept is not absolutely necessary. For example, it is possible to design the arrangement of an aircraft cockpit without considering the mission that aircraft will fly, but in that case the designer is more likely to make design errors. It is a reasonable hypothesis that in system development, whether military or civilian, system-type thinking is required, but that such thinking is not necessary (although perhaps desirable) in the design of objects not directly related to a system. However, an object that may be used as part of a larger system, such as the CRT in the air traffic control system referred to previously, should be designed in terms of the potential needs of that system.

Types of Systems. The concept that human factors is merely a matter of matching personnel needs and desires to system characteristics or rather making system characteristics conform to those needs and desires, is a simplistic notion. This kind of thinking ignores the fact that there are different types of systems and that in at least one of those types the system closely controls what its personnel do, and that what they do is what the system (or rather its developers) wants them to do.

In other system types, the people functioning in relation to the system have much more freedom in what they do, but the general outlines of what they do are still limited by system characteristics. Take an office building as an example of a system type. The people who use the office building may come and go as they please, but when they occupy an office the configuration of that office determines, however slightly, the things they do—for example, how far they can walk from wall to wall or what they can see out the window. Human-machine systems and subsystems vary in terms of a number of characteristics (see Chapter 5 for additional detail), but most important for the application of human factors is their "service orientation", the extent to which system design is directed by consideration for its personnel and for its users or clients. There are three types of service orientation: service-oriented systems, mission-oriented systems, and mixed systems. In service-oriented systems, examples of which are hotels, parks, theaters, and office buildings, user desires can and should be accommodated because these systems are designed specifically for "pleasure" users. Such users play a passive role in the functioning of these systems; they sit or watch or perform in their own subsystems, but do not interact (except possibly in an emergency) with the normal functioning of the total system. Service-oriented systems have their own workers, but these systems are not designed to please *them*.

In mission-oriented systems—most obviously weapon systems, but also production (factory) systems—user considerations are much less important; there may even be no users, in the sense of people for whom the system functions. Personnel in mission-oriented systems are the people who exercise the system and whose wishes are subordinate to the requirements of the system; in mission-oriented systems the mission is all-important.

Mixed systems combine characteristics of both the other types of systems. They have a mission, but the mission is at least partly to serve users. Examples are transportation systems (e.g., aircraft), welfare organizations, police, and hospitals. Here one can take client desires into account, but only partially, because the mission must be accomplished, not to the detriment of clients but disregarding their desires if necessary.

We run into difficulties when we fail to differentiate among these system types. In mission-oriented systems, we attempt to match system demands with personnel resources and limitations, but we do not consider user desires. In mixed systems (most systems are mixed) one considers user desires but only within mission constraints. To maximize system performance, it is necessary to take personnel limitations into account. The goal of human factors is to optimize the total system, which means adopting indirect ways of accommodating personnel. We cannot ask users in advance what they want and then incorporate their desires in the mission-system configuration, because these desires may conflict with system requirements. We have done this in service-oriented systems, to a certain extent, but not in other types.

Human Factors System Characteristics. The relationship between human factors and the system has other characteristics that define the discipline:

1. The *physical object of study* with which human factors is concerned is the system and subsystem; its *behavioral object of study* is the individual operator and team linked to individual pieces of equipment and to the system and subsystem.

2. The *functional object of study* (unit of performance) for human factors is the interaction of the human with some aspect of equipment functioning (e.g., the operator with his or her equipment interface, procedures, and technical data).

3. The *reference situation* for human factors, the situation against which all other human performance situations must be compared, is the performance of personnel in the operational (i.e., fully developed and functional) system performing its assigned mission(s) in its designated (operational) environment. The reference situation is not ordinarily static; we use the generic term, but each operational system behaves slightly differently from other systems, and variably from time to time too, so that the reference situation even with specific systems is an abstraction.

4. The human-machine system is an artificial *construction* developed by humans. Although all systems fall into a few generic categories, each system is essentially individual because it can be designed in different ways to accomplish the same goal(s). For example, a system performing the same functions can be manual or highly automatized.

5. The system is composed of personnel, equipment (including hardware/software mechanisms), operating and maintenance procedures, technical data and documentation, and a purpose and functions and tasks. Some of these *elements* serve a support function, others specialize in achieving the system mission; often the same elements do both. Systems have attributes that derive from the nature of their elements. For example, systems may react quickly (e.g., aircraft) or slowly (e.g., nuclear power plants). Systems may be large or small, simple or complex, and so forth, and these attributes influence the performance of the operator or technician.

Assumptions. The following assumptions are part of the system concept.

1. Every system element influences all the other system elements. In some cases the influence is mutual, in others the element being influenced does not reciprocate. The functioning of equipment influences personnel performance and is in turn influenced by personnel performance, e.g., an error may cause a Chernobyl breakdown. The quality and quantity of technical data and documentation (e.g., technical manuals, circuit drawings) influence the operator's

performance, but the operator's performance does not influence technical data because the latter are fixed (except when an error is found or a modification is made). In other words, dynamic elements in the system may influence other dynamic elements, and static elements may influence dynamic elements, but dynamic elements cannot influence static ones. The amount of influence varies from very slight (perhaps unmeasurable with our crude instruments) to the very great (overt, perhaps obvious). Behavioral design is necessary because the operator and his or her equipment mutually influence each other. If there were no interaction between the two, it would hardly be necessary to consider the human in system design.

2. Operation of the system automatically creates a demand on each dynamic system element, to which that element applies available resources to satisfy the demand. Ordinarily, the energy level of humans increases—they become more alert, and depending on what they are required to do they may engage in thinking or problem-solving; their feeling of stress may increase too. Similarly, the equipment may be required to activate certain mechanisms, power volumes may increase, and so forth. The resources referred to are the mechanisms developed (built into the equipment, trained into the operator) to satisfy increasing demand. The resources may or may not be sufficient for this demand; if they are not sufficient, the human-machine unit may fail to complete its task

3. The system is directed by its goal or mission, as interpreted by system personnel. All system elements (including the human) are subordinate to that goal, which means, for example, that the pilot of an aircraft is not free to fly to San Francisco when the schedule calls for Oklahoma City. The system functions performed support the goal or mission; if they do not, the system has malfunctioned. Preliminary and terminal operations leading to accomplishment of that goal are controlled by information/control mechanisms built into the system. These continuously compare actual system performance with required performance and when properly designed, call attention to discrepancies or provide feedback.

4. To a certain extent, when they are exercised in their operational environment, the system and its elements behave differently from when they are exercised elsewhere (e.g., at a test facility). This makes it even more necessary to test and gather data in the operational environment.

The assumptions above can be made more specific as they relate to the human element:

1. System personnel in mission-oriented and mixed systems form a specific subsystem of that system; users of a service-oriented system do not.

2. Personnel performance interacts with machine functioning and in the process contributes to and melds with machine outputs.

3. Personnel performance occurs at individual and team levels. Personnel outputs at these levels are transformed into subsystem- and system-level outputs by physical processes.

4. System personnel who are an integral element of the system assume the purpose, goal or mission of the system; personnel who use the system but who are not part of it (e.g., Social Security system clients) will not adopt that purpose or perform that mission. The purpose or goal or mission is decomposed into subpurposes appropriate for the individual operator or team. Individual will is submerged in that purpose.

5. Because the system is organized hierarchically, relationships among the various levels are implemented by information transmission among personnel and between personnel and equipment.

6. In an optimally functioning system, all personnel performance is relevant to the system purpose.

7. Control over the system is exercised by personnel ("managers") acting to implement the system purpose. That control is aided by feedback information transmission from all system levels and from equipment and/or personnel.

8. Recognized failure to achieve the system purpose elicits compensatory performance on the part of personnel. That performance seeks to restore system functions in accordance with standards related to system goals.

9. Failure of system personnel to perform in accordance with the system goal results in ineffective terminal outputs.

10. Stimuli from systems other than one's own may impinge upon one's own system and require specific personnel responses.

Variables. There are two types of variables in the system to be concerned with: those that describe the functioning of the physical system and its subsystems, and those that describe the performance of individual and team operators. System and subsystem variables are physical, because at subsystem and system levels the contributions of the human at lower levels have already been combined with equipment contributions as a result of the transformation processes referred to previously. The functions and mechanisms at the operator or team level are much more familiar to behavioral specialists because they are more distinguishable as human or machine processes. This does not mean that there is no human input at higher system levels—someone must give the order to "fire!" or throw a switch that does the same thing, or make a corporate decision—but most of the behavioral inputs affecting the system have already been transformed into physical inputs.

Tables 1.2 and 1.3 are lists, respectively, of system and subsystem variables and individual and team variables. Items may overlap, and the lists may not be comprehensive. The interesting thing about the two lists is their similarities and differences. There are purely human variables in individuals and teams that have no counterpart in the subsystem and system: reward/motivation, fatigue, training, experience, aptitude. On the other hand, the system has certain attributes, certain goals, and a hierarchical arrangement that one does not find in individuals and teams. Other variables are the same, or are the same when the

Table 1.2 System and Subsystem Variables

1. The size and complexity of the system
2. The number of subsystems
3. The organization of the system
4. The number and type of interdependencies within the system
5. The number and specificity of goals and missions
6. The nature of the operational environment in which the system functions
7. System attributes—e.g., determinate/interdeterminate, sensitive/insensitive
8. The nature of the system terminal output or mission effects
9. The functions and tasks performed by the system
10. The requirements imposed on the system
11. The nature and availability of resources required by the system
12. The number and nature of information feedback mechanisms

Table 1.3 Individual and Team Variables

1. Personnel aptitude for tasks performed
2. The amount and appropriateness of training
3. The amount of personnel experience and skill
4. The presence or absence of reward and motivation
5. Fatigue or stress condition
6. The functions and tasks performed
7. The size of the team
8. Requirements imposed on the individual or team
9. The physical environment for individual or team functioning
10. The number and type of interdependencies within the team
11. The relationship between individual/team and other subsystems

difference of scale is accounted for—for example, the size of the team and the system, the number and type of interdependencies in both, or the functions and requirements imposed on both. Both the system and the operator or team must have available the resources required to carry out the mission. The nature of the environment in which both function is important, but the environment is different for each. For the individual or team, that environment is embedded in their own system (e.g., lighting, ventilation in the airliner cabin); for the system as a whole, the environment is outside the system (e.g., the sea, air, terrain). It is therefore apparent that even when variables that seem to be similar function at both individual/team and subsystem/system levels they are still subtly different.

Hypotheses. Most of the individual and team variables (Table 1.3) have already been the subject of studies, but not in a system context, which means that whatever has been learned about these variables is still only suppositious until verified in a system framework. Studies of system and subsystem variables (Table 1.2)—what Mattessich (1982) referred to as empirical systems re-research—are quite rare, at least from a behavioral standpoint, although one cannot ignore the research described in Parsons (1972).. Examples of the kinds of behavioral hypotheses that can be developed from the variables in Tables 1.2 and 1.3 are:

1. An increased number of subsystems in a system tends to slow system response because of the need to communicate information (orders, data, and inquiries).

2. In systems that are highly determinate—very proceduralized, little choice among response options—the influence of the individual or team is relatively slight. When the system is indeterminate—that is, when there are a number of response options and which one is selected depends on interpretation of stimuli whose meaning is ambiguous—personnel influence is quite important and the effect on system output is marked.

3. The performance of the individual or team is not related to the size of the system.

There are serious difficulties in testing hypotheses at the subsystem and system level because the sheer size of many systems makes it difficult to manipulate them. While it is not easy to measure individual and team performance in a system context, it is easier to do this than to work with total systems as the objects of study. Specialists have not generally attempted to test system-level hypotheses, leaving this to the organizational development psychologists, who have done a little (but not much) with them.

Three types of system-related research can be performed: studies of the effect of system variables on system performance; studies of the effect of system variables on personnel performance or the effect of personnel on system outputs; and studies of the effects of individual/team variables on individual or team performance. Only the third has been extensively explored in traditional human performance studies.

Implications of the System Concept for Human Factors Research

The implications of the system concept for human factors research are not implications for practice. System development, which has already been influenced by system engineering concepts, imposes its own requirements on human factors practice, and that practice has developed procedures to accommodate to those requirements (see Chapter 7). From a research or measurement standpoint, however, the system concept requires the following for human factors research:

1. Human performance must be measured in a system context (the whole) or a distorted picture of that performance will result, because the action of isolated variables is different from the action of the same variables in the whole context. This has implications for data collection, validation, and the way experimental studies are conducted. Because the real world is the operational system and there is a need to collect human performance data describing the total system, researchers must measure in the real world much more than they presently do.

In addition, experimental studies must be validated by operational data collection because the conclusions derived from experimental study, in which variables are almost always isolated from their total context, may be different from conclusions based on measurements in the real world. Furthermore, the results of experimental studies will be deceptive if the studies are not modified to include aspects of the real world; the alternative is to expand validation efforts.

2. Overall system performance becomes the criterion of the meaningfulness of human performance. If that performance does not affect total system output, it is insignificant from a system standpoint no matter how important it is from the standpoint of the individual. The common criterion of the importance of a behavioral variable—its effect on the human or on the team—is no longer adequate unless that effect is sufficiently strong to damage the human (in which case it will probably damage the system as well).

3. The system itself is an object of study. If one cannot disengage the human from the system in which he or she performs, one must study the total system. In this connection, human factors should now overlap with operations research and systems engineering to a greater extent than ever.

4. Our study cannot be confined to a single level (individual or team). Hierarchy is implicit in all systems, and all levels must now be studied.

These implications will be discussed in greater detail in subsequent chapters. For the present, it is sufficient to note how the system concept changes the research emphasis in human factors: the experiment on the individual is no longer sufficient unto itself; the unit of performance being measured—the system—becomes much larger, with all the attendant problems of increased complexity; there is much greater emphasis on gathering data in the field; and there is a new standard for the meaningfulness of human performance. These are truly significant changes, if they are implemented.

REMAINING THEMES

The following are themes that the remainder of the book will discuss in greater detail.

1. Human factors is a unique discipline with distinctive characteristics, although many disciplines have contributed to it. If the discipline is distinctive, it may be that concepts and methods carried over from the parent disciplines are not completely adequate to supply answers for the new one.

2. The goals of human factors are to describe, predict, and control human performance in the system context. *Description* implies the gathering of normative data, not only about human performance but also about systems as objects of study from a behavioral viewpoint. *Prediction* requires estimation of human performance in quantitative terms. Human factors attempts to exercise *control* over systems by applying behavioral principles to their development.

3. The central question for human factors is how the personnel subsystem

contributes to the performance of the total system and how the factors impinging on the personnel subsystem influence its performance. This requires investigation of the transformation processes within system development and operation.

4. If one accepts the point of view (the belief) that the system and system development are fundamental to our technological civilization, research on these phenomena is also fundamental. Human factors is the only behavioral discipline that transcends and melds both behavioral (personnel performance) and physical (equipment parameter) domains. The system concept is critical because it provides a unifying framework for human factors as a totality.

5. If the operational system performing an assigned mission in the operational environment represents "reality" for human factors, the validation of human factors principles and data derived from any source can be accomplished only by replication of studies in that reality and/or prediction to performance in that reality.

6. Evaluation is a critical aspect of human factors, but it cannot be accomplished without the development of human performance standards based on normative descriptive data—what operators ordinarily do in certain specified circumstances with specified equipment. Standards are linked to prediction of human performance because the standard describes what humans are likely to do in a particular situation.

7. If the discipline is to progress, it will be necessary to develop a number of behavioral taxonomies that can be used not only as a means of communication among specialists but also as organizing formats for research and predictive data bases.

8. The emphasis placed by human factors on the operational system as the reference situation requires consideration of research paradigms that are alternative to the traditional hypothesis-testing laboratory situation.

9. Measurement in human factors is complicated by the multidimensionality of human and system performance. Multidimensionality exacerbates the problem of deciding among alternative criteria and measures. The need to remain faithful to the reference system during measurement produces problems of operational fidelity. Much measurement data are obscure because the context of those data is unclear.

10. Because objective data that describe only simple, discrete dimensions are difficult to interpret, objective data must be supplemented by subjective data, which have more dimensions than their counterparts.

11. The physicalistic orientation in which system development proceeds creates problems for human factors: it is necessary to determine physical equivalents for behavioral processes, and engineers are reluctant to consider behavioral variables in their designs.

12. Human factors suffers from a variety of constraints that may not be significantly different from those faced by other disciplines but that have a

disproportionate effect on the discipline, because it is not as "robust" as the others. Some constraints, such as the inadequacy of supporting data, are inherent in the discipline as it is presently implemented. Other constraints stem from relationships with government, academia, and industry.

SUMMARY

The conceptual structure that underlies human factors research is based essentially on beliefs, although over time these become progressively differentiated into definitions, assumptions, variables, and hypotheses. There is a distinction between human factors as a discipline and the various special interest areas that compose it. The significance of the human factors belief structure is that it determines research purpose, the kinds of variables studied, and the manner in which research is performed in the individual interest areas. Because that structure is largely informal, it is possible for the discipline to accommodate contrasting viewpoints. This may be necessary because of the multidimensionality of the variables affecting human performance. Opposing beliefs in human factors center around the dichotomy of research and application, a dichotomy that produces a continuing tension between researchers and practitioners. Human factors professionals have only one relatively formal belief—the system concept—but they utilize it only very generally and occasionally. If the system concept is actually implemented in human factors research, it imposes certain demands that sharply change the manner in which that research must be performed.

CHAPTER 2

The Distinctive Characteristics of Human Factors

In this chapter we shall define what human factors is, its scope, what it is supposed to do, and what makes it different from other disciplines, including the special implications of the system concept for human factors. The distinctive characteristics of human factors require the discipline to adopt new concepts and methods.

It is important to differentiate between human factors and psychology because, despite their close relationship, if human factors is merely a special branch of psychology the human factors problems attacked and the methodology used will be those of psychology, and these may not be wholly appropriate for human factors. The closeness of psychology and human factors forces us, paradoxically, to call attention to the extremely important differences between them.

The concentration on psychology and engineering as primary predecessors of human factors is not meant to denigrate the contributions of medicine, biomechanics, time and motion study, physiology, safety, reliability, and other special disciplines that have made some contributions to human factors. It is merely that psychology and engineering have had by far the greatest impact on human factors. The importance of these two is reflected in the fact that the great majority of specialists belonging to the Human Factors Society (approximately 72 percent in 1986) were trained either as psychologists or as engineers.

Responses to earlier versions of the chapter suggest that the topic of the contributions of other disciplines to human factors is extremely sensitive. There are several points of view on these contributions. One could maintain that human factors is *sui generis* and was not influenced by other sciences, but that is nonsense; one could say that all contributions made by other disciplines influenced human factors equally; and one could maintain (my own point of view) that many disciplines contributed but that the contributions of some were greater than others. If this last is true, I would nominate psychology and engineering to have preeminent effects—psychology because it provided basic concepts and methodology for our research, and engineering because it provided the context in which human factors applications to design are made. This is not to denigrate the contributions of the other disciplines, such as physiology, biomechanics, industrial engineering, reliability, anthropology, safety and social psychology. After all, it is not a coincidence that another name for human factors is "engineering psychology."

HUMAN FACTORS AS A BRIDGING DISCIPLINE

Only human factors is required by the terms of its conceptual framework to incorporate both behavioral and physical elements within itself. Psychology incorporates physiological elements but not physical ones, and although individual engineers often claim that they take behavioral considerations into account in their design, they do so primarily to minimize the effect of behavioral elements on the functioning of equipment.

Because human behavior occurs in the context of physical objects, some might think that this accounts for a physical element in the behavioral sciences. But there is a great difference between performing in the context of physical elements and performing in interaction with those elements. Human factors alone does the latter. The need in human factors to mediate between the behavioral and physical domains creates the further need to provide transformation equations, ways of translating behavioral into physical equivalents, and vice versa.

The conversion processes referred to by Van Gigch (1974, and Chapter 1 of this book) are similar to but not quite the same as transformations. Conversion is the change of one physical or biological element into another physical or biological element of a different form. Transformation goes much beyond that because it crosses domains and is therefore infinitely more difficult than conversion.

This is not to say that we have learned how to make these domain transformations easily. Our techniques for attempting to do so (e.g., the human-computer interaction guidelines of Smith and Mosier 1986) are quite crude, which is why human factors has so much difficulty making its impact on system development felt.

Behavioral transformations are symbolic only; physical elements are not actually changed into biological elements, or vice versa. Instead it is a matter of determining the physical *equivalent* of a behavioral element or the behavioral equivalent of a physical element. This type of transformation is expressed in human performance data relationships; one should be able to say that such and such a behavioral design feature has been reflected in a gain or loss in operator performance of x units. If such equivalents could be established, they could be used for performance prediction, and they might also provide some idea of the mechanisms responsible for the equivalents.

HUMAN FACTORS AS A SYSTEM DEVELOPER

Among the behavioral disciplines, human factors is the only one that actively participates in the construction of new human-machine systems. If one assumes, as Chapter 1 did, that the natural object of human factors study is the system, and if that system has a life cycle that includes its design and development, then human factors must participate in that design and development. It follows that if human factors participates in design and development, it must also research design and development processes.

The relationship between human factors and system development has certain implications:

1. Although human factors has research interests other than system development, it is necessary to apply research findings to system development. This means that to some as yet undefined extent human factors research must be responsive to the kinds of behavioral problems arising in system development. The application of research findings raises the question of how research performed outside the system development environment can be made more readily applicable to that environment.

2. The transformation problem referred to previously stems directly from system development.

3. The analytic and evaluational methodologies that have been created by behavioral specialists (e.g., function and task analysis, test and evaluation) derive from system development requirements and are irrelevant in a purely research mode.

4. The interaction between human factors and engineering, both from a conceptual standpoint and as a cultural environment in which many human factors specialists work, would not exist without system development.

In summary, if the relationship between human factors and system development did not exist, the discipline as we know it today would not exist.

THE CONTRIBUTIONS OF PSYCHOLOGY AND ENGINEERING TO HUMAN FACTORS

Psychology has provided human factors with a research orientation, and engineering has provided the application mode, primarily with regard to system development. In part the tension that has arisen between the research and application aspects of human factors is derived from the major differences between these two contributors—psychology and engineering.* Most specialists are psychologists by training, and so the lessons learned and the ties to the

---

*There are empirical data that show that practitioners do not make much use of human factors research products because they consider most of these to be largely irrelevant to the kinds of problems arising in system development (Meister 1979). This reluctance or inability to use research outputs is considered to be an indication of tension within the discipline.

parent discipline are particularly binding. For these specialists there is no comparable engineering training. The engineering indoctrination is learned from the environment in which practitioners are placed, if their lot in life is to work in system development. Many of the lessons learned from engineering deal with constraints—the limitations of what specialists know, the difficulties of converting behavioral analyses into engineering equivalents, the obduracy of schedules, the necessity of fitting a behavioral orientation into a physicalistic milieu. The precision and control of the laboratory that were extolled as an ideal in psychological training are now opposed by the pragmatic "make do" attitude of the engineer.

It is dangerous to make categorical statements about what has been carried over from psychology to human factors. If one adopts a very stringent criterion of relevancy, many things that have had an effect on the discipline but that are not immediately applicable to the specialist's activity may be ignored. Almost everything in psychology has had some effect on human factors, acting in the first place on the original specialists, who then transferred their concept of behavioral science into the way in which their successors think and act. Among the aspects that are most specifically relevant are: the stimulus-response concept, by which is meant the way specialists conceptualize human performance as a sequence of stimuli that initiate responses; the physiology of the human body—its capabilities and limitations; an awareness of the importance of certain behavioral functions—such as information-processing, attention and vigilance—in explaining human performance; specific theoretical orientations, such as theories of learning, workload, and stress; data from research on such topics as perception, attention, fatigue, and transfer of training; the importance of experimental design and statistics; experience in performing behavioral research in a controlled situation, usually in a laboratory; some notions of the utility of theory and rudiments of a philosophy of science; specific data on performance maxima and minima, such as the toxic limits of gases in the atmosphere and the shortest possible response time to a single discrete stimulus; an acquaintance with the methods of collecting behavioral data—for example, experimentation, instrumentation, observation, interviewing, and questionnaires; and finally, information gleaned from specialized topics in psychology, such as industrial and applied psychology and perhaps even social psychology.

In addition the value of training in computer skills provided by the university should not be ignored. This training has been extremely influential in focusing the attention of human factors on computer technology.

THE DIFFERENCES BETWEEN PSYCHOLOGY AND HUMAN FACTORS

Some psychologists may feel that human factors is merely a special application of psychology. I contend that although human factors has been derived largely from psychology and influenced by many other disciplines, it is nevertheless a distinct, individual science. In support of this viewpoint we should describe the differences between human factors and psychology.

The Distinction between Behavior and Performance

Behavior can be defined very broadly as any activity—cognitive, physiological, psychomotor—of the human organism. Daydreaming is a form of behavior and so is kissing someone or playing chess. Performance. as we define it, is work-goal motivated and as such is only a part (although a large part) of the human's total behavior.

It may be an overstatement to say that human factors is interested in performance only, but the statement is largely correct. Obviously the worker's motivation, or lack of it, affects his or her performance, and theoretically the specialist should be interested in work-related motivation, but in practice so little is known about the relationship between work and motivation that pragmatically the specialist can do little about it. It has been suggested that equipment should be designed so that the operator's job is self-motivating, but that is beyond present capability. It is possible, of course, to develop incentive plans for increasing motivation and productivity, but this falls more properly into organizational development or industrial psychology.

In any event, psychology is interested in both performance and behavior, or rather in behavior as encompassing performance. The scope of psychology is therefore much greater than that of human factors. For human factors, performance is "instrumental" behavior—behavior attempting to achieve an overt goal directed in many cases by some agency other than an individual. This behavior is organized and driven by a purpose existing in the system of which the worker is a part. Nonperformance behavior is not only of no interest to the specialist, but actually detrimental to the achievement of the work goal because it diminishes the worker's allocation of resources to the goal. This is not as negativistic as it appears. System developers are aware that humans engage in behavior as well as in performance, that in order not to cripple that performance it is necessary to provide opportunities for the worker to engage in behavior: rest periods, the opportunity to talk to co-workers and so forth. Whether the concern is compassionate can be argued, but the effect is the same—concern that the worker not be overloaded, that stereotypical response patterns be accommodated, that the most effective work-shift pattern be utilized.

Because human factors restricts its interest to performance, and because performance is only a subset of behavior, the scope of theorizing in human factors is also restricted. Psychological fact and theory describing the fundamentals of individual behavior are accepted as valid for system personnel generally without question. For example, the specialist accepts the centrality of the neuron and the nervous system as the foundation of behavior—it is unnecessary to look for an alternative mode of explanation, one that would be more exclusively the domain of human factors. Except for those who are training specialists, a special theory explaining how learning occurs in a system context is unnecessary. Human factors researchers study the target acquisition process, not the more fundamental processes of perception. Those who study color in perception do so in most cases in relation to its coding properties rather than because of an interest in color per se.

If the scope of its study (i.e., performance) is only a subset of behavior, how can one claim that human factors is a fundamental discipline? It is fundamental because its subject (the system and its development) is critical to modern civilization and because the discipline can be studied independently of other disciplines—that is, it is possible to explain human performance in human factors terms without bringing in nonhuman factors concepts. This does not mean that one should not make use of concepts from other disciplines when they apply, it is simply that one need not do so.

The Importance of Purpose

Purpose is given to the system by its developers. This purpose then animates system personnel and directs what they do. Purpose is critical to human factors because literally everything—system operation and the worker's task—depends on it and is ultimately derived from it. Purpose has no such role in psychology, although it does in engineering. Indeed, purpose as an explanation of behavior is frowned on in behavioristic psychology. Although it is true that humans, even outside the system in which they work, behave purposefully, an explanation of behavior in terms of purpose is considered a tautology, because the human is not a fabrication, as is the system. A machine is given its mechanisms to achieve a goal established by its maker.

The implications of the central role of purpose in human factors are quite important. Any analysis of system and personnel performance begins with a single question: What is the action or performance intended to accomplish? Because every action of and in the system is designed to accomplish a purpose, it becomes necessary to determine whether that purpose has been accomplished, so testing and evaluation are necessary. Procedures for personnel to follow are developed to accomplish the same purpose. Feedback to enable the worker to correct any system deviations from the optimal accomplishment of the work goal is critical. Explanations are couched in terms of purpose or reflect that purpose.

Purpose is equally critical in the development of systems. Every step or process in that development is theoretically determined by the development purpose—for example, to achieve a given system capability. However, purpose in system development has a less clear-cut role to play than in the operating system. That is because the many activities in development take place over time, and the link between the overall (molar) development purpose and any specific (molecular) design action may be difficult to determine.

The system purpose is overt—or will be, if the system is designed properly—so there is therefore no need in human factors (as there may be in other behavioral disciplines) to use unconscious mechanisms as explanations of behavior or performance. The human may well have unconscious motivations, but these are no concern of the specialist unless in some way these unconscious forces interfere with the orderly attainment of the system goal. And even then we do not attempt to determine the unconscious mechanisms—we merely retrain or replace the worker when his or her performance degrades.

The Link with Technology

Because of its engineering background, human factors is the only behavioral discipline tied to technology. This means that, when technology shifts, the areas of interest that specialists develop shift. We have witnessed such a remarkable shift in the recent interest in the behavioral aspects of computers (Shackel 1985). No other technological shift—the change from the vacuum tube to the transistor, for example—has had such phenomenal effects in terms of directing human factors research interests into a new area.

Psychology is essentially independent of technology because context is only one of the variables influencing human behavior. In that connection, psychology is less fettered than human factors. One question with which we shall deal later is whether human factors research is determined solely or primarily by technological requirements, so that, for example, if the technology needs to know which menu format is most effective in computer software, some researcher will study the question. Alternatively, it is possible that there are research questions that do not ignore technology but that are centered more on systems, system characteristics, and system variables *in general*. These questions will be discussed in Chapter 4.

The technological orientation of human factors may also be a weakness because those who control technology and therefore decide which technological questions need answering are very often bureaucrats and pragmatists, not scientists. Behind the menu format question may be a more critical behavioral problem that will not be attacked because the technologist is not interested in it. Technology is important but many of its concerns are immediate and do not lead to a deeper understanding of the behavioral aspects of the technological phenomenon.

The problem ultimately resolves itself into a matter of allocation of resources. In a discipline that is not overly rich in personnel and financial support, concentration on one problem usually requires ignoring another. Again, we come back to value criteria and how to decide among competing research demands.

Job/Task Centrality

Almost every human factors analysis begins with a critical question: What is the operator supposed to do? (Note that this is not what his purpose is, but what actions he must take.) A major output of mission/function/task analysis is the description of the task, or what the operator is required to do. Correspondingly, test and evaluation are supposed to answer the question "Did system personnel do what they were supposed to do?"

No other behavioral discipline, with the exception of industrial psychology, concentrates as heavily on the task and the job, but industrial psychology has no responsibility for development of the primary system, which creates the task or job.

Evaluation and Standards

The system is designed to accomplish a specific purpose (goal or mission), but some human actions implement that purpose while others do not. It is necessary to determine by evaluation whether that purpose is being accomplished and which actions are erroneous or late, so that if the system is off-course, it can be brought back on course. Its performance can be evaluated only if required actions and performance values are specified. These are standards of effective performance.

Evaluation and standards are central to the system and to human factors. One can draw a direct relationship between the system with its purpose, and the notion of evaluation and behavioral standards; without the system there would be no need for them. Many standards are peculiar to the individual system, but it is possible also to develop general human performance standards representing not requirements for specific system performance but normative expected performance. An example of such a normative standard is the minimum number of television lines required for the human to resolve an electronically displayed symbol (between twelve and fifteen lines). One must have human performance standards so that the system can be designed in accordance with human capabilities and limitations. They are also necessary to evaluate the performance of system personnel, to know what these personnel should be able or unable to do.

Psychology has need of standards also—for example, in intelligence and aptitude testing—but standards do not play as significant a role in psychology as in human factors because humans in their non-work activities are not required to behave in a standard manner.

The need for performance standards in human factors has significant research implications, because that need requires a deliberate effort to collect empirical data to derive such standards. Unfortunately, present-day researchers avoid the responsibility because, as we shall see, the collection of normative data for standards—the description of what people do in particular situations—

does not fit well with the traditional hypothesis-testing research paradigm. Consequently, few behavioral standards are quantitative.

With regard to techniques needed to perform evaluation, human factors is in much better shape because data collection techniques utilized in psychology (experimental design, interviews, observations, ratings, etc.) transfer over quite readily to human factors. On the other hand, we cannot be completely satisfied with these methods because evaluation is sufficiently different from experimental research that the traditional techniques perform with less than optimal efficiency.

The Level of Explanation

When human factors attempts to explain human performance, that explanation is—or should be—couched in system terms. Whereas other behavioral disciplines explain human behavior in terms of the individual or group (psychology), as a unit of a cultural matrix (anthropology), or as part of a social unit (sociology), human factors views the human as an integral part of the human-machine system. The uniqueness of this interpretation is one thing that distinguishes human factors from the other behavioral disciplines. Although this level of explanation is logical for a system-oriented discipline, relatively few specialists utilize it in such bold terms. That is because few researchers have followed up the implications of the system concept. One rarely finds explanations in system terms in the individual interest areas, except possibly in discussing organizational dynamics.

Can the explanations that specialists provide for the phenomena they study be translated into system terms? This is quite difficult when the phenomena have been studied in purely individual terms. If one measures the performance of an individual batter in a baseball game without reference to the team's success or failure in that game, it is impossible to interpret the batter's performance except in individual terms.

One can attempt to explain human performance in at least two ways: at the individual or team level—that is, performance in terms of the mechanisms that are inherent in individual or team output and do not go beyond that output—and in terms of the relationship between the individual or team performance and the performance with which it interacts, that is, in terms of other system elements at other levels. Ideally, explanations should include both, but in practice researchers confine themselves to the first, in part because it is the "traditional" explanatory method, but even more because they have not included the system in their studies. One cannot translate performance studied in purely individual terms into system terms; to explain in the second mode requires that one collect data at more than the individual or team level.

The explanation of human performance in terms of the system requires answers to two questions: How significant—statistically and practically—is the contribution of personnel performance to terminal system outputs? and

What variables and mechanisms are responsible for the effectiveness, or ineffectiveness, of the personnel contribution to system performance? These questions underlie the essential point that human performance in the system framework cannot be understood unless it is related to that framework. This results from the overriding importance of "purpose." Human performance in the system must be interpreted in terms of accomplishment of task purpose, and that purpose is linked inextricably with the system.

The Individual within the System

The focus of attention in human factors is the individual or team—but always in relation to the work system, as part of that system. If human factors is concerned with Mr. X, it is in the activities that he performs on the job, with time out for lunch. Once Mr. X returns home after work, has dinner, converses with his wife, watches television, and retires to bed, he is no longer a subject of human factors study. Of course, if anything that Mr. X does off the job affects his work activity, we are interested in it.

Other behavioral disciplines, such as anthropology, sociology, or psychology, have a much wider scope than human factors does, in the sense that they are concerned with how the individual functions across all contexts. Psychology, for example, would be interested in everything Mr. X does. To a certain extent, pragmatism determines the scope of interest for human factors. Everything related to human performance on the job may be within the theoretical scope of human factors, but what one cannot do anything with is meaningless. For instance, there may be practitioners who feel that the social climate of the job at which Mr. X works is or should be a matter of concern for the discipline, but in the context of developing a new system there appears to be no realistic way of taking social climate into account in the new design—at least not without radically changing the nature of the system, which is usually not feasible.

Optimization of the System

Because humans are viewed as part of a higher-order system, the attempts of human factors to improve their performance are conducted as part of a more general attempt to optimize the total system. It is popularly supposed that the goal of human factors design application is to match system requirements with human needs and resources, the assumption being that a proper balance between system characteristics and human capabilities and limitations will optimize both the human and the system. The implication of this assumption is that one cannot maximize the role of one system element at the expense of another. Nevertheless, this fallacy persists. Engineers often engage in unneeded automation to exploit machine capabilities, and some specialists seek to maximize the role of system operators, because that magnifies the importance of human factors. An example of the latter fallacy is the statement by the National

Research Council Human Factors Committee, which says explicitly: "Systems exist to serve their users, whether they are consumers, system operators, production workers, or maintenance crews" (Committee on Human Factors 1983, pp. 2–3). The system exists to serve a purpose, which may or may not include personnel, but it is the purpose that is important, not the fact that personnel are involved.

It is only fair to say that there are those who disagree with my position. They look to the ultimate purpose of developing a system, which is some benefit to be derived from the operations of that system. From that standpoint the statement by the Human Factors Committee is correct. It is true that ultimately a textile weaving factory is designed to engender profits for its owners and shareholders, but in the more immediate sense its purpose is to produce textiles. If the purpose of all systems is to provide a benefit to their owners or developers, then all systems have the same purpose, which makes it impossible to use system purpose as an organizing framework for human factors concepts.

An unbalanced design solution results in less than optimal performance of the total system. The role of the human in the system is a role that optimizes total system performance, even though from a purely individual behavioral standpoint that role may not be the most desirable one. (It is assumed, however, that the system does not ask more of its personnel than they can safely or reasonably do.) In the ideal design situation, the designer considers all reasonable ways in which the human can be utilized and selects the one that enables the system, including its personnel, to perform at its maximum. Although engineering seeks only to secure reasonably satisfactory design solutions and human factors attempts to optimize these solutions, practitioners' efforts must often be compromised, so that the practical effect of human factors inputs on design is also less than optimal.

Since system personnel are controlled by the system, it is possible to adopt an extremely authoritarian point of view with regard to their use in the system. It may appear logical from the system framework (with its subordination of the human to that system) to maximize system output by demanding an excessive level of performance from them. Outside of a completely authoritarian political structure, such as Nazi Germany and its concentration camps or the Soviet Union, this kind of reasoning is fallacious. Since the system concept implies interdependency of elements, failure to treat personnel in a positive manner will ultimately produce a degradation of the total system that may cause the system to fail. One can see this in a sociological context: the management-labor adversarial stance so frequently found in the United States and other countries tends to reduce system output by encouraging strikes and other disorders.

THE GOALS OF HUMAN FACTORS

Human factors has three goals: to describe, to predict, and to control the performance of the human in the system structure. These goals are no different from those of any other scientific discipline, but their implications for human factors are distinctive.

Definition of these goals may be superficially simple, but it is actually complex. To describe something is to report what exists or what happens. The "what" being described must be specified before it can be abstracted from the matrix of all things existing or occurring. If one cannot describe everything, then what is it that we want human factors to describe? Because the operational system performing assigned missions in its operational environment is the human factors reference situation, what we want to describe is that system, the performance of system personnel, and the variables affecting that performance. The choice of the operational system is obvious because it is our reference situation. A less desirable but still acceptable situation is a highly realistic simulation of the operational system.

Before one can describe, however, one must have a conceptual orientation toward what one wants to describe. Only certain performances are of interest; only certain variables inherent in the system are hypothesized to be important. The parameters we are interested in were listed in Tables 1.1 and 1.2, but they must be tailored to the specifics of the individual system.

Examples are the success/failure rate of mission accomplishment, the contribution of personnel performance to the success/failure ratio, and the influence of various behavioral variables on the success/failure ratio. Unfortunately there is little description of this type going on in human factors today. Most researchers avoid the operational system because of the presumed "lack of experimental control," which is, however, largely irrelevant for descriptive measurement.

There are several reasons that specialists should describe or measure operational system performance. First, as a reference situation the dimensions of performance in the operational system are indispensable for establishing the dimensions of simulation fidelity. When we say that this or that measurement situation is more or less faithful to the operational system, our normative data will help tell us what we mean by that phrase. Second, measurement of the operational system will suggest variables for further investigation. For example, certain attributes of different system types—indeterminacy or sensitivity perhaps (performance changes in response to varying contexts)—may suggest particular variables to be studied in the laboratory. Third and most important, measurement and description will provide data (frequencies of actions taken, influencing actions, success/failure) that will lead to the development of predictive data bases.

The three goals—description, prediction, and control—are interrelated.

Description is the first step to prediction. Prediction is a form of control; if one knows what an operator in a subsystem will do in a particular situation, that knowledge permits one to exercise a certain amount of control over that operator. Prediction requires a taxonomy of systems, system variables and tasks, and specific performance measures (e.g., errors, time). If descriptive data utilizing this taxonomy are gathered, these fill in the cells in a predictive data-base table.

Control is defined as active intervention in a process, not the control of system personnel and users, although under authoritarian systems this type of control can be achieved. Human factors control is intervention in the system development process. In system development one controls the operator's responses when the human-machine interface is modified in ways that determine the nature of the operator's responses. Control is also exercised in training and testing. However, control by modifying the human-machine interface is exercised only weakly because the practitioner's knowledge of transformation mechanisms is poor. Specialists lose control when they are unable to predict the relationship between the human-machine interface and operator performance.

The three goals have significant implications. Description means that along with laboratory experiments there must also be measurement of the operational system in its operational environment (or a close relative), because that is the reference situation and anything else represents only an approximation of reality. Just as important, description implies data collection for its own purposes rather than solely for hypothesis-testing, although it does not exclude the latter. Because hypothesis-testing is engaged in demonstrating a point, its primary interest is not data collection, although some data must be collected by experiment. Description also demands a conceptual framework that suggests what is to be described and how measurement should proceed.

Prediction implies the development of a data base with which one predicts, and the compilation of quantitative data for that data base. Even before these, and as part of the conceptual framework required for description, it presumes one or more taxonomic structures to organize what is to be described and predicted. Control implies a significant increase in the amount of attention paid to system development, including the performance of studies to determine the relationship between system characteristics and personnel performance.

All these implications have been only poorly implemented in research and practice.

THE SCOPE OF HUMAN FACTORS

In defining a discipline it is necessary to ask what it includes, because scope in part determines the research and application activity that the discipline pursues. It would be easy to say that every aspect of technology as it relates to personnel performance becomes the responsibility of human factors, but this may be overly broad. People draw graffiti on buildings—does this mean that there is an interest area that can be called "graffiti human factors"? Clearly we need a more concrete accounting of responsibilities.

A more reasonable definition of scope might be that human factors includes (1) analysis, measurement, research, and prediction of any human performance related to the operation, maintenance, and use of equipment and systems; (2) research on the behavioral variables involved in the design of equipment, jobs, and systems; (3) the application of behavioral knowledge and methods to the development of equipment, jobs, and systems; (4) the analysis of jobs and systems to assist in the optimal allocation of personnel roles in system operations; (5) research on the experiences and attitudes that equipment users and system personnel have with regard to equipment and systems; and (6) study of the effects of equipment and system characteristics on personnel performance. This listing is quite comprehensive, although it merely suggests a *range* of activities. Within this scope are a surprising variety of topics and methods. For example, Salvendy (1987) includes in his *Handbook of Human Factors* both selection and training, each of which has its own provenance but both of which are usually associated with human factors in system development.

It is fair to say that anything involving the interaction of people and technology could be within the scope of human factors. This tendency to include as much as possible in its area of responsibility was fostered early in the development of the discipline in order to achieve a recognized substantial role, particularly in system development.

The reality has been far more constrained. For example, at one time in the 1950s specialists claimed there was a need to review all procedures written during system development to ensure that they satisfied behavioral criteria. In practice, except for a few critical procedures, practitioners did not evaluate procedures because the task was too onerous, and indeed they lacked a formal method of evaluating them. The discrepancy between what the discipline claimed as its right to perform and what it actually did and could do was marked. Every beginning discipline attempts to enlarge its scope as do even more settled ones.

The difficulty with all this variety is that it creates a lack of unity within the discipline. This is more marked in research than in practice. The application of human factors to system development has a unity imposed on it by the natural sequencing of development activities. A common purpose—to develop a specific system—and a chronology that imposes itself on all developmental processes, including the behavioral, creates a unity in practice, despite the idiosyncrasies of the individual system. As an example, regardless of whether one is developing hardware or software systems, the analytic processes required to determine functions and tasks, for example, are much the same. In research, on the other hand, the only common thread linking the individual interest areas is experimental or scientific method, which is a rather weak thread because of its abstractness. What do biomechanics, visual perception, and training research have in common? Specialists in these areas are unlikely even to read one another's study reports. So from the research standpoint one must ask whether human factors is more than an umbrella phrase for a collection of unrelated research activities.

This heterogeneity gives individual researchers little incentive to consider their work in any light beyond the limits of their interest areas. Researchers usually do not often speak to the practitioner or work in system development, so they are hardly aware of a world beyond their special interests. This is one reason that human factors research may lack utility—it is phrased very largely in interest-area terms. Earlier a distinction was made between human factors as an umbrella discipline and the many individual research interest areas (e.g., workload, shift cycles, anthropometry) associated with human factors. What does one have to do with the other? Could one not, for example, as one of the Chapter 1 survey participants suggested, do research in the area of human-computer interaction quite apart from the concept of human factors?

Presumably specialists in the individual research areas feed the results of their work into human factors channels—journals and reports—and the discipline uses and applies these results, mostly in system development but also in measurement and operations. From that standpoint human factors is preeminently an application discipline. One might also think of human factors as a transmission medium for application of research results. In the course of doing so, human factors (the term really means its specialists) may modify those results by developing data bases, reformatting data, designing guidelines for its use, and so on. Although empirical studies of the process do not exist, it is quite probable that research results in the course of human factors utilization are modified by being extrapolated beyond their original study conditions (generalization) or by having unsupported inferences drawn from the data. Thus, in addition to being a transmission medium human factors also serves as a transformation mechanism. Human factors also becomes a selection medium because only some of the research results are utilized; many are ignored except by researchers working in the same field.

It is apparent therefore that human factors plays a significant research utilization role and that without the discipline the work performed in the individual research areas would be negatively affected, especially if one assumes, as I do, that knowledge is to be used as well as added to the "store of knowledge" that is part of society's wisdom. One might even ask whether there is anything like a store of knowledge until that knowledge can be utilized in some fashion. Knowledge without an actual or implied use is merely a collection of facts. Human factors as a discipline provides the actual or implied use for the data secured by the special interest areas.

The relationship between the research areas and human factors is feed forward, but unfortunately not feedback. Ideally, human factors would set standards describing the data and principles it needed, and researchers would concentrate their efforts "to fill the order." Specifically, human factors would establish criteria of what is usable human factors knowledge, and these criteria, to the extent that researchers heeded them, would guarantee the relevance of their results. Unfortunately, because feedback from the utilization environment is very poor, the potential for a mismatch between what research users need and what researchers provide is unacceptably high. Recommendations for what can be done about this problem will be discussed at the end of the book.

IMPLICATIONS OF THE SYSTEM CONCEPT FOR BEHAVIORAL MEASUREMENT

Chapter 1 listed implications of the system concept for human factors research. Here we shall examine these implications in greater detail—first, in relation to the way in which measurement research is conducted, and second, with regard to the topics of that research.

Implications for Measurement in General

For human factors research, there are six implications for measurement in general. The first is that *the operational system is the model for human factors measurement because it is the reference situation for human factors as a whole.* That model affects measurement in three ways:

1. At the very beginning of the measurement process, the questions asked stem from that model. The two most fundamental research questions are: What is the effect of system parameters on personnel performance? and What is the effect of personnel performance on system output? Because the system has parameters peculiar to itself, the system model requires that the researcher ask questions that might not be asked if that model did not exist.

2. The operational system is organized around its mission—a sequence of tasks progresses purposefully to an end point defined in terms of an overall system goal. Individual tasks in that mission have no meaning apart from the mission. Every system, civilian as well as military, has a mission that can be described verbally in the form of a scenario. The implication of this point for research in all situations is that the measurement should begin with an analysis of the mission scenario and should endeavor to reproduce the essential characteristics of the mission as the directing force for subject activity. (This is much easier in the operational environment.) To do this: (a) Tasks must be purposeful in terms of a larger goal—that is, they must have meaning not only in and of themselves but also in terms of implementing a larger system goal. Part-tasks or subfunctions like simple reaction to descrete stimuli are not admissible in system-oriented research unless one is studying task *mechanisms*. (b) The significance of these tasks must be meaningful to the research subject, not necessarily in terms of the subject's own personal interests, but in terms of what the subject understands the goal of task performance to be. For example, if the

investigator wants the subject to count all the patterns in a dot mosaic, the latter might be told that the mosaic represents a new means of coding mail, that the ability of humans to "read" such codes for mail-sorting is presently very questionable, that each pattern found can be classified in terms of individual geographic areas, and that the subject should work as fast and accurately as possible because the U.S. Postal Service has specified time and accuracy standards within which the sorting task must be completed. Although none of this may be strictly true, it produces more meaningful data if the task is more meaningful to the subject. Introduction of such "realism" into a measurement situation other than the operational system would undoubtedly create difficulties for the investigator because it complicates that situation. Will the reseacher find more significant performance differences than if the subject merely counted dots? In other contexts task instructions have had a signiicant effect on performance.

3. Conclusions must be replicated (validated) by measuring the same phenomena in or with operational systems in the operational environment or at the very least by some approximation of the operational system—there will be times when it is impossible to use the operational system for validation purposes. If validation is defined as testing measurement conclusions reached in the laboratory against reality, that reality for the human factors researcher is the operational system.

The logic of the system concept also suggests that the operational environment is the most desirable environment in which to perform research if one is to study human performance in a system context. However, this ignores the serious difficulties in measuring performance in that environment.

Second, in human factors research *all system-relevant factors must be included in the measurement situation.* If every system element influences every other system element to some degree, then the researcher must collect data on all of them; one cannot ignore some while concentrating on others, unless the degree of influence would probably be very slight or one already knows what the effect of an element on performance is. This system requirement would be very difficult to implement in an experimental situation because it is hardly possible to vary everything simultaneously or to control all variables other than the ones being varied. It is, however, possible to implement the requirement in a nonexperimental situation, one in which data are collected primarily by passive means—for example, by observation. In the "real world," which is not manipulated by an experimenter, all factors are automatically included in the data and function without constraint. In collecting data passively, if one thinks that the operator's motivation might be affecting performance of a particular task, for example, one would measure task performance and *concurrently* attempt to measure the operator's motivation. One accepts whatever the state of a variable is at the time of measurement, but one collects data on every variable for which it is feasible to do so.

Experimenters endeavor to include—or at least control—all the factors they think will influence subject performance. However, because they deal largely with individual performance, they include only factors that are relevant to that performance. It is also true that, if what one is attempting to measure is very molecular, system factors may be largely irrelevant. Psychophysical studies—for example, determination of minimal visual angles—do not require a system context, although they should be validated in an operational context.

The system-oriented researcher endeavors to include not only individual factors but also factors that may affect system outputs. For example, if researchers develop a measurement situation based on an information-processing system model, they might include such factors as the number and type of information channels, the types of messages, and message frequency and familiarity. If the measurement is based on a visual surveillance system model, researchers might include types of stimuli, the intensity and complexity of the stimuli, classification rules, and the like. Unfortunately, the number of variables to be included in the system-oriented measurement is a multiple of those in a nonsystem situation.

For the experimental researcher studying tasks modeled directly on those of an operational system, the major characteristics of that system must be deliberately included in the measurement. If synthetic tasks are developed, the researcher must include enough system variables to represent the system. Whatever the synthetic task situation developed by the researcher, a system model or a concept of the system of which the researcher would want the results to be representative is implicit in the task or set of tasks created by the researcher. To develop the most effective set of experimental tasks, that implicit model must be examined. Because a system is defined in large part by the interactions among its elements, the task representation will lose its system character if there are too few such interactions. The researcher must avoid the situation in which only one variable is abstracted from the operational system and used as a model for the development of task materials. This was, for example, the situation in which Bavelas (1950) in his pioneering study of communication processes abstracted only the patterning of information channels and created a methodology based solely on the arrangement of networks (e.g., Star, Circle). This representation was so limited that the results of the many network studies Bavelas initiated have been largely sterile.

If all system elements affect one another, exclusion of some from the measurement will produce an aberrant set of results. In the traditional experimental design, if the researcher excludes undesirable (e.g., potentially confounding) variables from *all* the groups being contrasted, it cancels out the effect of these variables on the measurement situation. From a system standpoint, however, exclusion of the inconvenient variables changes the way the remaining variables behave. Exclusion creates a nonoperational, and hence potentially invalid, measurement situation. The system-oriented researcher pays a price for his or her orientation. Fidelity to the operational situation becomes an additional criterion of acceptable research. It is my contention, however, that although it is difficult to include all system-relevant factors fully in a laboratory study or system simulation, it is possible to include at least the more obvious ones.

Failure to include system factors in nonsystem studies tends to produce artificial task situations. The reader may have had the experience of attempting to model a synthetic task after a real world original. In the process of cutting it down so it will fit into a "reasonable" experimental situation, it is often simplified so that it will not require extensive prior training of naive subjects, compressed so that it will fit within a thirty-minute test situation, modified so it can be presented in a group rather than an individual session (thus again saving precious time), and deprived of the essence of the real-world task so that it becomes only a symbolic analogue of the original rather than a concrete task. Nonetheless, when the study is written up for publication the researcher will claim that the results throw light on the way the original task is performed.

A third implication for human factors measurement in general is that *the effect on system output is the criterion of significance for personnel variables.* Because personnel performance is designed to support the output of the system, that output becomes the ultimate evaluational criterion. This means that if a personnel variable does not influence system output significantly it is unimportant on a system level, even though it may be significant on an individual level. Suppose, for example, one conducted an experiment in which assembly-line production is contrasted under two conditions—with piped-in music and without. Two measures are applied: ratings of job satisfaction (individual performance level), and number of units produced (system output). The difference between the music-no music conditions is highly significant statistically in terms of job satisfaction ratings, but the output measure produces only small and variable differences. The conclusion would have to be that the variable was insignificant from a system standpoint. In applying the results of the study, job satisfaction would have to be traded off against the cost of supplying the music. In true system research the specialist must measure not only personnel subsystem output but also system output, and must compare the two to determine how they are interrelated. This means that in most traditional studies where only personnel elements are varied the data have limited significance.

One cannot assume that a variable affecting individual human performance will automatically have a corresponding effect on the system output. The effect may be reduced by intervening factors that cancel it out or reduce it significantly. This often happens in large, complex systems in which chains of activity must take place before the terminal output is achieved. What might be a significant effect in a single operator system may be insignificant in a multi-operator system. This does not mean that, if an individual variable is suspected of being unimportant to the system output, one should not measure that variable, but it does mean that measurement of individual variables should be accompanied by measures of system output, so that the meaning of the individual variable can be better understood.

Fourth, because *systems are organized hierarchically with intermediate as well as terminal outputs,* human performance must be measured at all levels. In the operational environment, performance at the individual level is often separated from the system output level by time and by intervening steps with their correlated outputs. If x_1 is the individual output, and y the system output, then if

$$y = (f) x_n \ldots \ldots x_4 \cdot x_3 \cdot x_2 \cdot x_1$$

the difficulty in relating x_1 to y increases as x_n increases. Where x must be correlated with y, the more the intervening steps between the two, the lower the correlation is likely to be. On the contrary, in the usual laboratory research the time intervals between stimuli and subject response are usually quite short because researchers often cannot afford lengthy time intervals and many intervening steps and because they know that if they expand their measurement situation they are much less likely to secure significant differences or high correlations. By abbreviating the measurement situation, the researcher finds it much simpler to demonstrate significant relationships among variables. Unfortunately, because of the abbreviations produced in the experimental test situation, these relationships often bear little resemblance to operational reality.

Fifth, for human factors research *the system concept emphasizes measurement in the operational environment* for several reasons: (1) the operational system is the measurement model; (2) it is difficult (but not impossible) to include total, functioning systems in more controlled (e.g., laboratory) measurement environments; and (3) efforts to reproduce system tasks in controlled environments often lead to highly artificial situations that bear little relationship to their operational models (although this need not be so).

In collecting performance data on the system it is necessary to become familiar in advance with that system in some detail. This does not necessarily mean learning how to operate individual items of equipment, but it should involve knowledge of how the system structure is organized; hierarchical levels; communications channels; the information that is transmitted up and down channels; functions to be performed by all individuals, teams and subsystems to be scrutinized; standards of acceptable performance; intermediate and terminal outputs; data automatically recorded as part of routine system operations; measures to be applied; and the mission scenario.

The sixth implication of the system concept for human factors measurement in general is that *the system concept emphasizes evaluation of performance.* Evaluation is inherent in the system concept because it is necessary to determine whether performance standards are being or can be met. Evaluation tests must be performed continuously during system development to guide its proper development, and after the system becomes operational they must be performed during its operations to control and stabilize effective performance.

Evaluation testing represents a category of behavioral measurement that is distinctly different from the traditional hypothesis-testing of controlled experimentation. The major difference is that in evaluation one compares performance with a standard or requirement that is irrelevant to hypothesis-testing.

Implications for Experimental Research

Experimental research in human factors must be performed so that it fits into the system orientation. The type of questions, simulation requirements, and the use of teams and training sessions are all important elements.

The questions asked. The questions asked in this research should focus on the relationship between individual parameters and system parameters. For example, if the study is on the effects on performance of varying delays in providing feedback to subjects, the null hypothesis would be reformulated to read: Does increasing or decreasing feedback delay make any difference to individual *and* system performance? In this formulation the researcher does not ignore the individual, but places him or her in context with the system. The system context is supplied by organizing experimental tasks into what corresponds to a mission scenario.

Simulation requirements. To study human performance in a system context, operational or simulated equipment is not an absolute requirement in the experimental situation, because system principles apply in all types of systems— manual as well as those that are highly mechanized. It is perfectly feasible for the researcher to develop an imaginary (synthetic) system that is defined by the following, as a minimum: a mission scenario and a system output or product that is required by the synthetic system goal and that is derived by integrating and transforming outputs from one or more sources.

The researcher can develop a synthetic system in which one subject's outputs are acted on by another subject, who makes use of those outputs to develop his or her own outputs. Each such transformation process can simulate, albeit symbolically, a subsystem. One reason for including such transformations in the study is to permit evaluation of the significance of individual responses in terms of their effect on a higher order output. Transformations can be effected by requiring some form of output coding or recoding or by making the first subject's responses one of the bases of a decision made by the second subject.

The researcher may of course run into difficulty in simulating the one-man system (e.g., a single-seat aircraft) in which the transformation occurs solely at the individual level. Transformations in one-man systems must be accomplished with the aid of machine functions that make it difficult to simulate such systems economically. Where the transformation is accomplished solely on a manual basis, it may be "cleaner" because the researcher need not take machine interactions with behavioral processes into account, but it is somewhat unrepresentative of the many transformations that do make use of machines.

Presumably, the more transformations in a system, the more complex the system and its synthetic analogue, but a very simple system can be represented by a single transformation.

Transformations can occur at all system levels, between levels, and within the same level. They often occur sequentially, as when information must be gathered from subordinate levels, and interpreted and integrated by superior levels. Transformations are related to the allocation of functions and superior-inferior levels of authority, but they are most likely to occur at points in the system at which different individuals (in a team) or different subsystems inter-act—that is, where an output from one function, team or subsystem must interact with another.

Teams. System simulation strongly emphasizes team situations, because most operational systems of any complexity are multioperator systems. Moreover, the simplest way of accomplishing a transformation experimentally is to have personnel operate on each other's outputs.

Training. Operational systems are exercised by relatively well trained crews. The common practice of employing subjects who are relatively unfamiliar with the tasks they are to perform is completely unacceptable to system-oriented research. Measurement of naive subject performance merely determines how long it takes subjects to learn new tasks. Often such subjects have not fully learned their tasks by the time performance is measured. The employment of naive subjects also requires construction of highly abstracted, simplistic tasks, which must be simple if they are not to require prolonged training sessions. Subjects' performance under these conditions cannot be extrapolated to that of operational personnel.

If the task to be performed is an actual operational one, then operational personnel trained in that task must be secured; if a synthetic, or artificial, task is employed, subjects must be given extensive training on that task before testing begins. A series of tasks performed in the context of a simulated mission means that the subject will have to learn several interrelated tasks, and because the tasks will be meaningful ones the usual practice of giving, say, a fixed number of training trials (e.g., twenty) or training to criterion when the criterion is something as absurd as one perfect trial, will not do.

SUMMARY

Although a number of disciplines have made significant contributions to human factors, the disciplines of psychology and engineering have been most important. Psychology is responsible for much of human factors methodology, data, and concepts; engineering is responsible for providing the context in which most human factors applications are made. Nevertheless, certain characteristics not only differentiate human factors from other behavioral sciences, but also make it a unique science.

Only human factors among behavioral disciplines incorporates both behavioral and physical elements and participates actively in system development. The need to act as a bridge between the behavioral and physical sciences has significant implications for human factors research and practice. Human factors distinguishes between behavior and performance and, unlike psychology, is interested only in the human being's work performance and what influences that performance. In contrast to psychology, human factors emphasizes purpose as an explanatory mechanism and is linked inextricably to technology. Evaluation, which demands standards, is central to human factors measurement, but not to psychology. Human factors is committed to the system as an organizing concept, but psychology is not. That concept has certain implications for human factors measurement that render human factors measurement practices different from those of psychology.

CHAPTER 3

The Role of Human Factors in System Development

System development is the major area of application for human factors. Behavioral principles are applied in other areas, such as safety (Adams, Barlow, and Hiddlestein 1981) and quality control (Harris and Chaney 1969), but these are only minor compared with applications to the design of equipment and systems.

This chapter covers the following as they affect the discipline: (1) The process of *system development* as performed in the United States and in military system acquisition. The major limitation of this description is that we have little or no information about system development in commercial industry or in Europe, which may be somewhat different. (2) The *design process* (the ways in which design can be conceptualized behaviorally) that is part of system development. (3) The *design transformation* process (deriving behavioral implications of and equivalents for system dimensions). (4) The *engineering environment* in which the practitioner interacts with the designer and how that environment affects the former's ability to apply behavioral knowledge.

THE RATIONALE FOR BEHAVIORAL DESIGN IN SYSTEM DEVELOPMENT

System development includes two concurrent processes: design of the primary system (the hardware and software) and its support subsystems (e.g., training, technical data, personnel selection), and testing and evaluation of the system. Behavioral design is the application of human factors principles to system and equipment design. The rationale for this application is that because systems are developed by and for people it is necessary to make those systems as behaviorally effective as possible.

The participation of human factors in system development has important implications for what human factors does in both research and practice. If human factors participates in development, the discipline is obliged to ensure that, whatever other utility its research has, that research must be performed in such a way that its outputs are relevant and useful to development. Logically, behavioral research should be translated into principles and data appropriate to system development. Otherwise, one has what is unfortunately the present situation—an unacceptable gap between the discipline's research and application functions.

An additional rationale for system development work is that behavioral design increases the scope of human factors. The analyses and evaluations applied to system development are the only methods indigenous to human factors, because its research methodology has been largely taken over from psychology.

HUMAN FACTORS APPLICATION

The practitioner applies behavioral principles, data, and methods to design. What is meant by application?

Application involves the transmission of information from the practitioner to the designer for inclusion in design outputs. This transmission takes place in two forms: as general behavioral information of value to design as a whole, and as specific inputs to individual design projects. The general information seeks to educate the engineer in the principles of behavioral design and thereby influence his or her usual design procedures. The input seeks to modify the design of a particular piece of equipment or system. In both cases the information provided can be utilized by the designer or not. Utilization determines whether the application is successful.

Most general behavioral information is provided in design handbooks describing human factors engineering (e.g., Woodson 1981; Van Cott and Kinkade, 1972). The audience for this material consists of engineers everywhere. The information provider has no idea of the impact that information will have because no design decision or change in response to that information is required of anyone. Such general information is often ignored by the target audience (Meister and Farr 1967). This type of application is very weak and is not application as most practitioners think of application.

The transmission of specific inputs to the engineer in form of analyses, evaluations, interpretations, and recommendations in order to influence a specific design is application (see Rouse and Boff 1987). However, merely providing a design input without knowing whether the designer has seriously considered it, represents only a slight step beyond general information. If the designer does seriously consider a behavioral input, we may think of it as application even though the input does not finally make it into design. There is no question about application if the behavioral input is incorporated into design or influences the final configuration of that design. One can distinguish between incorporation and influence; in the former, the practitioner recommends a specific design change which is accepted; in the latter, the practitioner reports, for example, a test result that eventuates in a design change, whether or not the change is recommended by the practitioner.

The distinction between information and input is important for human factors research. If application means merely the transmission of general behavioral information to engineers, whether or not they use that information, then the practitioner need not be concerned with the engineer's design process, his or her biases, the engineering context, or, most important, the relevance and utility of the information provided. "Here is the information. Take it or not. Do what you want with it."

This is the easiest attitude for specialists to adopt, because the question of research relevance to system development or the effect of behavioral inputs on design then need never arise. But this definition of application is clearly not sufficient, because the purpose of the practitioner's work is not to sell handbooks but to influence design.

If, however, the term *application* is reserved only for behavioral inputs that are specifically incorporated into design, practitioners run the risk that their efforts will be considered as having low utility. This is because only a minority of all engineering inputs are ordinarily incorporated into design and it is usually impossible to determine which design features were influenced by which input. A devil's advocate might say that it is the engineer's responsibility to make use of these inputs and that the practitioner has no responsibility beyond merely providing them, but this is incorrect. Once one attempts to apply something, one must be concerned about the success of the application and the reasons for that success. The advocate might also suggest that it is generally impossible to determine whether the engineer has seriously considered an input. However, formal inputs usually generate formal replies, and practitioners can usually infer from interactions with designers how much attention has been paid to their efforts.

Factors involved in success or failure in influencing design—practitioner-designer relationships and behavioral research relevancy—will be discussed later.

CHARACTERISTICS OF SYSTEM DEVELOPMENT

The development process starts from broad molar functions and works to progressively more molecular tasks and subtasks. Consequently, actions taken at earlier, more molar (system, subsystem) levels have profound consequences for molecular (task, subtask, component) levels. For example, if the developer decides in preliminary design that information will be presented via a CRT, the developer must in detail design face all the problems involved in using a CRT— including display brightness, resolution, ambient lighting, and the like. This is why human factors insists on being part of the design team from the beginning of development. Test and evaluation proceeds in reverse, from testing of components, modules, and equipments to testing of the total system—operational testing.

Unless the system being developed is very simple, the development process may appear to the practitioner to be confused and only indirectly related to its ultimate purpose. That is because design is not a linear process, no matter how it may appear when described in words. For example, during detail design the practitioner may do a workload analysis and discover that the operator will be overloaded. This may require a return to function allocation, perhaps with a view to automating certain functions that had not been automated. It is also possible that in considering training requirements and programs the practitioner and the system engineer may decide that training is too costly. This may require revisiting earlier stages of system design to make operation easier and so reduce training requirements. There are feedback loops in development—it rarely proceeds in a neat, straightforward way.

THE DESIGN ENVIRONMENT

The environment in which development takes place is vastly different from that to which most behavioral specialists have been exposed in their training. The training environment of most practitioners is the university, within which research is primary. Research is characterized by the slow, deliberate, systematic order of topics addressed and the accretion of knowledge that does not have to satisfy immediate utility requirements, but the engineering environment is frenetic, time-stressed, pragmatic, and utilitarian. Consequently, when novice practitioners are introduced to the engineering world they often experience a "culture shock" to which most eventually adapt but which they always retain to some degree.

The difference between the research environment and the application environment is important because it is in some degree responsible for difficulty in applying behavioral research to system development. The research product— the journal article or research report—is traditionally designed to be utilized slowly, deliberately, and systematically and is directed toward conclusions phrased in generalities. By contrast, the development environment requires a high degree of specificity—for example, numerical precision. There is consequently a dissonance between the research product and the environment in which it will be applied. In addition, this dissonance makes it more difficult to apply behavioral methodology, because that methodology has also been developed in accordance with research criteria and assumes that development is linear, single-thread, and systematic, whereas in most cases it is not.

SYSTEM REQUIREMENTS AS FORCING FUNCTIONS

System requirements drive the design tasks that are performed during development. A system requirement might say (although probably in many more words): "Develop a man-portable word processor that can also be used while traveling in an aircraft or train." The system requirement is usually a formal written document, which means that development requires translation of its words and graphics into hardware, software, technical data, and procedures. The practitioner, along with the designer, uses the system requirement both as the starting point for developmental analyses and to confirm the adequacy of design outputs.

Most system requirements emphasize physical performance; behavioral provisions are almost never included. This means that the practitioner's initial task is to deduce from the physical requirement what is expected of system personnel. Failure to describe behavioral requirements in the design specification or development contract also makes it more difficult for the practitioner to secure adequate consideration of his or her inputs.

SYSTEM DEVELOPMENT AS DISCOVERY

System requirements can be implemented in different ways. In one study (Meister, Sullivan, and Askren, 1968), six system engineers were presented with the same specification. Six different designs were produced, each satisfying the requirement, although probably not equally well, depending on the criteria each designer applied.

Because the same design requirement can be implemented in different ways, the design process involves selection of one of a number of alternative configurations that could best satisfy the system requirement. If the selection process is performed properly, it requires the application of human factors criteria—for example, one of the bases of selection should be how easy it will be for personnel to exercise or maintain the system.

Initially the behavioral implications of system requirements may be unclear to the practitioner. For example, the workload that personnel will be exposed to depends a great deal on the designer's choice of equipment mechanisms. An automatic system usually demands less of the operator than a manual system does. As choices among design options are made, the unknown aspects of the system are clarified until, after the system is installed, almost everything about it is known.

SYSTEM DEVELOPMENT AS TRANSFORMATION

System development is the transformation of system requirements into physical mechanisms to satisfy those requirements. For the engineer, the transformation is solely within the physical domain. For the practitioner, the transformation is somewhat more complex—from the physical requirement to the behavioral implications of that requirement to the physical mechanisms for implementing those behavioral implications. Behavioral requirements must be inferred from a concept of how the system should function ideally—for example, the system should not impose too heavy a burden on its personnel, or the pilot of an aircraft should have adequate visibility outside the cockpit.

An absurdly simplistic example of a behavioral implication is as follows: The practitioner asks himself or herself, What does it mean that a hand-held display must be operated under water by divers wearing heavy diving clothing? Diving gloves are large and clumsy, so it would be advisable to make controls larger to accommodate the clumsiness. And visibility under water will be sharply restricted, so displays should be as bright as possible. This example is relatively obvious, but others are by no means so simple. For example, operators in a command and control system may be required to correlate several channels of information presented in overlapping fashion. Will they be overloaded? What is the probability that significant error would result from the correlation requirement? What physical mechanisms should be recommended for reducing the likelihood of errors resulting from this requirement? The practitioner is engaged in this process of implication/transformation throughout system development.

THE SYSTEM DEVELOPMENT CYCLE

The phases that system development follows are quite logical and derive from the manner in which design is carried out. The Department of Defense has special names for these phases, but we will use those that inherently describe what goes on in them: system planning, preliminary design, detail design, test and evaluation, production, and once the system has been turned over to the owners, operation. Consumer system development follows much the same sequence, again with the caveat that much development is nonlinear. Sometimes it is necessary to back up and start again.

In *system planning,* the major activity is identification and definition of the need for the system, including surveying available technology to identify areas of technical inadequacy in the proposed system.

In *preliminary design,* alternative system concepts are identified. System design and developmental tests are initiated, a test and evaluation master plan is created, requests for proposal for downstream engineering development are written, and prototypes of equipment being developed are constructed.

In *detail design,* full-scale engineering development of the system is performed and production planning begins. The developmental tests of the preceding phase are continued.

In *production and deployment,* the complete system is fabricated. The first production items are exposed to highly realistic *operational testing* to determine whether the system satisfies performance requirements. If these requirements are satisfied, the system is turned over to the owner and it goes into *operation*.

BEHAVIORAL ACTIVITIES DURING DEVELOPMENT

Behavioral design involves a series of analyses and evaluations that parallel and interact with analyses and tests performed by engineers. Department of Defense document MIL-H-46855B entitled "Human Engineering Requirements for Military Systems" (1979), requires that, *as appropriate* for a particular project, the following be undertaken: definition and allocation of system functions; information flow and processing analysis; estimates of potential operator/maintainer processing capabilities; identification of human roles; task analysis; analysis of critical tasks; workload analysis; studies, experiments, laboratory tests; development of mockups and models; dynamic simulation; application of human factors to preliminary and detail design; and test and evaluation of design.

The Army's MANPRINT program (Elton 1986), which has only recently been initiated, requires much the same set of activities but requires them earlier in system development. The term "as appropriate" used with reference to the Defense Department's MIL-H-46855B was emphasized because it describes a major qualification to these activities. The type and number of human factors activities in any single development project will vary according to the complexity of the project, whether there is a predecessor system for the one being designed, and which behavioral analyses and evaluations performed on that predecessor system generalize to the new one. For minor developments that represent only modest changes in design, some human factors activities might be inappropriate—a very new, complex system might well demand all of them. The selection of appropriate activities is a matter of practitioner judgment, need perceived by development management, funding, and time availability. How much the practitioner will do often depends on management attitude toward the discipline; the qualification in MIL H-46855B can be used by an ill-disposed manager to restrict human factors activities unduly.

The tasks specified in MIL-H-46855B are required because each system development phase raises behavioral questions that must be answered (see Table 3.1). The activities performed to answer these questions are listed in abbreviated form in Table 3.2. Those who want to know more about the analyses and evaluations in Table 3.2 should refer to Meister (1985b). The behavioral questions in Table 3.1 have certain implications for human factors. The activities discussed below follow Table 3.2.

Table 3.1 Behavioral Questions Arising in System Development

System Planning
1. Assuming a predecessor system, what changes in the new system from the configuration of the predecessor system mandate changes in numbers and types of personnel, their selection, their training, and methods of system operation?

Preliminary Design
2. Which of the various design options available at this time is most effective from a behavioral standpoint?
3. Will system personnel in these options be able to perform all required functions effectively without excessive workload?
4. What factors are potential sources of difficulty or error, and can these be eliminated or modified in the design?

Detail Design
5. Which is the better or best of the design options proposed?
6. What level of personnel performance can one achieve with each design configuration, and does this level satisfy system requirements?
7. Will personnel encounter excessive workload, and what can be done about it?
8. What training should be provided to personnel to achieve a specified level of performance?
9. Are (a) hardware/software, (b) procedures, (c) technical data, and (d) total job design adequately engineered from the human point of view?

Test and Evaluation
10. Are system personnel able to do their jobs effectively?
11. Does the system satisfy its personnel requirements?
12. Have all system dimensions affected by behavioral variables been properly engineered from the human point of view?
13. What design inadequacies must be rectified?

Source: Meister 1982.

HUMAN FACTORS ACTIVITIES IN SYSTEM DEVELOPMENT

A major activity during system planning is to determine which novel characteristics of the follow-on system will have a significant effect on personnel. This requires the practitioner to examine the relationship between system characteristics and human performance. At present this relationship can be expressed only qualitatively—that is, in terms of more or less or a greater or smaller effect. For example, it is impossible to say that characteristic x will have the effect of slowing operator response by 18 percent or of increasing workload by 15 percent. The practitioner's inability to do this results from a failure of research to support the practitioner.

In preliminary design, the practitioner contributes to and analyzes initial design outlines. Along with Rouse (1985), the author conceives of that design as a problem-solving process. Because the optimal system configuration is not immediately obvious when one begins design, the process has four major stages: formulation of the design problem, generation of alternative design solutions, analysis and evaluation of these alternatives, and selection of a preferred alternative.

Table 3.2 Human Factors Activities in System Development

System planning
1. Review engineering planning documents to ensure that behavioral factors have been considered
2. Review predecessor system behavioral analyses and other documentation
3. Compare predecessor system and proposed system in terms of number and type of personnel required, new training needed, and other behavioral factors
4. Predict areas of significant behavioral impact and difficulty
5. Perform the following analyses (optional):
   a. Mission analysis
   b. Determination of functions

Preliminary design
1. Continue performance of mission and function analysis
2. As required, perform the following analyses:
   a. Function allocation
   b. Behavioral trade studies
   c. Task description/identification
   d. Task analysis
   e. Special analyses (e.g., information flow, workload)
   f. Develop human factors section of test and evaluation master plan
3. Review and critique proposed designs

Detail design
1. Review and evaluate human-machine interface design drawings and procedures
2. Perform detailed behavioral trade studies
3. Recommend equipment features and control/display hardware to designers
4. Participate in design reviews
5. Make quantitative predictions of personnel performance
6. Update human factors section of test and evaluation master plan
7. Develop training requirements and program
8. Construct mockups and conduct mockup tests
9. Participate in developmental tests

Production
1. Conduct human factors part of operational tests
2. Evaluate and recommend system improvement modifications

Source: Modified from Parks and Springer 1975.

The conceptualization of a new design should be accompanied by a mission/function analysis. The centerpiece of mission analysis is development of a scenario or description of the sequential events in system operation, assuming the new design is implemented. The scenario as initially developed in preliminary design is essentially a broad outline of how the total system and subsystems function; later, as design becomes more molecular, it is expanded and the details describing equipments and modules within equipments fill in the gaps. In preliminary design, the scenario describes functions and gross tasks; in detail design, the scenario will describe more molecular tasks and subtasks. The practitioner's analytic activity is paralleled by a comparable engineering analysis. For the engineer, the scenario describes physical (e.g., electronic) processes. For example, control of multiple signals transmitted over a fiber-optic cable in the system is hypothesized in terms of how a microprocessor distribution network functions.

Ideally, the practitioner is part of the design team formulating the design problem and generating alternative solutions. Much of this formulation occurs informally in brainstorming sessions, and the practitioner contributes to the extent that his or her engineering knowledge and creativity will permit. On a more formal basis, the practitioner is responsible for determining which design solution is best from a human performance standpoint. This requires an analysis of the alternatives in terms of the human performance to be anticipated with each alternative. The alternatives will take one of the forms described in Table 3.3. Given alternative mechanisms for performing machine and human functions, what human/system performance can be expected of each alternative? The practitioner would like to be able to assign a success or error probability to each alternative, but this is impossible because the capability to predict human performance or to determine the quantitative relationship between system characteristics and performance is lacking. The most the practitioner can do is look for system activities that may overload the operator and point these out to the designer. The analyses listed in Table 3.2 (e.g., information flow, workload) help identify these, but again largely in qualitative terms that limit their usefulness. The practitioner is able to answer the question, "Will personnel perform effectively?" only in very general terms. If there are no obvious behavioral discrepancies in the design, the practitioner will say, "Yes, personnel will be able to perform." This promise is, however, based on very inadequate evidence.

There have probably been some design drawings in preliminary design, and in detail design the number of these will increase as design becomes more molecular. Again, the major question the practitioner must ask is: Which is the best design, behaviorally, and will system personnel be able to perform effectively? This question requires the behavioral analyst to define what is meant by "effectively." The only reasonable way to answer a question dealing with effectiveness is in terms of a quantitative performance metric (e.g., number of errors or predicted probability of mission success), because system effectiveness is performance-oriented. To say which of several design options is best from a behavioral standpoint is to ask: "What will be the effect of this (or that) design feature on operator performance or on personnel reacting to that feature? Given that operator performance, what will be its effect on task or system performance?"

When one attempts to determine factors that are potential error sources, this implies that there is some sort of quantitative relationship between design features and operator performance. Very often data for these relationships do not exist, and so in evaluating a design drawing the practitioner uses a checklist of desired characteristics to judge whether the equipment has those characteristics. Such checklists are useful primarily as memory prompts for the practi-

Table 3.3 Illustration of Alternative Human-Machine Configurations in System Development

Alternative 1 (Operator Primarily)	Alternative 2 (Human-Machine Mix)	Alternative 3 (Machine Primarily)
Sonarman detects target signal on scope, examines brightness, shape, recurrence, movement, etc., and reports "probable submarine" target or "nonsubmarine" target	Sonarman detects target signal on scope. Associated computer also detects signal, records it, and searches library of standard signals. Computer displays to sonarman original signal and comparison signal on sonar gear, together with the probability of its being a submarine. Sonarman decides on basis of his own analysis and computer information whether target signal is submarine or nonsubmarine and reports accordingly.	When a signal having a strength above a specified threshold is received by the sonar array, a computer associated with the detection apparatus automatically records the signal; analyzes its strength, brightness, recurrence, etc., according to preprogrammed algorithms; compares it with a library of standard sonar signals; and displays an indicator reading "probable submarine."
Operator Functions 1. Detection of signal	*Operator Functions* 1. Detection of signal	*Operator Functions* 1. Take action on receipt of "probable submarine" signal
2. Analysis of signal 3. Decision-making 4. Reporting of decision	2. Analysis of signal 3. Decision-making 4. Reporting of decision	
Machine Functions 1. Display of signal	*Machine Functions* 1. Detection of signal 2. Recording of signal 3. Searching for comparison signals 4. Analysis of signal 5. Display of information	*Machine Functions* 1. Detection of signal 2. Analysis of signal 3. Decision-making 4. Display of conclusion

Source: Meister 1971.

tioner, but unless a deviation from "good" human engineering practice is relatively obvious in the drawing, this kind of evaluation does not really evaluate. These qualifications suggest that the human factors activities performed in response to the questions in Table 3.1 are performed somewhat inadequately.

The one area in which human factors can feel relatively confident is in test and evaluation (measurement) because there one is dealing with relatively concrete events. The aim of test and evaluation, especially in operational testing of the entire system, is to provide a quantitative evaluation of personnel performance as it relates to system output. This means that the practitioner should be able to assign a probability of correct performance to all human activities in the system. Ideally one should be able to say that the personnel subsystem contributes 25 percent or 50 percent or ―― to system output.

Human factors cannot do this. Quite apart from problems of developing criteria and measures, which will be discussed in a later chapter, the practitioner lacks the ability to quantize performance at levels higher than the individual or group task. What the practitioner does most often in operational testing is check whether individual tasks are performed correctly and observe whether personnel manifest obvious performance difficulties. The behavioral part of most final test reports usually describes only human engineering discrepancies and the performance incidents associated with them. If human factors research is to aid in the analyses and evaluations of Table 3.2, its central theme must be the relationship between the physical and behavioral domains. More specifically, that research (whatever the specific topic studied) must address the effect of equipment or system design features on performance. Currently behavioral design is a matter of recommending as a design input one or two discrete molecular features, such as those found in Schneiderman (1985) or Smith and Mosier (1986), for example, computer menus should contain no more than N choices. We lack a set of fundamental behavioral design principles which would permit the practitioner to look at design in a holistic manner. Although function analysis views the system holistically, this analysis is too molar to affect physical processes directly.

System development catalyzes and enforces the relationship between research and application; it reinforces the value of controlled experimentation to study the relationship between individual design features and personnel performance, while emphasizing the importance of making that experimentation similar to operational testing. It can be argued that the special aspects of the human factors concept structure are distinguishable from general scientific concepts only, or largely, because of system development, that the peculiar characteristics of system development endow the human factors conceptual framework with its most distinctive characteristics.

DEVELOPMENTAL CONSTRAINTS

System development is often performed under severe constraints, the most important of which are *time* and *cost*. Because there are so many unknowns that must be clarified, system development is time-driven. There is never enough time for the practitioner to do the analyses, studies, and evaluations he or she would do if unrestrained. In this respect, system development must be considered a degraded process. The implication for human factors is that the behavioral methods it applies to system development must be capable of functioning in a much less than optimal environment and must be robust, relatively insensitive to variations in engineering conditions, and capable of supplying useful results with contaminated or insufficient information.

With regard to cost, if project money is tight there may not be a human factors program at all, or it may be severely curtailed. There will be fewer analyses and evaluations than desirable. Alternatively, the human factors program may be aborted early in order to reallocate the money to another—supposedly more important—development effort that is suffering financially. Moreover, a behavioral recommendation cannot be too costly to implement lest it be automatically rejected (unless it is critical to development).

These constraints cause practitioners to develop an attitude of pragmatism ("make do") that tends to conflict with their concept of what they ought to do as "scientists."

BEHAVIORAL INPUTS

Behavioral inputs during development may consist of four types; the word *may* indicates that the practitioner may not be required or may not be able to provide all these inputs. Top priority in the list below is always given to inputs that are related to a specific design problem, followed very closely by test results. Behavioral inputs include:

1. Inputs affecting the design of the system hardware, software, and procedures, the intent being to ensure that these development products satisfy at least minimal standards. These inputs can include design recommendations and/or review and evaluation of human-machine interfaces (usually displays and control panels), computer software, job procedures, and technical data; specification of required working environment characteristics (e.g., lighting and workplace layout); and prediction of personnel performance.

2. Inputs related to evaluating the operational effectiveness of personnel—writing test plans, including specification of personnel performance criteria and measures; statistical and experimental designs; design, review, and evaluation of test scenarios; conduct of personnel performance tests; analysis of test data; and development of conclusions and writing of test reports.

3. Inputs relating to the selection of system personnel—determination of the number of personnel required by the system, description of the jobs to be performed in the new system, description of the skills and skill levels required of operating and maintenance personnel.

4. Inputs relating to personnel training—specification of the curriculum content and its length in time; number of students in the course; equipment facilities (e.g., trainers, simulators, plant) and instructors needed for training.

Inputs to development come from several sources: the engineer primarily responsible for the design of a particular equipment, other engineers supporting the primary engineer, and nonengineering support sources (among which one finds the practitioner). These inputs compete with one another, sometimes because they are incongruous but more often because of their demands for the designer's attention. They are examined by the responsible designer or the design team, if one is involved, to ensure that they add some increment of performance capability and do not conflict with the system requirement or some other feature of the system or involve a constraint that must be taken into account in design. Because behavioral factors are considered constraints by designers, they are important because engineers are very sensitive to constraints. For example, unless the pilot's eyesight is accommodated in the design of his instruments, performance of the aircraft will be degraded. Behavioral factors must impose a significant constraint on system performance or they will not be accepted; minor constraints receive short shrift.

Physical design characteristics in which designers are most interested must be linked with anticipated operator performance, preferably in quantitative form. Human factors in its application to system development can be very broadly, albeit simplistically, summarized in an equation:

Operator performance $= (f)$ system/equipment design features

The equation should be phrased quantitatively because the design engineer is much more likely to accept behavioral inputs when they are phrased quantitatively. If the practitioner says, "This design feature will produce better performance," the engineer will probably respond, "*How much* better performance?" The designer is even more likely to ask this question if there is some cost, however trifling, to pay for including the recommended design feature in the system; design is very often a matter of trading off one feature for another, or paying for that feature in terms of space or complexity or money, for example. Unless designers can be convinced that a behavioral recommendation will produce some value—primarily in equipment performance but at least in human performance—they are not likely to accept that recommendation.

THE DESIGN PROCESS IN SYSTEM DEVELOPMENT

The characteristics of the design process significantly influence the practitioner's success in ensuring that design inputs are accepted. It is difficult for human factors to aid design effectively without understanding how the engineer designs, because any aid provided must interface with and match the engineer's design strategy. Difficulties in getting the engineer to incorporate behavioral inputs into design result in part from a discrepancy between these inputs and that process. Unfortunately, much of what the engineer does when he or she designs is unknown, because the process is largely cognitive and thus covert. The effect is that there is a random element in the behavioral input to design— sometimes it matches the designer's cognitive process, sometimes it does not.

It is impossible to be confident about describing the design process. Any conceptual model of that process, however apparently reasonable, must be highly speculative; empirical data describing how the engineer designs are sparse. A few data about the role of human factors in design have been collected by the author, his associates, and others (see Lintz, Askren and Lott 1971; Meister 1971; Meister and Farr 1967; Meister et al. 1968, 1969a, 1969b), but we need to know much more. An excellent source, but one which still leaves much unanswered, is Rouse and Boff (1987).

Some analyses that designers perform are almost unconscious. In any event they are very often informal. In fact, engineers may be only partially aware of how they think because they tend not to analyze their own processes. Consequently, some design steps may be skipped or compressed, certain design questions may remain unanswered, and the engineer's biases are allowed a freer rein than would otherwise be the case.

Engineers are experience-oriented. They will, all other things being equal, tend to repeat design approaches and solutions previously found effective. This tendency is exacerbated by the fact that most new design is not revolutionary but builds incrementally on past technology in the form of predecessor systems. There is nothing unusual or wrong with the experience orientation, but it may cause the designer to focus on particular design alternatives because they fit his or her experience and to ignore other possibilities because they do not. Engineers also are often intuitive in their thinking, failing to think out design solutions fully. The criteria used to analyze candidate solutions usually or often do not include behavioral aspects, and this may result in the selected alternative being inadequate from a human factors standpoint. In addition, the engineers' urge to come to grips with the hardware or software-specific aspects of design as quickly as possible often causes them to short-change the analytic aspects that should precede hardware or software design. Moreover, when designers lack necessary information, they often do not know where to find it. (See also Klein and Brezovic 1987). All this does not mean that the designer will necessarily develop an inadequate design—although this has happened, particularly from a behavioral standpoint—but the existence of such tendencies makes an effective design solution more difficult to achieve.

The engineer usually functions as a leader of a team of designers, together with support personnel, such as practitioners, who have a relevant interest in that design. The engineer generates design solutions both individually and as a team member, and also receives inputs and critiques from other team members. The team leader receives and passes upon these inputs, acting almost as a goalie in a hockey game, batting away (rejecting) all inputs except those that he or she judges will make a significant difference to the performance capability, reliability, cost, or development time of an equipment item. It is important to realize that the more criteria the designer has to apply to these inputs, the more difficult design decisions become. Consequently, the designer would prefer to ignore inputs that are least relevant to the primary design problem. Although engineering is based on quantitative foundations, design is at bottom a highly judgmental process in which all the engineer's biases and predelictions have the opportunity to influence the final configuration.

The designer tends to divide design inputs into two categories: those that pertain to the primary hardware/software system being developed, and those that relate to any auxiliary subsystems or system aspects that merely support the primary system. The latter, among which are counted human factors, are considered of lesser importance and therefore receive lesser attention.

What this means practically is that whatever the designer is provided with (information, data, principles) should be related as much as possible to the design of the primary system. Such inputs achieve greater credibility in the engineer's eyes if the specialist manifests in the input a certain degree of familiarity with the physical processes and considerations involved in the design. Practitioners consider that this gives the input "credibility," which biases the designer to accept that input. Developing this credibility may be difficult if one lacks an engineering background. In any event, the kind of behavioral inputs the engineer understands best—even though he or she may not like them—are those that constrain the design (e.g., a maximum number of personnel for which equipment is to be designed) or that deal with concrete system operations. A behavioral input that has implications only for personnel selection or training would be considered by most designers to have only slight relevance to their primary design problem. Such inputs should be related to the performance of the primary system.

Engineers apply these criteria of relative input importance on their own because they are not part of system requirements (i.e., not written down anywhere). But engineers also take their cue from management. If the latter emphasizes the importance of behavioral design, engineers will adopt the same philosophy. The practical result of the designer's characteristic response to behavioral inputs is that the behavioral material provided often tends not to be used. As a result, the specialist, having usually been trained in a university tradition, which emphasizes verbal indoctrination, tends to feel that indifference to behavioral design can be overcome by verbal indoctrination of the designer.

How does one find out more about how the engineer designs? Studies performed so far have used three methods: First, in the structured design exercise, or simulation, a design problem developed by the researcher is presented to the individual engineer for solution. The major variables in studies using this technique (e.g., Meister and Sullivan 1967; Meister, Sullivan, and Askren 1968; Lintz, Askren, and Lott 1971) were the presence or absence and nature of human factors data made available to the engineer subjects.

In the second method, as utilized by Meister and Farr (1967), Rogers and Armstrong (1977), and Rogers and Pegden (1977), engineer subjects are presented with selected types of behavioral data. Typically this information has been extracted from existing data documentation (Van Cott and Kinkade [1972]) and developed in alternative formats (Meister and Sullivan 1967). The variables in studies using this technique have been types of information and formats. Measurement consisted of assessing the engineers' preferences for alternative formats and their ability to extract the "correct" information from the various types of data presentations. The results of these studies suggest that designers are more receptive to data phrased in quantitative, graphic, or tabular terms than to data that are qualitative and verbal, and that they resist complex verbalisms, probably because they are not verbally fluent. In addition, because engineers are relatively indifferent to abstract, general inputs, preferring that all inputs relate very specifically to their design problem, most general written human factors materials are in effect rendered useless for engineering indoctrination purposes.

In the third method, groups of "experts" are asked about the importance of behavioral factors on system design or operation (see Whalen and Askren 1974; Potempa, Lintz, and Luckew 1975). Skill is one of the most important of these factors because a high skill requirement on the operator of equipment drives up the personnel cost associated with the system. These studies demonstrated that operational personnel can estimate the impact of certain types of system/equipment characteristics on the numbers and types of personnel required (Potter, Korkan, Dieterly 1975; Potempa, Lintz, and Luckew 1975; Whalen and Askren 1974). On the other hand, engineers appear to have relatively few and nondifferentiated concepts of skill, although they consider that equipment maintenance requires a higher level of skill, oriented primarily on cognitive capabilities, whereas operating tasks require lesser psychomotor abilities.

Does behavioral data have an impact on designers? Meister, Sullivan, and Askren (1968) concluded that manpower quantity and personnel skill constraint data do have an impact on the equipment configuration, but not as much as one would wish.

Lintz, Askren, and Lott (1971) found a negative correlation ($-.32$) between utilization of human factors data by designers and experience, which suggests that younger, less experienced engineers are more receptive to behavioral concepts; data related to costs and numbers were considered almost three times more valuable than data related to skill type or personnel availability. However, these authors consider that although designers will include behavioral data in engineering design trade studies, the trade-off process depends on the personal style of the engineer.

Design has been conceptualized (Rouse 1985) as the formulation of a problem (What can be done to satisfy system requirements?), the generation of alternative solutions to that problem, analysis of these alternatives, and selection of the most effective one. During this process, which is repeated throughout development, designers ask various questions of themselves. For example, in problem formulation: What is the new system or equipment supposed to do? What functions and tasks must be performed? What system elements are fixed—that is, already determined by fiat? What information about system elements is needed? Does the problem resemble one the designer has previously encountered? In analyzing the alternative solutions that have been generated, the designer should ask: What criteria apply to the problem? What constraints have an impact on the alternatives? What alternative parameters can be traded off? What are the similarities and differences among alternatives? In selecting the preferred solution, the designer asks: What are the advantages and disadvantages of each alternative?

The engineering answers to these questions, which are asked in large part informally and unsystematically, are provided largely by engineering knowledge and designer experience. These questions must also be answered by the practitioner, but through formal analyses. The mission, function, and task analyses referred to earlier help determine what the system must do and what functions and tasks must be performed. The practitioner supplies behavioral information about criteria and constraints and the behavioral parameters that can or cannot be traded off for equipment characteristics. The practitioner attempts to indicate the behavioral advantages and disadvantages of each alternative.

From the standpoint of the questions to be answered, design can be viewed as a process of information-gathering and transmission. It is also one of problem-solving, creativity, and decision-making, but in all these functions information is the one crucial element.

The designer relies on practitioners as an information source. The information that the latter are expected to provide describes equipment and human performance relationships. In turn, practitioners depend on research performed by others for that information because they have neither time, money, nor opportunity to perform the research themselves. As we have seen from earlier discussions, those research outputs somehow miss their target. Rouse (1985) insists that for information to be perceived as valuable it must reduce uncertainty, and there is much uncertainty during the design process. As long as the practitioner's information is qualitative, it reduces uncertainty only very slightly, and the engineer discounts its value.

DESIGN TRANSFORMATIONS

Because transformation is the essence of engineering design, it is also at the heart of behavioral design. There are three types of behavioral transformation: dimensional equivalence, behavioral analysis, and developmental transformation.

Dimensional Equivalence

We assume that each piece of physical equipment or job dimension has an individual probability of error or probability of successful performance associated with it. The dimension does not necessarily cause the error or operator response; all we know about it is that the dimension is associated with the error or the response. A *dimension* is a parameter or characteristic of a piece of equipment, task, or procedure. For example, the parameters or dimensions of

Table 3.4 Sample Data Store Card

		Joystick (May move in many planes)

Base time = 1.93 sec.

Time Added (sec.)	Reliability	
		1. Stick length
1.50	0.9963	a. 6–9 in.
0	0.9967	b. 12–18 in.
1.50	0.9963	c. 21–27 in.
		2. Extent of stick movement (extent of movement from one extreme to the other in a single plane)
0	0.9981	a. 5°–20°
0.20	0.9975	b. 30°–40°
0.50	0.9960	c. 40°–60°
		3. Control resistance
0	0.9999	a. 5–10 lb.
0.50	0.9992	b. 10–30 lb.
		4. Support of operating member
0	0.9990	a. Present
1.00	0.9950	b. Absent
		5. Time delay (time lapse between movement of control and movement of display)
0	0.9967	a. 0.3 sec.
0.50	0.9963	b. 0.6–1.5 sec.
3.00	0.9957	c. 3.0 sec.

Source: Munger, Smith, and Payne 1962.

the joystick in Table 3.4 include stick length, control resistance, time delay, and so on.

In Table 3.4, taken from a very early human performance data base (Munger, Smith, and Payne 1962), each physical dimension or characteristic of the joystick has associated with it a probability of correct operator performance (1.0, minus the error rate in operating the joystick). This is the "human re-liability" of the operator's performance of joystick movement; the joystick in and of itself has no human reliability, nor does it have a "base time," which is the average time required to make the movement. Some of the dimensions apparently require more time, added to the base time, to make that movement.

Dimensions that are critical to performance, such as the location of impor-tant displays or the speed with which stimuli appear, may cause large changes in operator performance, whereas others that are less important, such as am-bient lighting or the size of the work station, seem not to affect performance significantly except at extreme values. What makes a dimension important to performance is the task with which it interacts. For example, the task of main-taining altitude in an aircraft makes the location of the altimeter important. If the altimeter is located peripherally, the probability of pilot error increases. The determination of human performance equivalents requires performance measurement in a controlled research setting. Because these equivalents can be determined only by research, human factors applications to design are absolutely dependent on research outputs. To be relevant to this need, the research must be directed by design requirements.

The problem with dimensional equivalence is that it is only that—an equivalence. These performance equivalents may be meaningful in terms of predicting human performance (more on that later), but they do not help us understand the mechanisms producing the equivalence. Because the parameters in Table 3.4 are very simple, unidimensional parameters, it is possible, although not easy, to explain a larger error rate when, for example, control resistance is greater (i.e., when it is harder to move the stick). However, if we had the performance equivalents of tasks and functions, such simple explanations would probably not satisfy. If there are indeed performance equivalents that can be associated with design and job elements, we need a theory to explain these correlations. To develop such a theory, which would be very desirable, we need many more performance values associated with many task, equipment, and system elements, and we do not have them. It is highly probable that behind these dimensional equivalents there are intervening variables that serve as the mechanisms producing these equivalents, but do not have any idea what these are.

Behavioral Analysis

Behavioral analysis is the practitioner's analysis of the behavioral implications of the physical features of the equipment or job or system. The transformation here is from the physical feature to the operator task performance inferred to result from that feature. This type of logical transformation, which is qualitative, although it may be based on quantitative data, is not as difficult to accomplish as dimensional equivalence.

Behavioral analysis is performed when, for example, the practitioner examines the potential effect of the underwater environment on display visibility (reduced) or that of extreme cold on manual operations (the need for larger controls because gloves will be used). More will be said about this later.

Developmental Transformation

Interface transformation, the interaction between the operator and the equipment during system operation—as, for example, throwing a switch (a performance) that turns a transformer on (physical output)—is a type of transformation that is implemented mechanically or electronically and is outside our consideration.

Developmental transformation, which does concern us here, is the development of a system from a set of written, conceptual requirements to physical equipment, procedures, and technical data. It is the ultimate, highest-level transformation. Within that transformation, which may take months or years, there are many more molecular transformations. When the engineer imagines various ways in which a piece of equipment could be constructed to satisfy a requirement—generates alternatives—the transformation is from the requirement to a design. Similarly, when the practitioner analyzes the system requirement or a design drawing and extracts certain behavioral implications from these, he is transforming the object of the analysis—the drawing—into something else, its characteristics or attributes.

It is possible that an important mechanism involved in design transformations performed both by the engineer during design and by the practitioner during behavioral analysis is the creation of a *performance scenario*—a description of how a required system or mission output would be achieved if a certain design configuration existed. The scenario can be utilized at all physical and behavioral design stages, ranging from the most molecular (e.g., circuit analysis, where the *performance scenario* is of electrical flow) to the most molar; the scenario may involve either physical components alone, as in the circuit analysis, or combined physical and behavioral units, as in the behavioral analysis. Along with the scenario, the analyst considers the factors in the scenario that could determine the accomplishment or nonaccomplishment of the system or mission output.

If the scenario is unwritten its effectiveness is reduced because designers may forget to include necessary details. Alternatively, the procedure can be much more formal, as illustrated by Table 3.3. The practitioner, who in many cases is more verbal than the average engineer, tends to write the scenario out. In any event, if one wants to apply quantitative performance values to the equipment items or events in the scenario, the alternatives must be written down.

Because of the importance of the performance scenario in transformations, behavioral analytic methods (see Meister 1985(b)) rightly emphasize the development of mission, function, and task scenarios. Although the creators of these methods may not have been considering transformations when they developed these methods, they intuitively developed procedures appropriate for design transformation. The transformation we are most interested in is the relationship between the physical object or characteristic and its behavioral equivalent— that is, human performance in accomplishing a task involving that object or characteristic. If practitioners understood this relationship quantitatively, it would enable them to aid design much more than they can now.

The operator is part of a system, so it follows that the operator's performance is influenced by other system elements and their dimensions. Since that influence or effect is manifested by a change in task performance, it should be possible to equate these dimensions with a change in operator performance, which would then enable us to predict performance from the dimension. This was the logic behind the development of the Data Store (Munger, Smith, and

Payne 1962) and could conceivably be the logic behind the development of fundamental design principles. We hypothesize, for example, that an increase in the number of displays at the work station will be responsible for some reduction in operator performance. Because of the resulting diversion of attention, it should be possible to equate various numbers of displays with either an increase in error or a reduction in task success probability. Something like Table 3.4, although somewhat less molecular, listing the relationships between the dimensions and the change in task performance, would be extremely valuable if it existed, because one could presumably select the dimensions producing the least loss in operator performance for inclusion in design.

This is of course very reductionistic because it is necessary to decompose the system element into its dimensions to determine their influence. This reductionism may seem to violate the assumptions of the system concept discussed in Chapter 1; however, design has been conceptualized as a process of both decomposition and (followed by) composition (Rouse and Boff 1987). Moreover, it is the system concept—the assumption that all elements of the system influence each other—that leads us to the notion that element dimensions can influence operator performance.

It can be hypothesized that every dimension serves as a stimulus to the operator and that the operator reacts to that stimulus by modifying task performance. This response to system stimulation can occur only through the task, because the operator interacts with the system only when he or she performs a task. The operator must be aware of the element dimensions in order to respond to them; if the operator is not aware of them, they will not exercise an effect on performance. This is why many equipment dimensions have only a theoretical effect on task performance; a dimension is so minor, or other dimensions are so much more compelling, that the operator overlooks the less compelling one. Ultimately, to predict performance at the equipment level it will be necessary to reconstitute the decomposed individual dimensions into their original whole. This presents serious problems because the relationship among the individual dimensions is unclear.

In Chapter 1 it was suggested that the system imposed some sort of demand on its personnel when the system was functioning. Each element dimension of which operators are aware imposes a demand on them (for attention, at least) that requires them to increase psychological or physiological effort to deal with that demand. For example, increasing the number of displays at the work station beyond some point makes the operator subdivide attention excessively, requires greater effort to keep up with the display stimuli, and leads to increased performance error.

A first step in the development of dimensional equivalents is to pinpoint characteristics of the equipment, the task, the system, the environment, and the individual that might have an effect on task performance. So far specialists have not done an adequate job of conceptualizing these characteristics. Table 3.5,

Table 3.5 Dimensions for Which Performance Equivalents Are Needed in Behavioral Analysis

Equipment Variables
Work station dimensions (e.g., size, shape, height, width, chair dimensions)
Control/display variables:
- Type of component (e.g., switch, meter)
- Component parameters (e.g., joystick length, display brightness)
- Number of controls and displays
- Spatial arrangement of controls and displays
- Number of characters per line, and number of lines on CRT screen
Computer response time

Task Variables
Major behavioral functions performed in the task
Task characteristics (e.g., discrete, step-by-step vs. branching alternatives)
Stimulus characteristics (e.g., frequency, speed, complexity, number)
Amount of operator involvement in task performance
Response requirements (e.g., precision, speed, memory, perceptual resolution)
Speed with which scenario unfolds
Task duration
Work methods
Rewards/punishments
Shift schedules
Procedural characteristics
Availability of tools, supplies
Task loading
Risk involved in performing task
Monotony
Manning parameters

Output Variables
Output characteristics (e.g., covertness, number, speed of emission)
Output consequences (e.g., feedback presence or absence, amount, timing)

Environmental Factors
Lighting, noise, temperature, vibration, acceleration

System Factors
Type of system (e.g., determinate, indeterminate)
Complexity (defined independently of operator performance)
Number of subsystems
Number and type of communications channels
System organization
System policies
Supervisor/manager actions
Team structure
Distractions from outside the system

Personnel Variables
Skill
Amount and type of experience
Motivation
Internalized stress/fatigue
Intelligence
Physical condition
Work attitudes

which was taken in part from the list of "performance shaping factors" developed by Swain and Guttmann (1983), is a very preliminary attempt at such a taxonomy.

Table 3.5 shows that the dimensions range from very molar to very molecular, from the physical (condition) to the psychological (motivation). It is extremely unlikely that each dimension listed is equally important in influencing task performance—and this too is a great gap in our knowledge, because we should at least be able to rank order the variables in Table 3.5 in terms of general importance. On the other hand, it is possible that all Table 3.5 variables are equally important in varying contexts, so that, for example, in one situation intelligence is most important and in another procedural characteristics are most important. Alternatively, one could hypothesize that generally—and as long as we are not talking about extreme conditions—the ordering of importance runs from closest to the individual to farthest from the individual. If this last were the case, individual factors would be most important, and system factors least important, with equipment and task variables about equally important, and more important than environmental factors. But all this is mere speculation because no one has performed the studies needed. Table 3.5 lists independent variables that could occupy a laboratory or institute for a lifetime.

THE ENGINEERING ENVIRONMENT

The application of behavioral principles to system development takes place in a sociocultural environment that has a significant impact on the effectiveness of that application. The two major elements in that environment are the system development process, about which we have spoken at some length, and the engineer, with his or her requirements, biases, and modes of operation, to which we now turn.

The critical element is the engineer, because the engineer is the one the practitioner must work with and through to make his or her inputs. The relationship between the practitioner and the designer is only slightly less important than the data, principles, and design guidelines that support and direct what the practitioner does.

Engineer Attitudes toward Human Factors

Many engineers have a set of concepts that they use to justify their lack of interest in behavioral design. These are not formal assumptions, but rather inarticulate belief structures that can be deduced from designer actions and arguments. If asked to agree or disagree with statements describing these beliefs, designers might well disagree, because these beliefs are relatively unconscious.

The following are the common misconceptions among engineers: (1) The designer is already occupied too fully without having to worry about human factors. (2) To consider behavioral design means shuttling between the physical domain, in which engineers feel reasonably comfortable, and the behavioral domain, about which they know very little. Like most people, engineers are reluctant to engage in situations in which they may be less than adequate. (3) Many designers believe that the effect of the human on equipment or system performance is minimal and that the system will overcome any behavioral deficiencies. In this concept, the system "buffers" or compensates for the effects of personnel inadequacies (e.g., errors, increased response time, reduced performance quality) so that inefficient human performance does not really have a significant negative effect on the system. If this is true, there is no need to consider personnel in design of a system, except for selection and training. (4) Whatever design deficiencies of a behavioral nature are not picked up as design proceeds—and the designer is certain they will be and that they will be rectified—the operator will be flexible enough to compensate for them. This is probably a reflection of our historical self-confidence that Americans are resourceful, innovative, and inventive. There is partial support for this—minor inadequacies can be overcome by operators, but this is not true of more serious ones. Moreover, it is probably possible to overcome design inadequacies as long as system personnel are unstressed. Stress tends to rigidify personnel and magnify system weaknesses. (5) There is nothing one can do to rectify the notorious incapability of the operator; he will inevitably make mistakes, so it is useless to take precautions about this—that is, to design specifically to avoid or eliminate behavioral limitations. (6) There is in fact no real problem requiring behavioral design, because "good" engineering design includes human factors, so special efforts are not needed. In practice, however, this is usually not the case. (7) Including behavioral inputs in design will not solve the human-system mismatch problem—that the discipline is ineffective. Great efforts have been made to counter this argument by compiling case histories documenting behavioral contributions to design and system efficiency (e.g., Price, et al. 1980a; Sawyer, et al. 1981). However, when inputs of various disciplines enter into the design process, it is difficult to single out any one contribution that was significantly more important than another. As a result, convincing empirical evidence testifying to the worth of the human factors contribution to design does not yet exist.

Designer Characteristics

Comparatively little research has been done on the relationship between the practitioner and the designer (but see Perrow 1983). As a consequence, whatever we do know is based mostly on personal experience and is largely anecdotal. However, these anecdotes have been around long enough that one must take them seriously.

What we do know can be summarized in a series of statements: (1) Most designers are indifferent to human factors. They do not read behavioral material, and they accord human factors a low priority in the design process. (2) Their attitudes toward the discipline are bolstered by a series of beliefs or assumptions that are largely erroneous or simplistic. (3) The engineer's design process is extremely conservative, not completely systematic, somewhat primitive, and based on the principle of least effort. (4) Many practitioners tend to be somewhat reactive toward the designer because they believe there must first be a design option before it can be examined for behavioral aspects. It is of course theoretically possible for the practitioner to initiate a new design, but realistically this is almost never done. Most practitioners lack the engineering knowledge to develop their own design, and in any event this would probably be regarded by the designer as an invasion of his or her prerogatives. Consequently, many designers tend to view the practitioner merely as a design critic. (5) Because of the designer's attitudes toward human factors, the practitioner spends much time in efforts at indoctrination.

The paucity of data on the designer and design situations is frustrating. Most of the few behavioral studies performed are from the 1960s and early 1970s. Since then, there has been nothing. We still have only a very unclear idea of how the engineer designs, and this is not only disappointing from a research standpoint, but it also hampers human factors efforts at behavioral design.

SUMMARY

Because human factors has a responsibility to contribute to system development, the discipline must ensure that its research products are relevant and useful to development. The application of behavioral principles to design is accomplished in two ways: by providing general information, as in the form of a handbook, and by making an input to the design of a specific equipment or system. The latter is more important than the former. System development begins with broad molar functions and works down to more molecular tasks and subtasks. Testing of the equipment and system proceeds in reverse order. System requirements drive design, but unfortunately these requirements rarely include human factors. System design involves the analysis and selection of alternative design options. It also involves transformation of requirements into hardware and software, and for the practitioner the transformation of physical requirements into their behavioral implications. The system development cycle proceeds from planning to preliminary design, detail design, testing, production, and deployment. During development a variety of analytic and evaluational activities may be performed by the practitioner, depending on design requirements, availability of financing, and time schedule. Behavioral inputs provided to the designer include those that have a direct impact on design, those that result from testing the equipment or system, and those that deal with selection and training of system personnel. A number of transformations are at the heart of behavioral design, the two most important being *dimensional equivalence,* in which for each physical equipment or job dimension there is a human performance value that represents the effect of that dimension on performance, and *behavioral analysis,* which is the examination of the behavioral implications of a physical requirement. The critical element in the development situation that largely determines how effective the practitioner will be is the engineer, whose attitudes toward human factors are all-important. Those attitudes are at best neutral and at worst negative. In general, the engineers feel they can "handle" the human factors of their design on their own.

CHAPTER 4

The Special Requirements
of Human Factors Research

The special features of a system-oriented human factors create distinctive requirements for its research.

TYPES OF HUMAN FACTORS RESEARCH

Human factors research can be divided into four categories, none of which is peculiar to human factors:

1. Knowledge-based research, whose purpose is to add to the stock of knowledge about a particular topic. An example is a study of the minimum number of television lines needed for a human to resolve a target (Erickson 1978).

2. Development research, which is performed to answer a specific question arising out of and needed for the development of a new system or the operation of an already installed one. An example is the comparison of the effectiveness of various devices (e.g., typewriter, light pen, joystick) used to enter data into computerized systems (Whitfield, Ball, and Bird 1983).

3. System evaluation, which is the measurement of personnel performance in the operational testing of a new or old system and may be considered a special form of development research.

4. Methodological research, which is designed to assist in the implementation of the other three categories or, more generally, in enhancement of the discipline. The development of a taxonomic structure to support development of a human performance data base is an example.

The reason for dividing human factors research into four parts is to emphasize methodological research as a distinctive category. Most human factors research is either knowledge-based or developmental. Because of the newness of the discipline and the comparative crudity of its methodology, methodological research demands much greater attention than it has so far received. Methodological research should actually precede the other two types because it "feeds" them. Weak methodology hampers both knowledge-based and developmental research, because the measurement methods that are needed by both are not available.

One could say that both knowledge-based and methodological research are basic research, as the term is used, but the basic versus applied dichotomy is not very helpful in developing a research program (see McGrath and Brinberg 1984). Those who adopt the viewpoint that human factors is wholly an applied discipline will perhaps not accept that it could perform basic research; if, however, it is a fundamental discipline, as this book maintains, it performs both basic and applied research.

There are other ways of looking at human factors research that overlap with the preceding classification but that may be more meaningful. In this view human factors research consists of:

1. Human-centered research, which studies the functioning of the individual or team without particular regard to the equipment or system context of that functioning

2. Human-machine centered research, which relates personnel variables and performance to the immediate human-machine interface

3. System-centered research, which emphasizes study of the reciprocal relationship of personnel variables with system variables

The distinctions represent a progression of hierarchy, size, and complexity— from the individual or team by itself (which would be human-centered), the simplest and most molecular of the levels, to the individual/team interaction with its equipment interface (human-machine centered), which is intermediate in hierarchy, size, and complexity, and finally, the personnel subsystem in relation to all other system elements (system-centered), and the most complex and molar of the levels. System-centered studies may include aspects of the human-machine relationship but not the human-centered, because the latter has no equipment context.

Most human factors research is of the human-machine variety. There is a substantial amount of human-centered research, but comparatively little of the system variety (but see Parsons 1972 for a history of system-centered research in the 1950s and 1960s). There are several reasons for the comparative lack of system-oriented research. The most important reason is that most specialists do not think in terms of systems. Another reason is that system-oriented research must by its nature involve relatively large study objects and relatively abstract attributes, which make it difficult to insert these devices into confined environments, such as the laboratory or a simulator. Even when performed by human factors professionals, human-centered research is psychological but not human factors in nature, because it lacks the equipment interaction that is the distinguishing aspect of the discipline. Nonetheless, a great many people who think of themselves as human factors researchers do human-centered research because they are unable to differentiate human factors from psychological research.

Needless to say, the three types of research above are variously applicable to system development and operation. System-centered and human-machine interface research are directly applicable—human-machine research is most applicable because the practitioner usually works at the interface level—whereas human-centered research is only indirectly applicable, where it is applicable at all.

Examples of Research Types

It may help to provide examples of the three types of research taken from the 1986 proceedings of the annual meeting of the Human Factors Society.

First, human-centered research is exemplified by Ackerman's (1986) study on skill acquisition, individual differences, and human ability that explored a theory of ability/skill relations. Information-processing consistency, mission load, and stimulus novelty were varied experimentally. Taxonomic category labels were presented verbally or as dot figures. "After a 5 sec. display of the memory set items, subjects would see a choice among probe words (or figures), one of which would correctly match a member of the memory set. Subjects indicated the position of the correct probe stimulus with a key-press on a standard CRT keyboard" (Ackerman 1986, p. 271).

Human-machine research is exemplified by Zwahlen and Kothari's (1986) study of the effects of positive and negative image polarity visual display terminal (VDT) screens. Eight experienced typists worked two full days at a VDT work station using either a hard-copy-screen or split-screen data presentation on a light or dark character CRT display. The task was to enter data and maintain a file. A computerized system collected eye-scanning and pupil diameter data. It also recorded keystrokes per minute and errors per file. At the beginning and end of each work session, subjects answered ocular and musculoskeletal comfort/discomfort questions.

An example of system-centered research is a study by Shaffer, Shafer, and Kutche (1986) to validate predictions of workload by measurements taken in a scout-attack helicopter. Videotapes of cockpit activities during operational exercises were analyzed to determine the relative workload contribution of communication and crew station activity of the pilot and copilot.

A balanced research program would include all categories of research, with greater emphasis on system and interface research, but this rarely occurs. It would also be desirable for the various types of studies to be linked—by common tasks, for example.

Research and the System

Human factors research has so far been described in very broad categories, some of which overlap with other disciplines. One overriding characteristic differentiates that research from research in other behavioral disciplines: its relationship with the system. This relationship has certain implications for research characteristics: involvement with an actual system or a physical or symbolic surrogate of that system; consideration of human performance at (as a minimum) two levels, one representing the personnel subsystem, the other representing a higher-order system level with terminal outputs; inclusion in the study of at least one system element or job characteristic other than personnel—for example, equipment, procedures, technical data, and work-related tasks.

Ideally, measurement of human performance in the context of an actual operational system epitomizes human factors research. There are those who distinguish between research and measurement and who maintain that measurement is research only when variables are controlled and hypotheses are tested, but this distinction is labored and meaningless if one assumes that all data, however gathered, adds to the knowledge base. The reason for emphasizing operational measurement is that human factors at this stage of its development requires much data of a nonexperimental, descriptive nature that ideally should be gathered in an operational setting. Where measurement in that setting is impossible, a physical substitute (e.g., a simulator or test vehicle) or a symbolic version (e.g., computerized or paper and pencil) is acceptable.

Two levels of performance—one representing the personnel performance level, the other representing a system output level—are required, because systems are defined in part by their hierarchy. Because of this hierarchy involving multiple levels, a critical question for human factors research is: What is the the effect of personnel performance (at one level) on system output (at a higher level)?

To be applicable to system problems and questions, human factors research should include in its test design not only personnel factors but also at least one other system variable. The inclusion of system variables enables the researcher to answer the other critical question for human factors research: How do system characteristics influence personnel performance?

TECHNOLOGY AND HUMAN FACTORS

One element critical for human factors research is not found in the research of other disciplines. By its nature, human factors research must be responsive to technology and must include it or related variables in the research. When a technological innovation arises, one must test to determine whether human performance and behavioral variables are affected by the innovation. The most outstanding example of this is the increase of research related to the human-computer interface (Shackel 1985). Three questions in relation to technology must be answered:

1. To what extent are human factors research problems determined by technology?

2. If technology changes radically, do human factors research problems and methods of application change correspondingly, and, if so, then what does one

do about the "old" but still unresolved problems of the "old" but still existent technology?

3. Are there any human factors research questions that transcend technology?

The Nature of Technological Change

Technological change occurs constantly, but often in such small increments that we may hardly be aware of them. In this magnitude such changes do not have an impact on human factors to any great extent. What specialists mean when they refer to technological change is a change sufficient to bring about a significant modification of personnel work behaviors and a significant change in the way in which systems are developed, tested, and operated.

Certain technological changes that were significant for engineering have not had an appreciable effect on human performance. A prime example of this is the development of the transistor, which succeeded the vacuum tube. This change profoundly affected engineering, but it had no significant impact on human factors because the change was reflected in internal circuitry only and not in the operator-machine interface. It may have had a major effect on maintenance technician performance, but there are no data to verify this hypothesis.

Behavioral Effects of Computerization

Within the past ten years, however, we have witnessed what many have called the "computer revolution"—a revolution that has presumably created a new set of behavioral processes and human factors problems. The effect of computers on human factors professionals has been so significant that one of the respondents in the survey described in Chapter 1, someone prominent in the discipline, suggested that the human-computer interest area might even split off from human factors as a whole and develop its own discipline.

Has computerization actually changed most jobs as radically as it appears? Only if the answer to that question is yes can we say that human factors problems of attempting to explain job performance have also changed significantly. There is no question that computerization has changed the nature of some jobs—not all jobs—but many. One need think only of the postal sorters of the past who took a batch of envelopes in one hand, read the address on each one, and shoved each one by hand into appropriate pigeonholes. Contrast that with what postal sorters do in a semiautomated post office: letters are flipped mechanically in front of the operator at a machine pace, and the operator has only to read the zip code and key it into the system. Or compare the task of the World War II combat pilot who did all sighting by actually seeing a target, with that of the modern pilot who watches a CRT and maneuvers one blip on the screen onto another blip.

However, merely to say that jobs have changed is superficial. We must ask ourselves what this means in terms of the human processes involved in these jobs. Have the functions and tasks involved in computerized jobs changed significantly? The computerized job requires fewer motor and psychomotor functions, and many more perception and cognition functions. Has the nature of the operator's perception and cognition changed radically because of the computer? Is watching two blips come together on a CRT significantly different from aiming an arrow at a bird in flight? Is studying a circuit diagram on a CRT significantly different from studying the same diagram on paper? At a *function* level, the processes do not appear to differ so greatly, because functions (e.g., to analyze, compute, or compare) are so general that they can apply equally well to a wide variety of tasks that vary widely. The *task,* being largely determined by context—that is, the characteristics of the equipment being used, the environment in which the task is being performed—does change when it is computerized, because much of the effect of computerization is a matter of context. An example of this is the difference between typing a manuscript at a computer terminal and typing it on an electric typewriter. It is entirely reasonable that context should influence task characteristics; the context is part of the overall system in which the task is performed, and system elements influence other elements.

It is also possible that computerization levies different demands on the operator. One can conceive of computerization as requiring many of the same behaviors that noncomputerized jobs do, but abbreviating their duration and hence reducing the load on personnel, because automation speeds up the entire job.

It is possible too that what has happened in computerization is that the *frequency distribution* of underlying processes required by the task over the range of jobs performed has changed markedly. Instead of gross motor acts, for example, we now perform fine perceptual or cognitive tasks. With previous, noncomputerized jobs we may have used the same more complex processes, but fewer of them.

Much of the change that is so striking in computerized jobs results from the automation of task *outputs.* For example, I observe a colleague who uses a computer program to lay out control and display panels—that is, he uses the computer to draw circles to scale, to label components, and to rearrange modules in testing one location against another. In the past he did all this manually. His analysis of what the displays should depict and his mental arrangement of components on the panel face are still done manually; only the output of the job has been affected, but this part is so overt and so dramatic that it overshadows other behaviors that remain much the same as before.

Whether one sees major or minor technological changes in computerization may depend on the system level from which one is viewing. At the individual human-machine interface (e.g., function keys, alphanumerics), it may appear as if technology has changed markedly, because the input-output devices comprising the interface are particularly subject to technological change. It is possible that there is not quite so much change if one examines computerized systems in terms of the internal processes that the task now demands.

Computerization does change the nature of jobs, but more in degree than in kind. The more important questions are: How does this job change affect human factors research and practice? Have the questions human factors decides to investigate changed significantly? Has human factors application to system design changed significantly? Do technological changes, such as the introduction of computers, produce differences in human performance so great that "new" human factors problems requiring new research emerge?

Imagine that extra-sensory perception (ESP) were so developed that psychokinesis replaced all mechanical devices for moving objects, and telepathy were used instead of electronic sensors for scanning far distances. Would human factors switch from its present emphasis on human-computer interaction to ESP? The answer is, of course, yes. The change from conventional psychomotor and perceptual functioning to ESP cognitive functioning would be so great that it would almost completely eliminate traditional psychomotor and perceptual functioning in a technological context. The critical question is whether people operating computers either alone or as part of a larger system utilize capabilities radically different from those they utilize with non-computerized systems. There are vague hints in the literature (e.g., Eggleston 1987) that computer usage produces a different mentality. If true, are new behavioral principles required?

Persistent Questions

There is also the question of what one does with remaining noncomputerized or partly computerized systems and the behavioral questions that were raised with those systems. Do these questions also remain? In psychology, problems related to thinking, problem-solving, decision-making, and the like have persisted over one hundred years of psychological research. It is true that psychology has little involvement with technology and technological change, but I believe that we have a similar persistence of behavioral problems in human factors. This assumes, of course, that we have not completely answered the earlier questions (and who would want to defend the position that we have?) and consequently that these earlier questions are still valid.

Illustrative of a continuing problem is that we still do not know *quantitatively* the relationship between equipment complexity and performance, between (1) the number of traditional controls and displays at a work station and requirements for operating them and (2) operator performance. Because computerization has now become important, should researchers ignore the problem of control-display and performance relationships? Our knowledge of the relationship between controls, displays, and performance, despite thirty years of research, is slight. The skeletons of old, unresolved questions like that still litter the human factors landscape and encourage cynicism. If researchers have failed to resolve these old questions, are they more likely to resolve any new ones produced by computerization?

Researchers can simply declare by ignoring them that the unresolved problems are really solved—knowledge by fiat, as it were—but that merely sweeps the difficulty under the rug. They could also transfer the previous set of problems from the old technology to the new. For example, if they are concerned about operator performance as a function of the number of displays on a console, they could address the same problem in terms of the number of alphanumerics on a CRT screen at any one time (display density). They could also claim that no problem is actually "solved", that there is always more to be known about it but that at some point one must go on to the next set of problems.

If one is going to dispose of a human factors problem, one must know when such a problem exists. It exists when a question is asked to which no answer is available. The relationship between operator performance and number of controls and displays is a problem because there is no quantitative equation relating the two variables, although it seems logical that operator performance should degrade as some function of increasing numbers of controls and displays. This problem will be solved when an equation is developed to describe the relationship and when that equation has been validated.

Problems that Transcend Technology

The last major question we must deal with is: Are there human factors problems that transcend technology or persist regardless of that technology? The following questions do not seem to have disappeared:

1. What qualities make the computerized human-machine interface "user friendly" or describe "good" human engineering? These might be attributes like provision of aids for the novice user; avoidance of procedures that, if performed erroneously, would shut the system down inadvertently; or the software's capability of being able to tell the user, upon request, where he or she is in the system process. Research performed at this attribute level is akin to the rather molecular research performed early in human factors—for example, concerning which of two altimeter readouts, digital or analog, gave better pilot performance.

2. What is the effect of experience and skill on operator and system performance in the computerized systems? What types of skills are important? How does one develop computer software and systems that are compatible with different experience levels? These questions were also asked in relation to noncomputerized systems, but we still lack acceptable answers.

3. What is the effect of fatigue, stress, motivation, and the like on operator or system performance? The same questions have been asked of noncomputerized systems.

4. How does one measure operator performance in computerized systems, and how does one evaluate alternative design options? Tests of software and computerized systems have apparently not changed significantly from testing of noncomputerized systems (Meister 1985b), although there may be exceptions for "expert" systems (Meister 1987).

It is possible that most behavioral problems do not change, but appear in a new guise only when one concentrates on the molecular hardware/software interface details in which they are wrapped. There may be few "new" problems, if one analyzes these problems at a higher system level.

It may be too cynical to argue that the rise of a new technology appeals to researchers, younger ones in particular, because it apparently presents "new" problems and cancels out the older ones that show a discouraging resistance to solution or that represent an unfulfilled agenda. Specialists can now approach previously intractable problems in a new context that makes them appear to be fresh. For example, work station design is still a problem, but now it can be addressed in terms of a "flexible" CRT terminal at a computer work station, in terms of CRT display brightness, ambient illumination, and so on instead of the older meters, joysticks, or transilluminated displays.

If technological changes are only moderate and gradual, human factors research problems appear to be constant. This suggests that certain research topics transcend technology, unless that technology is significantly different from what has gone before, and even then only the form of the problem has changed. If one looks at systems as systems, which requires some abstraction from technological details, certain problems persist despite technological change. The two most important are contained in the two questions: What is the effect of the personnel performance and behavioral variables on total computerized system outputs and performance? and What is the effect of computerized system characteristics (e.g., the type of system, its hierarchy, communications channels, nature of system outputs, complexity) on personnel performance? Because these problems are inherent in every system, they have existed throughout the history of human factors but may not have been recognized as problems. Human factors research is therefore not completely defined by technology, because major questions cut across technology or persist despite technology.

Although it is necessary to perform research to see how the new technology affects these general questions, research determined solely by technology may trivialize itself because the amount of system output variance accounted for by minor technological details (such as the alphanumeric font on CRT displays) may be very slight. Although performance is multidetermined, many of the variables supposedly influencing that performance, even the ones that turn out to be statistically significant in experiments, may have only a very small effect on overall output. From a design standpoint, research is needed to determine that only one or at most two variables are primarily responsible for a performance effect because engineering design options can take into account only one or two such variables at any one time.

Technology provides the *context* in which system relationships exist and must therefore be included in studies, but what is important is the system within which performance occurs, and the relationship between personnel performance and the system output. This suggests that we should examine what, other than technological details, differentiates one system from another.

In concluding this section on technology and human factors, it is only fair to indicate that it is very difficult to be satisfied with this or any other treatment of the effects of technology on behavior. This topic cries out for more empirical investigation.

FACTORS INFLUENCING SELECTION OF RESEARCH

Why is research performed to answer certain research questions and not performed to answer others? The system-oriented specialist will pose this fascinating and important question because compared with research on human-machine interfaces and to a lesser extent human-centered research, system-level human factors research is quite sparse. This can be seen by analyzing Table 4.1, in which the percentage of system-oriented research is indicated as a function of all human factors research citations in the journals (the items are not supposed to add to 100 percent). To obtain these data, the Dialog Citation System (a computerized document citation reference system) was asked, first, the total number of reports and papers on the topic "human factors engineering" published since 1967 (as far back as Dialog goes), and the number of those reports and papers published in system-related categories. The numbers were then transformed into percentages of the total to indicate relative emphasis in research topics. Citations in the literature were categorized by "keyword" or descriptors. The categories selected for examination were human factors engineering, systems analysis, man-machine system, system design, system concept, controls, and displays. These categories were considered most relevant to system design and development. The five sources searched were: *Psychological Abstracts,* encompassing all nongovernmental behavioral reports; *National Technical Information Service* (*NTIS*), which searches all governmental, nonclassified literature; and the journals *Human Factors, Applied Ergonomics,* and *Ergonomics.*

The reader should examine Table 4.1 with certain reservations in mind. The percentage of reports published in a category depends in part on how broadly or narrowly the category is defined. Moreover, the categories are only grossly descriptive of report content. The relatively low percentage of studies of the system concept, design, and analysis, contrasted with the relatively high percentage of studies of displays in all the sources, suggests that greater attention is

Table 4.1   Topics Addressed in Human Factors Research

Topic	Psychological Abstracts	National Technical Information Service	Human Factors	Applied Ergonomics	Ergonomics
Human factors engineering	100% (1,710)	100% (1,848)	100% (1,042)	100% (889)	100% (200)
System analysis	1.2%	4.0%	1.0%	1.0%	0.0%
Man-machine system	14.0%	15.0%	4.0%	3.0%	4.5%
System design	13.0%	3.0%	4.0%	3.0%	11.0%
System concept	0.0%	.001%	0.0%	0.0%	0.0%
Controls	2.0%	4.0%	2.0%	3.0%	2.5%
Displays	15.0%	3.0%	17.0%	8.0%	12.0%

Source: Data gathered by Marie McDowell of the Navy Personnel Research and Development Center Library.

paid to more molecular design elements than to research on design of the system as a system. Only among the *Psychological Abstracts* and *Applied Ergonomics* articles is much attention paid to system design. The "man-machine" system descriptor is prominent both in *Psychological Abstracts* and in *NTIS* but is so broad that classifiers tend to use it indiscriminately.

Rationale for Research Selection

Because there are not enough resources to perform every study that could be performed—even if they were of equal merit, which they rarely are—it is necessary to make choices. Choices imply both scientific and idiosyncratic criteria, which usually function in combination. The two types of criteria may coexist peacefully or in conflict. The individual researcher does not have complete freedom to select what he or she will study; job requirements, peer pressure, the need to satisfy authority, the researcher's inherent interest in a topic, and so forth, all figure in the selection decision.

One reason that there is a relative lack of system-oriented research in human factors is that researchers are ambivalent about the *implementation* implications of the system concept—that is, it is acceptable to talk about the concept as long as one does not have to research it. Another possible explanation is that the training most specialists receive in university focuses on human-centered research, or that the amount of effort required by system-oriented research may appear too great to the researcher. A perhaps even more important reason is that system-oriented research is difficult to perform, time-consuming, and expensive and that relatively few researchers have the resources to pursue it. But that simply regresses the problem back to research sponsors (providers of money) and to the government, which sponsors almost all human factors research (see Chapter 8).

Research topics can be selected for many reasons. First, a critical point in theory may have been reached. Occasionally some hypothesis suggested by theory needs to be verified or rejected because it will help determine whether the theory is viable. Because, relatively speaking, there is not a great deal of theory in human factors, this research motivation is exercised relatively infrequently. Second, there may be unresolved issues that research can help with. Normal science, to use Kuhn's (1970) phrase, proceeds by researching issues or problem areas that have not been resolved either by theory or by collection of empirical data. Researchers perform studies to confirm that the predictions based on theory are rooted in fact; if they are not, other researchers engage in further research to determine why the discrepancy has occurred. Again, because human factors is not heavily theory-oriented, this motivation is exercised only rarely. Third, research may be undertaken to fill up gaps in knowledge. Specialists in a certain area may feel that too little is known about a particular topic. Most knowledge-based research is performed in response to the general question, "What is the possible effect on performance of this or that variable?" Fourth, an answer may be needed. Because some research is a precursor to other research, preliminary data may be required to answer a question further down the line. Thus, the future research creates a present demand to secure this information. Fifth, there may be an inherent interest in a topic or question. All other things being equal (which of course they never are), the researcher's inherent interest in a topic or question should determine which research topic will be investigated. What produces an inherent interest—in workload, for example, as against system design—is shrouded in the biases produced in researchers by personality, training, and attitudes (see Chapter 1). One hopes that the researcher's inherent interest in certain topics will coincide with the discipline's interest, but in the case of system-level research this has not occurred. Sixth, authority-driven problems may give rise to research. All research must be paid for, and those who pay for the research can require that the research areas in which they are interested are the ones studied. Research is bought and sold like any other commodity (see Chapter 8). The realities may be swaddled in a blanket of words about science and research, but they exist nonetheless, and they reveal themselves very quickly if the researcher attempts to sell something that is unfamiliar and hence unpopular. The researcher does what he or she is told to do, sometimes indirectly or subtly. This is not necessarily an undesirable situation, if the consensus of influentials, editors, and funding agency heads is correct about what should be studied, but that can be determined only subjectively and judgmentally. Seventh, practical problems may benefit from light shed by research. Developmental research is performed in response to problems encountered in the development of individual systems or types of systems. Most government-supported research is of this type. Because the problem is usually quite specific, developmental research (other than that dealing with computer variables) does not usually reach the general literature, although all the results reported, when combined, might well contribute to knowledge. Finally, peer attitudes and publication can be motivators for research. The opinions of recognized leaders in the discipline have a singular weight for researchers.

Research Utility

In all the factors determining the selection of knowledge-based and methodological research, one relating to utility ("Will the results of the study be useful in answering some questions other than the one specifically addressed in the research?") has not been included. The utility of developmental research is immediately apparent, but in knowledge-based research, utility is much less clear and may even be obscure in methodological research. Research utility is not defined in terms of answers to specific problems, which is the function of developmental research, nor is it defined with regard to enabling further research on a particular topic to be performed, because this last is an open-ended commitment to research on any topic for any length of time and mocks the notion of research selection. There are two possible definitions of research utility: First, a reasonable amount of human factors knowledge could be defined as the ability to create a quantitative and validated equation between specified behavioral variables and human performance, an equation of the type described by Finley, et el. (1975):

$$Y = a_0 + a_1 + a_2 y_2 + \ldots a_m y_m = b_0 + b_1 x_1 + b_2 x_2 \ldots + b_n x_n.$$

Any study that provides data for such an equation has utility. Second, alternatively, any study that provides principles or data that can be generalized across a spectrum of system types, not merely a single system, or that can be applied to a variety of system aspects, has utility.

How can this criterion be applied in the selection of a research topic because, after all, utility is a post facto criterion? Presumably one can tell how useful a piece of research will be only after it has been completed. Before a study is performed, however, the researcher might develop a sample of the anticipated data and conclusions from the future research—and consider concretely how these would be utilized. For example, the researcher might think of the anticipated data or conclusions as having to be transformed into the equation above or into data providing design guidance (e.g., minimum field of view for rapid detection).

Utility is an extreme criterion, but not if it is viewed from the standpoint of someone other than the researcher, such as a practitioner. Such a criterion might be applied last, after all others, but it should be determining. Then if a useful applicable study output cannot be visualized, the study should be canceled. One would hardly expect the individual researcher to be so hard-headed about his or her work, but the funding agency might be.

All research is arguable, of course. One cannot demonstrate program worth, at least in advance of the research, but it is possible to estimate the utility of an approach, because if one can specify a desired product of the research to be performed, one can anticipate whether the research proposed is a reasonable way of achieving that product. It is possible that if utility became an important criterion for research selection there might be a significant *temporary* reduction in the amount of human factors research. Would this be undesirable? There is no inherent natural right that any particular piece of research be performed.

A PROPOSED RESEARCH PROGRAM

Any one who enumerates all the difficulties and problems that human factors research faces is morally obligated to describe the research he or she would perform—given that appropriate resources are provided.

System-Oriented Research

The research proposed here is system-oriented, which means that it centers around system variables, system development, and the role of human factors in both. System-oriented human factors research is also goal-oriented, which means that one starts by setting a goal and then working toward that goal. If, for example, one wants to be able to evaluate systems adequately, then one needs to know the quantitative relationships between system characteristics and human performance. This is a fundamental difference from knowledge-based research, which sets no goal but the general one of seeking to enlarge knowledge. In all fairness to the reader, it is necessary to point out that the other categories of research mentioned at the start of this chapter are also goal-oriented and that a program of system-oriented research may at one time or another include one or more of the other varieties. Nevertheless, these other research types are not necessarily oriented toward systems and system variables.

Proponents of knowledge-based research point to the amount of understanding that will be achieved over time. This is an ambiguous criterion at best, because no one agrees on what constitutes understanding. By any criterion, however, it is likely that the great majority of studies make no significant contribution to the knowledge base. In contrast, the system-oriented approach points to the amount of control achieved by research results (for example, in terms of the ability to influence design). The dichotomy between knowledge-based and system-oriented research is something like Greenwald et al.'s (1986) contrast between result-centered and theory-centered methods in psychology.

Because system-oriented research specifies a relatively concrete goal it can be evaluated—first, as to the likelihood of achieving that goal, and second, following completion of the research, as to its actual success in achieving that goal. This is in contrast to the knowledge-based research orientation, which because its goal is general cannot be adequately evaluated.

Some may consider it impertinent to evaluate or predict research effectiveness on the principle that *all* research, whatever its character, is useful, but why should not research be evaluated for adequacy? In very pragmatic terms, research *is* evaluated continuously by the major funding agencies through their selection of research priorities and by their continuation or rejection of research grants and contracts.

System- or goal-oriented research represents a genuine "new" start, whereas knowledge-based research is the continuation of effort in study areas that have already been somewhat mined. This continuity works in favor of knowledge-based research because it increases sponsor confidence that the approach will produce success. Any "new" research proposed has greater difficulty convincing funding agencies of the worth of the effort, something the knowledge-based research finds easier to do.

System-oriented research is pragmatic, utilitarian, and quotidian in flavor; the traditional knowledge-centered research is formidable in the authority of those who perform it. One approach does not necessarily exclude the other, however. It is possible to have both, although with twice as much research to perform the traditional approach will have fewer resources to dispose of. Nevertheless, both will be more effective than either alone, because one can serve as a check on and backup for the other.

The importance of system development for human factors requires that research directly relevant to that development be performed. It is common knowledge that many of the massive systems developed in the United States have not been as effective as they should be (e.g., the "Sergeant York" system); there is empirical confirmation of their deficiencies (General Accounting Office 1981), but civilian systems are probably not a great deal better, although because they work to less stringent requirements their faults are perhaps more easily papered over. In the case of government-sponsored systems, political factors play a role, but ignorance of developmental processes is also just as likely to hamper system development.

Studies of past developmental history might be useful in uncovering remediable inadequacies in developmental processes, but there is likely to be opposition to studies of the development process. I was involved in one effort by an admiral to investigate the human engineering process in a new class of frigate, but the investigation was aborted before it began by the reluctance of research managers to become involved in such an effort. The few studies that have been performed (e.g., Schwartz 1981) have usually embarrassed both the system developer and the funding agency. The reader might expect that books written by engineers to describe design (e.g., Pahl and Beitz 1984) would have considered the developmental process, but engineering books are written from an engineering, not a behavioral, prospect.

The central question motivating research oriented around system development and operation is how behavioral principles can be applied in a physicalistic environment that is often negative with regard to behavioral considerations.

It is possible to do this if one assumes that design is largely information analysis and transmission and that much of what the practitioner has to do is to provide the engineer with relevant information for effective decision-making. This puts the responsibility for providing the practitioner with relevant information squarely on the back of the researcher.

Most researchers study human performance but do not deal specifically with the design variables (physical hardware/software or procedural) that determine that performance. For example, we have many studies of workload measurement and prediction, but none that investigates workload as a function of system design characteristics. From the standpoint of the practitioner, such research just misses the mark. In addition, each study is idiosyncratic—each utilizing a different methodology, a different metric, and so forth. Data in individual reports are quantitative, but as individual items, not combined with data from other reports, not formatted in data-base terms. The utility of journal data is very limited, unless the data happen to be specifically relevant to the practitioner's immediate problem. Because data from a single report represent only a single instance, one can have only limited confidence in the validity of the data. There have been few studies specifically to gather data for inclusion in the generic equations referred to in the previous section.

A summary of the proposed system-oriented research is in Table 4.2. It should be noted that a proper investigation of any single research area will almost certainly require many individual studies carried on over a number of years.

Study of Factors Affecting Behavioral Design

The reason for suggesting the research outlined in Table 4.2 is that little is known, other than anecdotally, about the factors that affect behavioral design. It is extraordinary that, although at least half of human factors work occurs within or related to system development, we have few if any empirical studies of how behavioral design is actually accomplished. The development of large, computerized systems has raised new, unsettling questions about how such systems are and should be designed.

The goal of this proposed research is *to describe the system development process and the factors affecting the interaction between the engineer and the practitioner* as completely as possible. The major questions about system development and behavioral design are:

1. What types of behavioral inputs are actually made to the design or development process, how do they differ, and how are they integrated into design?

2. What factors determine whether an input is accepted wholly, accepted in part, or rejected?

3. How are questions 1 and 2 modified as a function of the various system development phases? What factors influence the designer during these phases?

4. How do organizational structure (e.g., the size of the engineering staff, or

Table 4.2 Summary of Author's Proposed System-Oriented Research

Research Area	Purpose
1. Factors affecting behavioral design	Describe the system development process and practitioner/engineer relationships
2. Equipment/performance relationship research	Determine quantitative relationships between equipment/system design features and operator/task performance
3. Human performance data base	Develop human performance predictive tables and graphs
4. Human performance–system output relationships; effect of system variables on personnel performance	Determine influence of behavioral variables on overall system performance and effect of system variables on human performance; validate laboratory-derived conclusions in system context
5. Methodological improvement	Evaluate adequacy and reliability of analytic/evaluational methods and practitioners

its communications channels) and other nontechnical factors such as funding and schedule influence behavioral design?

5. How does the relationship between the engineer and the practitioner affect the efficiency with which behavioral inputs are made?

6. What methods does the practitioner use to influence system design, and how adequate are they?

7. How does management and technical information flow affect system design? How does the practitioner provide information to the designer?

Answers to these questions call primarily for descriptive data—the researcher seeks to determine what is happening. This is longitudinal research, with data collected in an engineering facility and at the test site throughout the development of specific systems.

Depending on whether one can cut out a slice of the design activity for more detailed examination, traditional laboratory testing might also be of value. For example, if one wanted to explore the engineer's design strategies, it might be useful to create a controlled situation, as the author did (Meister, Sullivan, and Askren 1968), and present engineers with a set of design problems and ask them to solve them, while observing their performance. On the other hand, if one wanted to study management-employee relationships as these affect design solutions, it would probably be necessary to conduct the study in the engineering facility, because such conditions could not otherwise be satisfactorily simulated or controlled.

The engineering or test facility during system development is a natural environment, as opposed to an artificial environment (e.g., a laboratory or simulator). There are few natural research environments, but they are always to be preferred as research settings if one can make use of them. Engineering during system development is one; the operational system functioning in the operational environment is another. The school or training facility can be considered another natural environment, but only for the learning process.

System development processes can be studied in two ways: by the historical approach and by the participatory approach. The historical approach relies primarily on archival documentation as source material, although it may be possible to supplement the written material with interviews with participants in the development project if the lapse of time between the development and the study is not too long. Any post facto investigation must accept gaps in evidence as the time between the development and its investigation grows. Moreover, the historical approach is inherently inefficient because it depends on documentation that may or may not be relevant and that in any case covers only highlights; it also depends on interviews, some of whose material may be consciously or unconsciously falsified. The historical approach is acceptable, however, if the participatory approach is not feasible.

Participant observation as a research technique is nothing new, having been employed in child psychology and social psychology settings. It has been used relatively infrequently in human factors research because it provides only descriptive data and because most researchers preferred studies with controlled situations. A classic example of an observational study is by Grings (1953). The special value of the technique is that it reduces the deficit resulting from memory loss and enables the investigator to observe as events occur.

The participatory approach is reminiscent of the documentary volumes by Theodore H. White (e.g., White 1973) on the presidential election campaigns of recent decades. All White's reportage was on an individual basis—based on what he personally saw and had others tell him. The same process applied to the study of system development would require, at least in the case of large-scale systems, multiple observers with defined, formalized objectives and methods of data collection to ensure data validity and reliability. The investigators' role would not have to be concealed, but the details of what they observe and their conclusions could not be revealed to engineering management. Data could be collected through observation of engineering activities, such as design reviews and engineering conferences, interviews, examination of drawings, and review of documents (e.g., memorandums and test reports)—all this occurring as the system passes through various stages of its development. The participatory method encompasses the historical approach because it too makes extensive use of documentation, although this occurs while the documentation is being developed.

Because the participatory study is longitudinal, it is necessarily prolonged in time, perhaps as much as three to four years for complex systems. Daily surveillance would probably be unnecessary, however desirable; it would be necessary only to sample activity and to focus on the most significant aspects of the development, because it would be practically impossible to supply data collectors for every development facet.

The focus of the participatory investigation, as with the historical investigation, is examination of the interrelationships between equipment design and behavioral design. It is assumed that these two function both in parallel and in interaction. What one wants to do is correlate these two tracks. Investigators ought to be particularly alert to points at which equipment design and behavioral problems arise. What was done to solve these puzzles? What inputs were made, and what happened to them? All behavioral inputs would be analyzed in terms of their effectiveness and utility.

Two questions of importance to the investigator would be: "How are design transformations accomplished? and How does the organizational and social context affect system processes?" Transformation can be studied in two ways: (1) as part of the overall participation investigation and (2) separately, under more controlled conditions in a laboratory situation. The investigation of the system development process will inevitably cause the researcher to encounter design transformations, because every proposed design represents some form of transformation. Examination of design drawings will be supplemented by questioning of designers, with emphasis on why certain design actions were taken, what factors influenced the choice of design, the questions the designer sought to answer, the information requested, and so forth.

From a social-organizational standpoint, one wants to determine how design decisions are made. Interviews with designers suggest that design is a highly social problem-solving process, with decisions made by consensus among participating engineers in meetings that often resemble brain-storming sessions. No special methodology is needed to investigate organizational and social influences on system development, because these are an inherent part of system development as a whole. The researcher would, however, have to be alert to the possible effects of organizational variables on critical design decisions.

The variables involved are contextual, interacting only indirectly with developmental processes. It may be difficult to draw a direct relationship between the organizational-social context and any specific engineering decision, because the first is molar and covert and the latter is discrete and more overt. One might have to find technical decisions where there is considerable uncertainty about which way to go—decisions that have significant implications for the entire system—and to examine the factors affecting that decision, to discover how contextual variables had affected the decision.

Equipment-Performance Relationship Research

Research on the relationship between equipment and performance attempts to quantify dimensional equivalence, a form of transformation in which equipment/system/job and personnel dimensions are equated with an operator performance metric (see Chapter 3). Design is dominated by the engineer's need to secure relevant data, which from a behavioral standpoint is essentially the question asked by this research: What is the relationship between equipment and system design features and operator/task performance?

If the practitioner is to advise the design engineer, he or she must know what that relationship is in *quantitative* form. Neither the practitioner nor the designer is interested merely in the general conclusion that there is a relationship between a particular parameter and operator performance; they both need to know the quantitative values making up that relationship, or at least the relative importance of parameters to performance. The need for quantitative data in design is not universally accepted. For example, Rouse (1987) maintains that the questions designers ask of practitioners do not require data for their answers. These are questions such as "What would happen if feature X were replaced by feature Y?" and "Why should feature Z be included in design?" The answers to these questions may not be phrased in numerical terms, but one cannot answer them without having data that relate feature X to feature Y or provide a quantitative rationale for feature Z. To provide these data, researchers performing controlled studies must systematically measure their variables at several points along the continuum that describes those variables. Thus, in studying the effect of number of displays on performance, for example, it is not sufficient to contrast simply two displays vs. twenty, but two, six, twelve, twenty, thirty, forty, and so on, so that the shape of the curve relating the number of displays to performance is fully articulated. This means much more work for the researcher, but that cannot be helped.

In view of the centrality of equipment or system design to performance, it is surprising how little is known about this relationship. For example, out of 2,000 or more documents reviewed by the developers of the Data Store (Munger et al. 1962), only 164 usable reports were found. Studies performed by most researchers have investigated human performance, but not specifically in relation to design variables. Moreover, because research traditionally emphasizes hypothesis-testing, only the extremes of a distribution are usually measured, which means that the nature of the distribution is unclear.

Studies of human-machine interface dimensions must be performed in the laboratory because these require controls that cannot be exercised in the operational environment. The variables to be studied in the laboratory are those of Table 3.5, with the possible exception of system factors that may require a more expansive setting. The experimental methodology will not differ from that of other experiments. For example, if the researcher were testing joystick dimensions (see Table 3.4), he or she might compare three stick lengths, three stick movement extents, and so on.

One study output would include conclusions as to whether the variables tested produced significant differences in operator performance, but the major output would be twofold: the performance data associated with each dimension, and the significance of the dimension in terms of the performance variance it accounts for. To determine that a dimension accounts for little variance is as important as finding that it accounts for a great deal. Because the variables and dimensions to be studied are relatively molecular, the classic experimental study is highly appropriate. The study of equipment-performance relationships will therefore not require any significant changes in methodology, except for the purpose of the study.

Initial research will deal with single dimensions only, but eventually it will be necessary to test dimensions in interaction with each other. This may require the development of a system simulation, still within laboratory controls.

Development of a Human Performance Data Base

Something that some researchers might not consider original research is the development of a task and design-related human performance data base, an extension of the equipment-performance studies previously described. The data base would serve as a tool not only for predicting personnel performance in exercising operational equipment but also for making design decisions during development of the human-machine interface. Much of the data needed for such a data base could be derived from the preceding studies of the relationship between equipment and performance. Indeed, one of the requirements for that research would be to translate the study data into a form suitable for data base use.

However, the laboratory studies of equipment-performance relationships are only one possible data source. What is needed is a systematic, continuing effort to compile whatever data already exist in the literature and supply it to users in the form of tables and graphs. Journal sources of data should be supplemented by efforts to gather data from military-naval operational exercises (and civilian too, if possible), by measurement of operator performance in routine system operations, and from the development and exploitation of human-machine mathematical models. What some call data bases have been published (e.g., Boff and Lincoln 1988), but these are not designed to predict. The recently established Department of Defense Crew Systems Ergonomics Information Analysis Center at the University of Dayton may help (see Hennessy and McCauley 1986).

The popular concept of research is the so-called "original" study, which although it builds on previous research still explores new vistas, even if the variables may be somewhat shopworn. Consequently, the research community has been reluctant to compile previously gathered research data as a predictive tool, even while individual researchers make use of the data for their further studies. This reluctance assumes an innate superiority of the individual study, as if the value of a study were reduced once the study has been compiled with others.

The collection, organization, and integration of data from the general behavioral literature and from other sources require just as much scientific talent as the performance of the original experiments. The requirement for talent arises because of the need to compromise the great variability among different studies—because to demonstrate their individuality and originality, researchers insist on performing studies in a largely idiosyncratic way, which in turn leads to differences that must be reconciled if their data are to be integrated.

It is only fair to say, however, that there are those like Rasmussen et al. (1987) who reject the notion of a historical performance data base on the ground that human performance varies so much that such a data base cannot validly predict future performance. But if not a data base, what? Moreover, the effort to develop a formal data base will show where research is needed. Until one does something with data, such as attempt to predict performance, it is difficult to determine where data gaps exist.

The initial task in the development of the data base is to develop a taxonomy with which to organize data. Applying selection criteria to the published reports is the next task, because not all studies will satisfy requirements. Extracting the data from their sources, making use of the taxonomic categories, follows. Integrating the data (e.g., applying weighting factors to the data for special measurement conditions) and mathematicizing them—that is, reducing data to a common metric and transforming data into probability statistics—completes the task. This process must be repeated because data-base development is a long-term operation; new data must be added and old data must be refined. Continuing efforts should be made to validate the data base by measurement in the operational environment.

The preceding assumes that the data are derived from published reports (the procedure used by Munger et al. 1962), but a parallel task may be that of collecting data from the nonresearch sources mentioned previously. The great mass of human performance data that might be available for scientific purposes is not now recorded and/or utilized for predictive purposes. Data that simply reside in journal articles must be heavily discounted. The fact that a human performance data base, however crude, was developed twenty-five years ago (Munger et al. 1962) demonstrates that, given the will to do so, the research suggested is perfectly feasible.

Study of Human Performance-System Relationships

A critical problem for a system-oriented discipline is to determine the influence of human performance and behavioral variables on overall system performance and the reciprocal effect of system variables on personnel performance. There is a scholarly reason for investigating this topic, but there is also a very practical one: until operator performance and behavioral variables can be shown to affect system outputs significantly, most managers and engineers (perhaps even scientists) will be skeptical of human factors as a useful discipline. If personnel performance does not affect overall system output or mission success, it is essentially irrelevant to the system and can be ignored. Specialists assume that the relationship exists, but this is a matter of logic and inferences from records and must be demonstrated empirically.

Behavioral variables exercise their effects on performance at the individual or team level. What is suspected but not as yet demonstrated is that operator performance and behavioral variables have an effect on outputs at a higher system level. Catastrophically erroneous and incompetent human performance obviously affects the system, but apart from catastrophic situations the question is, Does human performance really matter? Because at least one system level separates personnel performance from system output, the relationship between the two may be difficult to demonstrate. If the system is a large, complex one with many operators, the relationships among system levels may be especially obscure. Differences of scale enter in. For example, what is the influence of a single maintenance technician aboard an aircraft carrier on the success of the carrier's mission?

The effect of personnel performance and behavioral variables on system output is one question. The other question is the effect of system variables on human performance. The assumption that all system elements influence one another suggests that human performance should be affected by system variables, such as the type of system, its size, and the complexity and type of output of the system.

Answers to some questions will make it possible to develop a model for how behavioral variables and human performance affect system output:

1. What is the relationship between personnel performance and system characteristics for example, the size, complexity, and communications structure of the system?

2. Is the effect of behavioral variables and personnel performance influenced by the type of human-machine system?

3. Do variables associated with individual performance (e.g., experience, stress, fatigue, feedback, motivation) function in the same way—or express themselves in the same way, because function and expression are not the same—when they are included in the system context?

4. What is the influence of molar system characteristics (e.g., complexity, indeterminacy, dependency relationships) on performance at the individual or team level?

The model developed from answers to these questions will be a contingency model. A behavioral variable or dimension acts as a stimulus to the operator or team. The latter must become aware of the stimulus and respond to it. If there is no awareness, the behavioral variable has no effect; if the strength of the variable is too slight, the operator or team will not respond. If the operator/team responds, the effect will be to cause an error (the term represents any nonoptimal performance) or not cause an error. If the former, the error must be such that it can affect the machine component of the system. If not, the error is of no consequence. The effect of the operator's error on the equipment must be great enough to cause the equipment to perform differently from ordinary operation. The deviation in equipment functioning must be sufficient to change the nature, quantity or quality of the system output. This means that any buffering mechanisms in the system will not be strong enough to prevent the effect from occurring. Obviously, many conditions must be fulfilled if a behavioral variable is to have any effect at all, which is why the probability of the effect occurring is usually very low (e.g., .0003). If this were not the case, systems would be highly unreliable.

To conduct such studies, it is necessary to develop methods of demonstrating the relationships described previously, to actually perform the demonstration, and to quantify the impact of behavioral variables and performance on outputs at higher system levels. Because we are dealing with system interrelationships, it will be necessary either to gather data in actual systems or to create a synthetic system that can be exercised under researcher control. Actually it will be necessary to do both because even if one began with a synthetic system the conclusions derived from the study would have to be validated with actual systems.

Developing a synthetic system is perhaps an even more creative activity than conducting that study, because the simulation must encapsulate and represent all the critical features of a real system. The very act of creating such a system may illuminate many interrelationships that have been obscure. Creation of the synthetic system may require a preceding study of actual systems, which would be valuable in its own right. Questions of how large and complex the synthetic system should be must be considered. It is theoretically possible to create a synthetic system consisting of only two operators—one of whom feeds information to the other, who then integrates the information and produces something different from that information (this last represents a system output). If one complicates this situation by increasing the number of operators and the number of levels through which information must pass, will a different performance result be achieved? The effects found in the previous studies of equipment-performance relationships should be included in the synthetic system study to see whether effects found at the individual or team level generalize to higher levels by producing significant changes to system outputs. The synthetic system is an abstraction, of course, but it must be realistic enough that test subjects feel confident that they are performing meaningfully. The synthetic system is not a simulator, which is a controlled representation of a specific system. A synthetic system is a replica of systems *in general,* which contains characteristics found in many systems; this is precisely right, because the researcher will be studying general system characteristics. If the synthetic system is considered too costly, the answer may appear to be to study the same variables on an already available simulator, but this is a false answer because the peculiarities of the simulator will submerge the general attributes to be studied.

The characteristics of the synthetic system must be flexible enough that variations in system features can be studied experimentally. For example, it would be desirable to have the capability of making system outputs either specific, precise, and objective, or general, indeterminate, and subjective. The advent of the computer may make the synthetic system more feasible, because the work stations could be CRT terminals and all inputs could be presented graphically on the CRT screen. All personnel responses could also be automatically recorded and measured—truly an ideal situation for the researcher.

Studies of Methodological Improvement

Concern for the effectiveness of behavioral design in system development causes specialists to ask "How can we improve our analytic and measurement methods?" Present methods are both analytic and evaluational: mission, function, and task analysis; operational sequence diagrams; information-decision analysis; time lines; workload prediction and assessment; design checklists; design evaluation methods; and developmental and operational testing. For a description of these in greater detail, the reader is referred to Meister (1985b) and to Chapter 7.

To improve these methods, it is first necessary to find out how effective they are. Judgment on this point is highly subjective. All we actually have is insufficient anecdotal evidence.

Determining Effectiveness Criteria. The first problem in attempting to evaluate methodology is to determine effectiveness criteria. This is not easy. Presumably a method is effective when it produces desired results. The overall result to be achieved from these analyses is incorporation of a recommendation in design. Because many factors beyond the technical adequacy of a recommendation may cause that recommendation to be rejected, it is necessary to retreat to a less demanding criterion.

The purpose of the analyses is to supply behavioral implications of system operations. One criterion of analytic effectiveness might be the number of design, selection, and training deductions that one can extract from the analyses. The amount of detail in these deductions might be another criterion. But neither criterion is completely satisfying. The question of methodological effectiveness criteria remains open and should be studied intensively.

The analyses and evaluations to be judged must be derived from actual system development projects, so it would seem reasonable to make use of the previously suggested studies of system development to secure raw material for this study. For a large enough sample of the analyses and evaluations, it might be necessary to secure them from system development projects other than those being immediately observed. To make the practitioners' judgments meaningful, it would be necessary to supply a context for the stimulus materials (e.g., information about the nature of the development and the questions the analyses or evaluations were intended to answer).

Another important criterion is how reliable practitioners are in utilizing these methods. A small study performed by the author many years ago (Meister and Farr 1966) suggested low interpractitioner reliability in the application of design checklists for evaluation of equipment drawings. There is a possibility that all practitioners are not equally skillful in the use of behavioral methodology, and if this hypothesis were verified the methods might be improved and/or special training developed and provided for practitioners in utilizing these methods. Reliability measurement is comparatively easy: the same or similar problems (questions the analyses are supposed to answer) are presented to practitioners, they are asked to perform the analyses, and each one's consistency over a number of problems (intrapractitioner reliability) is determined. In additional, several practitioners would be required to solve the same problems (interpractitioner reliability). Any studies of practitioner reliability must be centered on analytic methods, because the practical problems (e.g., the cost) of repeating developmental and operational tests are insuperable.

Validity. There is no effort in this study area to include validity considerations. For the analytic methods, validity has little meaning, because these methods are simply tools and do not produce data directly, although they may produce more or less useful recommendations. In addition, there are rarely any external indices of analytic correctness, although Siegel and his collaborators (Siegel et al. 1964) did attempt to validate certain techniques they developed. It might, however, be possible to determine the validity of operational test data because these presumably predict the performance of system personnel when the system is in routine use. One could compare system performance in the operational test with system performance a year or so later, but the comparison would require performing another test of personnel performance on the operational system—something that may be difficult to arrange. There are, moreover, contaminating factors in any such comparison—changes in system configuration occurring over time, differences in training and skill level of system personnel, and so on. Comparisons might be indicative but not conclusive.

Methodological Utility. The ultimate criterion for evaluating the adequacy of human factors methods is utility. If application of these methods makes it easier for practitioners to accomplish their tasks, they are worthwhile, no matter how many reservations one has about the correctness of the methods or the outputs they produce. It would be highly desirable if practitioners, the users of these methods, could provide reports (ratings, observations, etc.) about the frequency with which these methods are used, their utility, and the ease with which they can be applied. A previous study by the author (Meister 1986) of measurement techniques used by test and evaluation specialists indicated that utility and ease of use in combination determine how frequently individual evaluation methods were employed.

One would have to be an optimist to expect that a program of testing the reliability and skill level of practitioners in the use of behavioral techniques would meet with general approval, because negative results could have undesirable consequences. However, the lack of interest in improving human factors techniques is inexplicable when contrasted with the extensive testing and calibration of physical instruments and paper-and-pencil achievement tests.

Study Qualifications. Certain points should be noted about the five research areas. There has been no attempt to classify the research topics in terms of priority. All the research areas are highly interrelated, and each can throw additional light on the others. However, each can also be performed independently of and concurrently with the others. This research can be performed either in the laboratory or with operational systems. Each research area requires the performance of several studies. One would expect immediate and practical outputs from the research.

Both knowledge-based and system-oriented researchers contribute to the store of knowledge, although because their focuses of interest differ the former contributes more to knowledge about individuals in relation to themselves, whereas the latter will provide more knowledge about the performance of personnel in relation to the system.

SUMMARY

The system orientation of human factors creates distinctive requirements for human factors research. That research can be conceptualized in a number of ways: as knowledge-based, developmental, evaluational, and methodological, or as human-centered, human-machine-centered, and system-centered. Most human factors research is human-machine-centered; comparatively little is system-oriented. The system orientation in research requires involvement with an actual or simulated system, consideration of human performance in a hierarchical structure, and inclusion in the study of at least one system element or characteristic. One critical element in human factors research is technology. Three questions that must be answered in relation to technology are: To what extent are human factors problems determined by technology? Do these problems change when technology changes? and Are there research questions that transcend technology? The answers to these questions are: technology—and in particular technological change—determine research problems, but some research questions transcend technology. A human factors problem exists when a quantitative equation relating operator performance and some system or job aspect is lacking. Many of the same human factors problems that were unsolved before the computer "revolution" are still valid, although they may have been transformed into computer-related problems. Because there is a lack of system-oriented research in human factors, a research program oriented around system variables and system development has been proposed. This program includes five areas focusing on factors affecting behavioral design, the relationships between equipment and human performance, the development of a human performance data base, human performance-system output relationships, and improvements in behavioral methodology.

CHAPTER 5

Taxonomy, Prediction, Data, and Standards

Taxonomy, prediction, data, and standards are all attempts to organize and control the many aspects of human factors. Taxonomy organizes the way one views behavioral elements; it is the initial building block for the analytic and evaluational techniques described in Chapter 7. Prediction is an attempt to anticipate how well the system and its personnel will perform after it has been constructed and staffed by trained personnel. Prediction enables the system developer to control the course of development, but it is nothing without quantitative data—a special kind of data refined for application purposes. The starting point for developing a data base is a taxonomy for each of the elements whose performance is predicted. So we are right back to taxonomy again. Standards are another means of controlling system development by establishing performance minima and required system characteristics. Standards also depend on the same data needed for prediction. In summary, taxonomy leads to data, and data lead to prediction and standards.

TAXONOMY

A taxonomy is a conceptual system for classifying objects, events, or objective and subjective phenomena—anything that one can react to as distinctive. Fleishman and Quaintance (1984) define a taxonomy more formally as "the theoretical study of systematic classifications including their bases, principles, procedures, and rules." They define a classification as "the ordering or arrangement of entities into groups or sets on the basis of their relationship based on observable or inferred properties" (p. 22).

Rationale

First, taxonomies underlie not only such human factors tools as task analysis and human engineering checklists, but also the very way behavioral scientists conceptualize the objects, events, and phenomena with which they deal. The analytic methods applied to system development—for example, mission, func-

111

tion, and task analysis—were initially taxonomies or lists of concepts, or depended on implicit taxonomies. The system and equipment components and parameters that we evaluate when the practitioner examines design drawings are reducible to and in fact stem from such taxonomies as the one implicit in the human engineering checklist.

Classification is inherent in behavior because it rests on the human ability to differentiate entities. If we cannot categorize these entities, can we recognize them as what they are? For example, human engineers would like to be able to classify equipment characteristics in terms of the strategies engineers use in their design. An example of a strategy might be to design for, remove, and replace maintenance. If it were possible to make such classifications, one could correlate levels of technician performance with these strategies; engineers might then be asked to adopt design strategies that are more favorable to personnel performance. However, because it is impossible to get engineers to describe these strategies adequately or to get practitioners to conceptualize (i.e., taxonomize) them, it has been impossible to develop dimensional equivalents for these design strategies.

A second and even more important reason that we should be concerned about taxonomies in general, and a task-descriptive taxonomy in particular, is that our ability to describe human performance is seriously circumscribed by our lack of taxonomies for that performance. The task, along with the system, is the single most important unit of performance in human factors. All our experimental studies involve subjects performing tasks that we cannot describe adequately. Our descriptions of human performance are, unfortunately in one respect, all verbal and hence somewhat suspect. When one imagines the totality of tasks that form the subject matter of our science, and the difficulty we have relating one task to another except in such very gross terms as "cognitive" or "psychomotor," one is overcome by a feeling of helplessness. If scientists are unable to classify the objects with which they are dealing, do they have the right to consider themselves scientists?

On the other hand, some might object that because the discipline has functioned, however well or poorly, without accepted taxonomies, we can get along without them. There is little evidence that the specialist's ignorance of taxonomy has any substantive effect on the way the specialist conducts research and practice, but we must ask whether we want to carry on the discipline like an automobile whose engine runs on only four cylinders out of six.

Factors Inhibiting Development of Taxonomies

It is relatively simple to develop a taxonomy. One starts with a topic, for example, controls, displays, or types of human-machine systems. Each topic has an organizing principle based on its parameters. A taxonomy can be developed on a purely descriptive basis (e.g., What systems with which I have been in contact have what characteristics?) or on a theoretical basis (e.g., Gagne's

[1965] eight principles of learning); in many cases taxonomies depend on both. Each taxonomic category is broken down into finer detail on the basis of similarities and differences within the subcategory until one can think of no way to break down the categories further or until the purpose of the taxonomy is satisfied.

If taxonomies are so simple to develop, why has human factors not developed a multiplicity of them, one for each evident need? There are five possible answers. First, the need for taxonomies may not be very evident to human factors professionals, possibly because most researchers are experimentalists and development of a taxonomy is largely an analytic effort. Second, it is so simple to develop one's own taxonomy, when the need for one is apparent, that the notion of setting aside research effort and time to develop a "univeral" taxonomy may seem ludicrous. Third, it is difficult to determine which of the many factors influencing human performance should be taxonomized. The apparently endless number of factors might seem to require more effort to taxonomize than is justified. Theoretically, every one of the performance-shaping factors noted by Swain and Guttman (1983) and listed in Table 3.5 should be taxonomized—a daunting concept—but the list can be pared down, as we shall see. Fourth, specialists may be uneasy about the idea of taxonomies because it is not clear how a number of taxonomies can be interrelated or under which conditions a taxonomy should be employed. The individual taxonomies could of course be treated as essentially independent, but this presumes that the system elements on which the taxonomies are based are also independent, which is incorrect. A fifth difficulty arises after a taxonomy is developed: How is one to know whether a taxonomy is "valid" or to be preferred over another taxonomy? And how does one determine taxonomic validity?

There clearly are many serious difficulties in pursuing a taxonomic effort, but these difficulties do not justify a rejection of the notion. The potential benefits of taxonomy more than compensate for all the difficulties.

A Framework for Taxonomic Development

Let us turn to the question of which taxonomies should be developed and, in particular, how they relate to each other. The starting point for the development of behavioral taxonomies is the notion of *the task,* which, along with the system, is the fundamental unit of performance in human factors. The function, exemplified in such terms as "detects," observes," and "codes" (Berliner, Angell, and Shearer 1964), is too broad and general for us to do much with it. For that very reason, perhaps, there is general acceptance within human factors of the Berliner et al. scheme as a taxonomy of *functions.*

The task is not unitary but multidimensional, which complicates behavioral concepts tremendously. The basic task is essentially a statement of a purpose— to aim at a target. That purpose acts as a shell or body to which certain modifiers are added. The task of aiming at a target with a bow and arrow is different from the task of aiming a missile by lining up one pip with another on a CRT screen. The basic task purpose is modified by equipment and procedural characteristics, so we need both a generic task taxonomy, exemplified by Table 5.1, and taxonomies for equipment and procedures. The task is performed in a system context, so we also need a system taxonomy (see Table 5.2). If we are interested in understanding the underlying processes that implement the task, we also need a taxonomy of underlying processes—for example, short-term memory or hypothesis-generation.

All this suggests that we need a taxonomy for every factor that influences task performance significantly. The key word is *significantly*. Most of these effects are probably minor, so the factor causing those effects could be disregarded for taxonomic purposes. Unfortunately, every factor at some time or another may have a significant effect on how the task is performed. The cause of variations in task performance is the effect of some task modifier that is allowed to exert a strong effect. For example, under ordinary circumstances the effect of work-shift cycles on task performance might be minimal, but if an emergency requires an abnormal shift cycle (e.g., daily shift changes), the effects on task performance could be devastating.

The starting point for taxonomic development is then the development of a generic task taxonomy, followed by one for equipment components and characteristics as well as one for procedures, because these exert the strongest effect on task performance most often. A system-level taxonomy should also be developed because the system is the higher-order context in which the task if performed. The individual taxonomies are linked together in terms of their role as modifiers of the generic or basic task, although how they do this is unclear. Ultimately the human factors theorist will have to explain how taxonomic effects modify task performance.

Uses of Taxonomies

In addition to its most important use—task comparison—a taxonomy may be used to structure a research program, as the basis of analytic and evaluational techniques, and as a structure for gathering and organizing collections of human performance data.

Table 5.1 A Generic Task Taxonomy

Perceptual/Visual Tasks (scanning displays; physical or natural objects)
1. Detect or verify the appearance of stimuli*
2. Note or detect the movement of stimuli*
3. Detect a change in stimuli*
4. Detect a change in stimulus characteristics*
5. Identify/categorize/recognize stimuli in terms of known data*
6. Compare stimulus characteristics*
7. Identify stimuli that deviate from standards or from other stimuli*

Table 5.1 *(Continued)*

8. Locate the position of stimuli or objects in terms of a standard
9. Change the position of stimuli
10. Change the characteristics of stimuli by motor action*
11. Count or calculate stimuli*
12. Introduce/input new stimuli by motor action
13. Delete or remove stimuli (the reverse of no. 12)
14. Read where reading is the sole function involved

*Found also in auditory and tactile perception.

Discrete Motor Tasks
1. Activate controls to positions without displayed information
2. Activate controls to positions in accordance with or as a result of displayed information
3. Connect or disconnect objects either directly or with tools
4. Carry objects
5. Open/close door or enclosure
6. Mark position of objects
7. Aim at an object
8. Lift object
9. Drop object

Continuous Psychomotor Tasks
1. Adjust position of objects without reference to displayed information
2. Adjust position of objects in accordance with or as a result of displayed information
3. Adjust position of controls to change the position of moving stimulus (as in tracking)
4. Record information manually
5. Input data by activating controls (e.g., as by typewriting)
6. Input data manually (e.g., as by writing)
7. Walk from one point to another
8. Swim from one point to another
9. Run from one point to another
10. Throw an object
11. Remove objects from or install them in designated positions
12. File objects

Cognitive Tasks
1. Perform quantitative computations
2. Compare calculated values
3. Develop hypothesis
4. Decide between two or more hypotheses
5. Analyze information
6. Hypothesize causal relationships
7. Verify that a hypothesis is correct or incorrect
8. Code/decode stimuli
9. Predict the occurrence of an event
10. Recall/remember stimuli/events (short-term, long-term)
11. Estimate the occurrence or characteristics of phenomena
12. Note a change in displayed information

Communications Tasks
1. Request instructions/information using a device
2. Request instructions/information face-to-face
3. Communicate instructions/information using a device
4. Communicate instructions/information face-to-face
5. Supply/listen to information using a device
6. Supply/listen to information face-to-face

Source: Revised from Meister and Mills 1971.

Table 5.2 A Taxonomy of System and Subsystem Variables

1.0 System/Subsystem Types and Functions
    1.1   *Mission-oriented systems*
         Weapon device (e.g., fighter plane)
         Military unit (e.g., squadron, brigade)
         Information collection/assessment (e.g., combat information center)
         Communication (e.g., radio, TV)
         Training (e.g., school, training facility)
         Coordination and decision-making (e.g., board of directors, headquarters staff)
         Management (e.g., company directors, stock exchange governors)
         Production (e.g., factory, steel mill, mining, farming)
         Judicial (e.g., law courts)
         Support (e.g., warehouse, word-processing center)
         Transportation (e.g., trucking, rail freight)
    1.2   *Service-oriented systems*
         Product distribution (e.g., supermarket, department store)
         Product servicing (e.g., repair shop)
         Entertainment (e.g., theater, fair, museum)
         Health provider (e.g., hospital, clinic)
         Habitation (e.g., hotel, office building)
         Environmental (e.g., park, beach)
    1.3   *Mixed systems*
         Communication (e.g., residential phone service, publishing)
         Governmental (e.g., fire, police, welfare)
         Personnel transportation (e.g., steamer, train)
         General education (e.g., public school)
    1.4   *System/subsystem functions*
        1.4.1   Maintain
        1.4.2   Distribute (e.g., products)
        1.4.3   Combat
        1.4.4   Analyze (e.g., information, products)
        1.4.5   Communicate
        1.4.6   Fabricate
        1.4.7   Train
        1.4.8   Entertain
        1.4.9   Service
        1.4.10   Transport (e.g., humans, products)
        1.4.11   Grow (e.g., food, animals)
        1.4.12   Mine (e.g., earth products)
        1.4.13   Manage (e.g., organizations)
        1.4.14   Study (e.g., science, research)
        1.4.15   Succor (e.g., humans, animals)
        1.4.16   Control (e.g., law enforcement)
        1.4.17   Rescue
        1.4.18   House (e.g., humans, animals, objects)
        1.4.19   Dispatch (e.g., personnel, objects)
        1.4.20   Compute (e.g., money, information)
        1.4.21   Fish
        1.4.22   Process (e.g., products, paper, information)
        1.4.23   Inspect
2.0 System Structure
    2.1   *Size* (large, small, intermediate)
    2.2   *Number of subsystems*
    2.3   *Number of personnel*
    2.4   *System organization*

Table 5.2   (*Continued*)

2.5   *Communications channels*
   2.5.1   Number
   2.5.2   Internal/external to system
2.6   *Complexity*
2.7   *Method of control* (e.g., autocratic, democratic, oligarchic)
2.8   *Number of hierarchical levels*
2.9   *Internal processes*
   2.9.1   Repetitive
   2.9.2   Nonrepetitive
   2.9.3   Fixed/proceduralized
   2.9.4   Flexible/nonproceduralized
   2.9.5   Automated
   2.9.6   Semi-automated
   2.9.7   Mostly manual
2.10   *Subsystem performance relative to mission*
   2.10.1   Continuous
   2.10.2   Intermittent
   2.10.3   Operation prior to mission
   2.10.4   Operation subsequent to mission
   2.10.5   Operation early in mission
   2.10.6   Operation late in mission
2.11   *Subsystem mission role*
   2.11.1   Performance of primary mission
   2.11.2   System support
2.12   *Subsystem boundaries* (division of responsibility)
   2.12.1   Well-defined
   2.12.2   Poorly defined
2.13   *Subsystem dependency* (ability to function regardless of other subsystem's performance)
   2.13.1   Completely dependent
   2.13.2   Partially dependent
   2.13.3   None (independent)

3.0 Outputs
3.1   *Output type*
   3.1.1   Fabricated products
   3.1.2   Repaired products
   3.1.3   Geographic movement
   3.1.4   Communications (messages)
   3.1.5   Weapons delivery products (e.g., bombs, rifle fire)
   3.1.6   Decisions (as in buying/selling stock)
   3.1.7   Information (as in newspapers)
   3.1.8   Services (as in selling products)
   3.1.9   Training outputs (e.g., skills)
3.2   *Output number*
   3.2.1   Single
   3.2.2   Multiple
   3.2.3   Fixed number
   3.2.4   Variable number
3.3   *Output frequency*
   3.3.1   Continuous
   3.3.2   Intermittent

(*continued*)

Table 5.2   (*Continued*)

3.4 *Outputs produced by*
    3.4.1 Equipment
    3.4.2 Personnel
    3.4.3 Both in interaction
    3.4.4 Both, but not in interaction
3.5 *Output effect*
    3.5.1 Change in other systems and/or environment
    3.5.2 Change in own system and/or subsystem
    3.5.3 Increase/decrease in inventory of objects
    3.5.4 Increase/decrease in inventory of personnel (as in combat)
    3.5.5 Change in nature of personnel (as in training)
    3.5.6 User satisfaction increased/decreased
    3.5.7 No effect
    3.5.8 Effect unknown

4.0 Environment
4.1 *Type of environment*
    4.1.1 Physical (e.g., air, water, temperature, noise)
    4.1.2 Psychological (e.g., degree of cooperation in team)
4.2 *Locus of environment*
    4.2.1 Within own system (e.g., space available)
    4.2.2 Outside own system (e.g., air, climate, ocean)
4.3 *Magnitude of environmental effect*
    4.3.1 None or almost none (e.g., sea state of 0.5)
    4.3.2 Slight to moderate (e.g., sea state 2.3)
    4.3.3 Great (e.g., sea state 5.0)

5.0 Inputs
5.1 *Type*
    5.1.1 Physical (e.g., illuminated display requiring action)
    5.1.2 Behavioral (e.g., verbal order to perform task)
    5.1.3 Combined physical/behavioral (e.g., verbal message over sound-powered phones
5.2 *Frequency*
    5.2.1 Continuous
    5.2.2 One-time (nonrecurring)
    5.2.3 Intermittent/variable
5.3 *Input characteristics*
    5.3.1 Input meaning unequivocal (requiring no analysis)
    5.3.2 Input ambiguous (requiring analysis and interpretation)
    5.3.3 Intense
    5.3.4 Weak (only slightly above threshold)
5.4 *Source*
    5.4.1 Multiple sources (requiring coordination)
    5.4.2 Single source
    5.4.3 Within own system (as in command from bridge)
    5.4.4 Within another system (e.g., message from base)
    5.4.5 From environment (e.g., clouds indicating approaching storm)

6.0 Communications
6.1 *Type*
    6.1.1 Provides information
    6.1.2 Requests information or direction
    6.1.3 Commands
    6.1.4 Asks question
    6.1.5 Coordinates team activity
6.2 *Frequency*
    6.2.1 Continuous

(*continued*)

Table 5.2 *(Continued)*

	6.2.2	Variable frequent
	6.2.3	Variable infrequent
6.3	*Source*	
	6.3.1	Communication within own system (i.e., subsystem to subsystem)
	6.3.2	Communication within own subsystem or team
	6.3.3	Communication to/from another system
	6.3.4	Up the command structure
	6.3.5	Down the command structure
	6.3.6	Lateral (one subsystem to another on the same level)

7.0 Feedback
- 7.1 *Type*
  - 7.1.1 Verbal
  - 7.1.2 Displayed
  - 7.1.3 Written
- 7.2 *Reference* (concerns performance by or relative to)
  - 7.2.1 Individual
  - 7.2.2 Team
  - 7.2.3 Subsystem
  - 7.2.4 System
- 7.3 *Characteristics*
  - 7.3.1 Specific
  - 7.3.2 General
  - 7.3.3 Rewarding
  - 7.3.4 Neutral (information only)
  - 7.3.5 Negative
  - 7.3.6 Immediate
  - 7.3.7 Delayed
- 7.4 *Frequency*
  - 7.4.1 Continuous
  - 7.4.2 Intermittent
  - 7,4.3 Very infrequent

8.0 Personnel Subsystem (PSS)
- 8.1 *Type*
  - 8.1.1 Individual (e.g., pilot)
  - 8.1.2 Team (e.g., tank team)

All other taxonomic categories in this table apply to the PSS as appropriate.

Task comparison. The most important use of taxonomies is task comparison. A taxonomy permits specialists to compare two or more tasks performed in the same or different contexts to determine whether the tasks are either the same, highly related, or quite different. If the tasks are different, the taxonomies can help determine what the differences are and what modifiers have been exercising their effects. This should allow us to compare data from different studies to aid in development of a human performance data base.

Structure for a research program. A research taxonomy is composed of categories that can be used as independent and dependent variables in research like that described in Chapter 4. Table 5.2 suggests a number of empirical comparisons—for example, the effect of system type (mission-oriented, service-oriented, or mixed) and such structural variables as size, number of personnel, and communications channels on personnel performance. The great value of the research taxonomy is that it organizes and structures the variables the researcher must deal with, thus expanding the researcher's understanding of the interrelationships among those variables. Because the taxonomy must be comprehensive, it forces the researcher to examine all the variables that could affect system and personnel performance. But the use of a research taxonomy is limited. It does not indicate which variables are most important nor how they should be studied.

A taxonomy of measures should always accompany a research taxonomy. I have reprinted an excellent one developed by Smode, Gruber, and Ely (1962) several times (see Meister and Rabideau 1965; Meister 1985b).

Foundation of analytic and evaluational techniques. Analytic and evaluational techniques would not exist if it were not possible to classify behavioral concepts and observed properties. The classification of system hierarchy (system, subsystem, team/individual, equipment, human-machine interface), for example, permits us to develop methods for use at the individual levels of this hierarchy. The features one can differentiate in the human-machine interface (the spatial arrangement of controls and displays, the relationship between controls and displays and sequence of operation, the manner in which software menus can be arranged, etc.) are transformed into a method (the human-engineering checklist) evaluating that interface.

Structure for gathering and organizing collections of human performance data. Whatever aspects of human responses can be observed and measured (e.g., response times, errors, successful task completions) have meaning only to the extent that they can be associated with a task and task modifiers. For example, what does it mean to say only that task X has been completed successfully by nine subjects in eight of ten attempts? Without a description of the task in generic terms—a task taxonomy—and a description of equipment components involved—an equipment taxonomy—the data are meaningless. Indeed, a prerequisite for data collection is a schema or taxonomy for differentiating data events from nondata events.

A taxonomy developed for one purpose can be used for other purposes as well. For example, a research taxonomy can also be used for performing analyses and collecting data.

Types of Taxonomy

Because classification is inherent in behavior and because the purpose determines the nature of the taxonomy, it is possible to develop a classification scheme for almost anything that can be broken down into distinguishable entities. A taxonomy can be developed for systems, tasks and subtasks, equipment and components, equipment characteristics, communications, inputs, outputs, generic measures, personnel skills, types of errors, principles of training, and types of data. The reader may be able to think of others. Many taxonomies may be found in Fleishman and Quaintance (1984) and in Meister (1985b).

A behavioral taxonomy attempts to classify what the human being does or has to do in a given task situation, the behavioral variables that affect human performance, and the internal mechanisms that direct human performance. The two subclasses of behavioral taxonomy are the descriptive taxonomy and the analytic taxonomy.

Descriptive taxonomy. A desciptive taxonomy describes what the operator does in performing his or her task (steers aircraft, tracks target, reads meter). It make no judgments about what cannot be overtly seen or described in explicit operations. To that extent, such a taxonomy is somewhat superficial, although very useful.

Analytic taxonomy. The analytic taxonomy, in contrast to the "simple" description of overt behaviors, attempts to classify the underlying mechanisms, attributes, or intervening variables responsible for the overt task behavior. Categories may include internal mechanisms, such as short-term memory, decision-making, coding, or monitoring. The taxonomy seeks to organize the causal factors behind the overt task behaviors.

Taxonomic Validity and Utility

Analytic taxonomies describe covert behaviors, capabilities, and mechanisms, so it is much more difficult to determine their correspondence with objective, real-world phenomena (but see efforts by Fleishman [Fleishman and Quaintance 1984] to validate his skills taxonomy). Under these circumstances, criteria of utility replace criteria of validity. Because each of the taxonomies describes a specific type of performance or performance variable, all are necessary. One cannot speak of a single taxonomy for human factors. Variations *within* a particular type of taxonomy are possible, and one variation may be superior to another (see, e.g., the comparison of taxonomies in Finley et al. [1970]), but in descriptive taxonomies the amount of variation in a given type is likely to be largely verbal variation.

Moreover, no taxonomy is inherently correct or incorrect. Fleishman and Quaintance (1984) discuss what they call internal and external validity, but when these are analyzed in detail they turn out to be utility criteria. Thus, for Fleishman and Quaintance validity is defined as the logic, parsimony, reliability, and exhaustiveness of the taxonomy. External validity is "how well the classificatory system achieves the objectives for which it is designed" (p. 84)—its predictive capability. This criterion is likely to be more important with descriptive taxonomies because such taxonomies describe entities that can be readily observed. With analytic taxonomies, which deal with complex, internal mechanisms, the criterion of correctness based on correspondence between the taxonomy and observed entities is difficult to apply. Nevertheless, a taxonomy will never be taken seriously unless users feel that its categories correspond somewhat to real-world entities.

How can one establish the validity of a taxonomy? Any phenomenon, object, or event has multiple aspects, and one can classify on the basis of each aspect. Taxonomic validity cannot be determined merely by passive observation, because the observer may use the same flawed concepts in conceptualizing the taxonomy and in observing what the taxonomy refers to. It is possible that validation arises because there are some consequences of the taxonomy—one can do something with it that is useful or appears coherent or meaningful to the observer. The central point, however, is that there is a referent to the taxonomy and that one must compare the taxonomy with the referent.

Taxonomic validity has in this way been redefined as utility. Because of this, the starting point for evaluation of taxonomies should be to examine the purpose for which the taxonomy was developed and see how well that purpose has been accomplished. If a taxonomy is to be useful, it must be possible for people other than its creator to use it reliably to classify, whatever the basis of the taxonomy. In addition, it should not require excessive training to make use of the scheme. If users find it difficult to differentiate one category from another or to assign empirical data to those categories, then the taxonomy is unreliable and will not be employed.

A major difficulty in developing behavioral taxonomies (e.g., functions, tasks) as distinguished from physical taxonomies (e.g., equipment components) is that in the former the physical reference for a behavioral category is based on quite subtle cues. For example, the difference between "reading" and "scanning" (if there is such a difference) may depend on the pattern of eye movements in both, something that is not easily observable and definable. The well-known lack of verbal precision, represented by the large number of associations most words have (even terms purporting to describe objective phenomena), introduces a certain ambiguity into any behavioral taxonomy and thereby reduces its usefulness. There seems to be a natural hierarchy in taxonomy, based on the amount of inference required by the categories. Descriptive taxonomies are likely to be simpler, requiring less inference to recognize an instance of what is being described. If success is achieved with the descriptive taxonomy, it may be followed by development of more analytic taxonomies, including those based on theoretical models and attributes deduced from more overt phenomena. It seems logical that taxonomies requiring the most inference should be the most sophisticated and hence most effective, but how can one know about this in advance of their application to the real world?

Data-Base Taxonomies

One or more taxonomies are needed for the development of human performance data bases. The reader will recall that two types of data bases are necessary. One type predicts the human performance associated with (1) decomposed equipment components (e.g., scales, alphanumeric fonts), parameters (e.g., CRT screen brightness), and dimensions (e.g., functional arrangement of controls and displays), a performance that describes the human-machine interface, and (2) task characteristics (e.g., requirements for precision). Another type of data base predicts the human performance associated with tasks, systems, and subsystems as a whole.

It may appear that human performance associated with tasks is the same as that associated with task characteristics, but this is not true. Task characteristics are the behavioral equivalents of equipment parameters. The human performance associated with tasks subsumes that associated with task characteristics, but does not explicitly extract those parameters. For example (all values are hypothetical), the human performance to be expected in the performance of task X when there are no constraining factors is .9851. The human performance expected of task X when personnel performing the task are very fatigued is .9644. It would be a mistake to assign the value of .9644 to fatigue as a task characteristic; the probability value is associated with the task as performed by a fatigued operator, not with fatigue as an abstraction or concept.

The Future of Behavioral Taxonomies

Development of behavioral taxonomies is an area that, with the exception of the work performed by Fleishman and his colleagues (see Fleishman and Quaintance 1984), has been largely ignored, although there have been and are continuing calls for further effort in this field. The failure to develop taxonomies is an example of how human factors professionals have attempted to leapfrog the fundamental processes needed to establish the discipline on a firm foundation. One can view the taxonomic effort as an attempt to establish a kind of regularity or order among the objects and phenomena with which human factors must deal. It remains to be seen whether there will be a resurgence of interest in taxonomies.

PREDICTION

To talk meaningfully about prediction, we need answers to four fundamental questions:

1. Why do we want to predict? This question was answered in Chapter 1— every science endeavors to describe, predict, and control.

2. What do we want to predict? Human performance, of course, but in two forms. The first is prediction of system, equipment, and task features that will lead to superior task performance—that is, the design characteristic (or combination of characteristics) that will produce superior performance. This form of prediction is directed at system design. The second form is prediction of personnel performance in the operation of human-machine systems. What is

predicted is how well or how frequently tasks required in that operation will be completed successfully. This form of prediction is useful not only in design but also just as much in system operation. These two forms of prediction require different types of data and data-presentation formats, which will be discussed later.

3. Can human factors predict at the present time? Some prediction is possible. For example, we can predict that vehicles equipped with high-mounted stoplights will be involved in fewer rear-end collisions than those that do not have such lights (Malone 1986), and that is admirable, but this is prediction for a relatively simple, unidimensional situation and is not prediction of absolute levels of performance, which is our ultimate goal. When it is necesssary to predict human performance in more complex situations, there are not so many available resources.

4. If we cannot predict, why can we not? And what can be done about this? The reason for our inability to predict is that we have neither theory nor data on the subject. Why this should be the case can only be hypothesized.

To anticipate further discussion, one cannot talk realistically about prediction without also considering *data*—the kind of data, where we get it, how we process it, how we present it, and so forth. Prediction depends on data. Prediction without data is not even theory, it is simply hot air. Prediction is also related to *validation*. One way to validate an empirically derived conclusion is to predict that the performance described by the conclusion will recur either in the same situation in which the conclusion was derived (this recurrence measures reliability) or, in a situation (presumably the operational situation) different from that from which the conclusion was drawn (this is predictive validation). Data and validation are mentioned only to indicate that human performance prediction is not isolated from other topics, such as validation, which will be discussed in the next chapter.

Difficulties with Prediction

Prediction is not unique to human factors. Test psychologists predict scholastic achievement, clinical psychologists predict mental behavior, and all researchers who conduct hypothesis-testing studies predict how their data will turn out. Prediction in hypothesis-testing is very narrowly focused. Because the hypotheses are drawn up in either/or fashion in advance of testing and because the test situation is designed to verify or disprove these hypotheses, the prediction is also either/or (the null hypothesis will be rejected at the .05 or .01 level). This is very different from prediction in a largely uncontrolled context. Uncontrolled prediction is much more difficult, because in contrast to laboratory hypothesis-testing, in which only variables of interest to the experimenter are allowed to exert an effect, in the uncontrolled situation all extant variables affect the performance being predicted. In the uncontrolled real-world situation, the basis for prediction will be either accumulated experience—which is the reason it is necessary to collect normative data—or a theory, or both, and human factors has little of both.

Prediction in the real world may also be more difficult because of what can be termed "contextual" variables—variables that influence performance but are not directly involved in the task itself. System organization, the personality of a supervisor, or the manner in which technical data are written are examples of contextual variables.

One must ask whether prediction from results secured in the laboratory to another laboratory situation is sufficient to satisfy the prediction goal. The answer is no, because the laboratory is a nonreference situation (the operational situation is defined as the reference situation; see Chapter 1) and prediction in human factors must always be relative to the reference situation. The simulator as a substitute environment for prediction is more satisfactory, but one cannot say that even that is completely satisfactory because there are still elements of the operational situation that one cannot replicate in the simulator.

Prediction must also be differentiated from replication. We gain confidence in our knowledge if we can replicate data in the same situation in which we gathered the original data, but prediction is the deliberate replication of a phenomenon or event in a different setting. We want to replicate, of course, but we also want to predict to a new setting. We must also differentiate prediction on the basis of theory from prediction based on experience. The former is preferable, but there must be a theory before one can predict from it. At the moment, most human factors predictions are based on historical data (what has happened before will happen again). Although this type of prediction is inferior to prediction based on knowledge of the functioning of critical behavioral mechanisms, it is not to be despised, because often what has happened before will happen again.

Predicting Relationships between Design Features and Performance

It has been pointed out that if a practitioner recommended addition or deletion of some design feature in a drawing or in a prototype equipment, it was because he or she felt that the human performance related to that feature would be increased or decreased by that feature. It is only an assumption, but a highly reasonable one, that what the designer and practitioner are mainly interested in is performance—of both equipment and personnel. Consequently, prediction of that performance is an essential element in design. It is possible for the engineer to design without seriously thinking of resultant human performance (some do, unfortunately), but design then becomes essentially a nonintelligent activity.

Prediction of relationships between equipment and performance is based on the common-sense assumption that if a task is simple enough for the operator, (e.g., pushing a single button when an unambiguous audio signal is received), performance of that task would be almost perfect (e.g., .9999), assuming continuing motivation and no fatigue. If this is true, then any complicating factor (e.g., an inappropriately small pushbutton or a more ambiguous audio signal) would reduce the probability of correct button-pushing or increase its error probability. Therefore, for each additional complicating dimension one would expect error probability to increase and success probability to decrease. So far this is logical.

What is not so logical is the implied assumption that each equipment or task parameter adds an error increment, which ignores the possibility that some parameters have no effect at all and that some parameters may even aid the operator, or the assumption that a configuration of parameters has the *same interactive effect* on human performance as that of each of the parameters when their individual effects are statistically combined. It is entirely possible that it is the *configuration* of parameters that determines performance, and therefore one has to measure the effects of varying parameter combinations. Swain (1967) attempted to demonstrate that operator performance with an item of equipment could be predicted by giving each parameter a nominal error probability of .0001, but one suspects that the matter is not solved that easily.

The consequence of accepting the assumption that each parameter has a measurable effect is that if one extracts all the parameters that *could* affect a particular task and combines them multiplicatively—as in reliability prediction—their success probabilities grow so low that the task has an unrealistically low likelihood of being accomplished.

There are two possibilities: (1) a configuration of parameters may have an effect different from that of single parameters statistically combined or (2) some countervailing tendency that is positive for task success will counter the error tendency of the individual parameters. If this last were true, it would be tremendously important to discover what that tendency consisted of. Perhaps training tends to nullify the presumed negative effect of added components and parameters. The Munger et al. (1962) data were derived from laboratory experiments whose subjects were, as is typical of most laboratory subjects, almost certainly inadequately trained for the tasks they performed. However, lacking normative data describing how well personnel ordinarily perform their tasks, we have no way of knowing what a realistic performance prediction consists of.

Our task is to determine which of the many hardware and software parameters are important for personnel performance. Theoretically every parameter exerts an effect on performance, but it is more likely that only a few are responsible for most of the variance in that performance. There is no a priori way to determine the relative importance—that is, the effect on task performance—of equipment components and parameters, because any component may have a number of parameters that could be critical to performance. For example, task performance using a CRT screen may be affected by, among other things, screen brightness, ambient lighting at the work station, screen color, symbol color, number of alphanumerics, and refresh rate. Only the controlled equipment-performance studies described in Chapter 4 will answer the question. The answer is much more complex than the simplistic notion that every parameter has an effect. At any rate, this was the conclusion suggested by the study performed by Mirabella and Wheaton 1974.

The problem of combining individual parametric effects is for later study. A more immediate problem is to determine the performance effects of single components and parameters, because data for even these are lacking. Except for the Data Store (Munger et al. 1962), which is hopelessly obsolete and flawed besides, there is no adequate data compilation even for individual components and parameters. (Some data have been developed by Swain and Guttman 1983, but these are appropriate mostly for nuclear power plant control activities.)

Predicting Task and System Operations in Mission Performance

Prediction of task and system operations in performance of a mission includes predicting the success rate of individual tasks performed by individuals and teams—that is, tasks 1, 2, 3, 4. . . n, none being combined, and predicting the success rate of operators and teams during mission operations. This prediction involves *all* tasks performed during the mission or operation—that is, tasks 1 + 2 + 3 + 4, . . . n (which does *not* mean that one adds performance values). The *combination* of all task performances in a mission represents the personnel subsystem output.

Task prediction is useful both in design and in system operation. Assuming that some minimum human performance must be achieved if a new, as yet undeployed system is to be effective, the developer would want to predict the actual performance personnel will achieve once that system is deployed. Such a prediction could be made either on the basis of the human performance associated with equipment components and parameters—that is, extrapolating from the effects of the combined physical features of the system (this is the discussion of the previous section) or on the basis of the tasks that must be performed if the system is to function adequately. The latter requires a data base of individual task performance. The first builds on performance associated with molecular equipment *characteristics;* the second builds on performance associated with *tasks,* but includes the equipment being operated during task performance.

Prediction by means of task performance avoids a major difficulty with predicting system performance on the basis of individual equipment features. The difficulty is the need to combine performance values associated with a number of design parameters. First, one must combine the human performance associated with individual equipment characteristics; this presumably gives one the performance associated with the equipment as a whole. Then one must do this for each phase of system operation. This is much more complex than combining performance associated with the tasks involved in the mission; the method of doing so depends on the dependency relationships among tasks, relationships that will require detailed analysis of tasks and missions.

The taxonomic categories around which task performance data can be gathered are organized primarily by the task description, including the equipment being acted on by the task. An example of a task description is "Adjust throttles to full power," where "adjust" is the action verb, "throttles" is the equipment acted on and "to full power" modifies the action verb.

The only thing the human performer can do is make (or avoid making) errors and complete a task successfully (or not), so the predictive metric is most likely to be either probability of error or probability of successful task completion. There are other potential metrics (e.g., response time or reaction time or number of units fabricated), but error and task completion are the primary indices. Since the goal is ultimately to predict task success, the error metric has limited usefulness unless an error is equivalent to failing the task (which is rarely the case). The error metric is more closely tied to specific equipment or task characteristics and thus can be of greater use in *diagnosis* of error causes and prediction of performance in terms of equipment parameters. Unfortunately, the error/task completion indices may be difficult to apply in continuous (as opposed to discrete) tasks and in tasks involving tracking (manual control).

Whatever metric is selected, definition of error and criteria of successful task completion must be determined in advance of data collection. Criteria are relatively simple in the case of such molecular tasks as throttle adjustment (failure to move throttles to full power setting) but more difficult for molar tasks, particularly those with cognitive elements. It may be necessary to use a subject matter expert to establish the criterion for such tasks or to serve as an evaluation judge in collecting relevant data.

Because the metric for predicting successful completion of the task is presently based solely on accumulated (historical) data, it is necessary to record the number of times the task has been attempted and the number of successes during these attempts, which translates to the percentage of times one succeeds in performing a task correctly. Clearly, the larger the number of task attempts, the more reliable the prediction based on those attempts will be.

For purposes of predicting team task performance, we consider only the output of the team and not the performance of the team members as individuals.

DATA

What kind of data do we need? Does human factors have enough relevant data to enable it to perform its necessary function? Where can one get needed data? How should the data be formatted?

The kind of data needed for prediction purposes has already been specified as either error or task/mission success completion data—however these are defined in a specific operation—because the only two things an operator can do are make (or not make) an error in performing his or her task, and complete (or not complete) the task satisfactorily. These are not alternatives—both occur in every task performance. In some tasks (manual craftwork or very creative work) performance quality is important, but this is often difficult to handle without a subject matter expert. Moreover, the precise decline in performance quality at which an error occurs is unclear. Certainly it varies with each craft.

Although task completion data are generally to be preferred to error data— one is ultimately interested in whether the task been completed—errors are more easily associated with discrete equipment parameters (as in the joystick example of Table 3.4), and available performance data have been derived mainly from experimental studies in which error was usually the one critical measure.

Data and Information

Data must be differentiated from information. Data are quantitative, information is qualitative. Data are inherent in task performance, information is contextual—it describes "something" about the performance. However, information related to task performance—such as task purpose, initiating cues, and time to perform the task—is highly desirable to permit more adequate interpretation of data. Although it may be first priority to know the probability that task X will be successfully completed, that datum will make more sense if we know in addition how frequently the task must be performed during the mission, the location of the task performance (if the system includes alternative locales), the difficulty level of the task, and so on. This additional information reduces the uncertainty inherent in the original data and makes the data more valuable.

Not all desired information is readily available. Occasionally specialists develop "wish lists" of the types of information that researchers, practitioners, and engineers want. An example frequently cited in the literature is Blanchard's (1973) study of information requirements based on interviews with data users. The resultant list of desired information was comprehensive—everything one would want to know about task performance—but it does not stand up well to the realities of actual data-gathering. For example, Blanchard's respondents wanted some indication of data validity, and nowhere in any study, no matter how highly controlled, will one find a judgment of data validity or indices on which a judgment of validity could be based.

Purposes of Data

The question of what purposes data fulfill is meaningful only if it is assumed that data *should* have value beyond archival and research or theory construction purposes. Data are necessary to analyze and evaluate new systems, equipment, and task design and to improve design, to predict the performance of new systems, and to prevent situations that could lead to errors and accidents in system performance.

A major reason for being concerned about using data for purposes other than research is that data for application are *qualitatively* different from research data because data for application play a different role. Research data are data in published journal articles or reports; application data take research data and compile, organize, and refine them in accordance with taxonomic categories and data selection criteria, extrapolate the research data when they are insufficient, and modify the data to take into account the characteristics that differentiate the research from the operational performance situation.

The reader may ask why research data cannot be used in its original form for application purposes. The answer is that most research data reflect the experimental situation from which they are derived—a highly controlled situation in which only a few variables are allowed to exercise an effect on performance without constraint. (The experimental situation is emphasized, not because this is the only situation from which data can be extracted but because it is *at present* the major, and almost the only, source of behavioral data.) Application data are applied to nonresearch situations and therefore must be compatible with the characteristics of those situations. It is necessary to modify research data because the application situation may, for example, be more or less stressful than the experimental one (and this greater or lesser stress in the experiment may have affected the performance results). It may be necessary to extrapolate data because the experimental situation did not include all the operational conditions to which the data may be applied. And certain experimental data may have to be rejected because of experimental inadequacies, for example. Should one use data whose validity has not been operationally demonstrated? There are dangers in producing application data: the researcher's extrapolations and modifications to fit the circumstances of the operational situation may introduce error, and it may not be too clear what factor one should add, subtract, or multiply to convert research data to the data that would have been secured had it been collected on operational systems.

Refinement of Data

To refine research data, several steps are required: The data-base taxonomy and data selection criteria must be developed, qualifying factors must be determined, and the common metric must be specified.

Developing a data-base taxonomy. The data-base taxonomy into which the compiled data will fit must be developed. The taxonomic categories specify the initial selection criteria for the data compilation. For example, if the taxonomy is organized around controls and displays (as the Data Store [Munger et al. 1962] was), the compiler will select the studies to be compiled in terms of controls and displays. If it is organized around computer interface characteristics, a different set of data will be required. The principles on which a data-base taxonomy is organized are determined by the compiler's interests and what the compiler intends the data base to be used for.

Developing data selection criteria. Not all data are equally useful, and some must be excluded. The conditions under which data were gathered must be reported explicitly enough that bias can be determined. This is often difficult to do; in attempting to summarize a large number of studies for my 1976 "case history" book (Meister 1976), I found that many published studies were unclear about experimental details. Other selection criteria might be whether a study has a reasonable subject N—that is, whether subjects "reasonably" approximate the characteristics of the population to which the data will be applied (e.g., anthropometric data on the elderly could not be applied to people of military age)—whether the experimental design included any biasing factors (it should not have), whether the statistical treatment was appropriate, and whether the tasks performed were reasonable approximations of those performed in real life.

Determining qualifying factors. Qualifying factors to modify the original data and/or to extrapolate it to cover a wider range of variable values must be determined. These "fudge" factors must be based on empirical studies that provide an acceptable rationale for modifying the original data.

Specifying the common metric. The *common metric* into which all original data must be transformed must be specified before the data are compiled, and the original research data must be capable of being transformed into the common metric.

Data Compilation and Availability

Once all these decisions are made, the actual data compilation can begin. This will not be an easy task, because the multiple criteria established must be applied one by one to each study and may result in the rejection of many studies, if previous experience is any guide. Payne and Altman (1962) used only 164 studies from more than 2,000 examined for developing their data. Indeed, even with computerized documentation citation retrieval systems to ease the selection process, collecting and examining prospective studies is an arduous chore.

Data Availability

It would be highly desirable to believe, as many specialists apparently do (see Chapter 1), that we already have sufficient data, but there is considerable ambivalence on this point. Even if human factors possesses sufficient data, there is no evidence that these data (with a few exceptions) are being used for prediction purposes. From an application standpoint, human factors is data-poor; the only major human performance data compilation is the Data Store

(Munger et al. 1962), which is obsolete. Topmiller, Eckel, and Kozinsky (1982) surveyed available data compilations (including those of other disciplines, including safety) and came up with very little. There may be masses of research data in journal articles and reports, but as long as those data remain unorganized and uncompiled, the data exist only for limited research purposes.

It is possible to have a reasonable amount of data even while admitting that there will never be enough data to satisfy scholars. The question then becomes: Does human factors have a reasonable amount of data? We define a reasonable amount of data as enough data to enable one to develop a quantitative equation between specified behavioral and system variables and human performance. If that definition is accepted, human factors does not have a "reasonable " amount of data.

Some specialists believe that if in a particular situation the data gathered might be less than optimal (e.g., less than complete or secured under less than the most rigorous experimental conditions and without trace of error), there is no point to collecting any data in that situation. For example, Price (1985) rejects the idea of allocating tasks between human and machine on a quantitative basis, because it would be too difficult to collect the required data. However, to reject less than "perfect" data is also to reject the research associated with those data. If this point of view prevails (and so far it seems to be a strong one), there may be no possibility of securing normative data, of predicting human performance quantitatively, or of coming up with quantitative standards. A more reasonable point of view is that data can be approximate, that it may even contain lacunae and errors, but that such data can be useful nonetheless. Moreover, continuing data collection efforts can make less adequate data more adequate.

To secure enough quantitative application data, it may first be necessary to change specialist attitudes. Specialists must recognize that compiling and organizing data for predictive purposes is as "scientific" a job as performing the individual "original" experiment. We have, after all, the example of such eminent scientists as Ptolemy and Copernicus, who spent much of their lives compiling astronomical tables.

Sources of Data

Experimental studies whose data on human performance are reported in journals have so far provided the largest part of our data. It is, however, sobering and somewhat depressing to realize that a great variety of work tasks are being performed every day without anyone recording the data from those performances for behavioral purposes. Much of those data are probably unavailable—for example, data from the operation of classified systems, data on jobs whose location, [e.g., mining], would pose great difficulty for data collectors)—but a certain amount should be within our grasp.

Formal exercises of military operational systems are a possible source. It is true that many of these exercises are "faked" in the sense that the systems are not allowed to function under completely operational conditions (because complete realism might demonstrate less than adequate performance), but with access to data collected by system managers and permission for specialists to collect behavioral data from these systems on their own, something might be secured. Data might also be collected from routine operation of military systems not engaged in formal exercises. Data from simulator training exercises could be extremely valuable. Operational tests of new systems could supply some data, although one would have to be careful in using these data because the systems from which they came had not yet been shaken down.

A prerequisite for any system data collection effort is that the people who control those exercises and those systems (mainly military and governmental functionaries) must be persuaded to permit and support the collection of data from their systems. Their concurrence will not be easy to secure, because government managers are reluctant to permit any measurement that might reveal inadequacies. (Civilian, nongovernmental organizations are unlikely prospects for data collection because they are motivated primarily by profit considerations; moreover, unions are suspicious of any worker measurement.)

One final source may have more potential than the others because it is more readily available—the subjective estimate by subject matter experts of error and task success probabilities for tasks with which they are familiar. Some studies (Seaver and Stillwell 1983; Comer et al. 1984) suggest that carefully made subjective estimates are quite reliable; validity has not yet been ascertained. Any use of subjective data, however, presupposes that subjective estimates would be a "first cut" and subject to revision and improvement by collection of additional empirical data.

Formats for Data

Human performance data can be formatted in various ways. The first type of data bank is what can be termed a *probability statement of task performance*. A sample item might be: "The probability of throwing a double-pole, double-throw switch correctly is .9968." This statement says nothing about the characteristics of that switch, other than its designation, and does not apply a probability statement to those characteristics.

A second type of data bank format, used by Munger et al. (1962; Table 3.4 in this book), consists of *probability statements associated with specific equipment characteristics*. For example, the probability of correctly operating a joystick control of stick length 6″-9″ is .9963; the probability of correctly operating that joystick with 5–10 pounds of control resistance is .9999, and so on.

A third type of data bank consists of the original *performance values* associated with particular parameters. The data are not presented in a probabilistic fashion, although presumably the error data could be transformed into probabilities. Data would be selected to illustrate the desirability of selecting one or the other design characteristics. For example, an item might report the percentage of correct responses to a television symbol with a certain number of scan lines per symbol height.

A fourth type of data bank could consist of *quantitative, nonprobabilistic statements* related to specific equipment characteristics. A sample item might be: "Display format X will produce 1.658 times more effective performance than display format Y" (X and Y differing in specified ways). The statement can be quantitative or qualitative; one could use an arbitrary set of scale values to represent relative performance, or one could use a rating scale or ranking.

A fifth type of data bank format would combine all the characteristics of the preceding formats. Such a format would provide the user with *all the data available* in whatever form it could be provided, whether or not the data could be formulated probabilistically or changed into a common metric. Thus, probabilistic values would be associated with certain tasks and task characteristics, where such values were available; raw performance data for other task parameters would be supplied when probabilistic information could not be supplied.

Currently, most human factors data are presented as part of a written paragraph (see, e.g., Van Cott and Kinkade 1972; Boff, Kaufman, and Thomas 1986). The reader might see little difference in utility between data in written form and data in tabular or graphic form. However, a tabular or graphic format imposes more rigorous requirements for organizing data; the more verbalism there is, the easier it is to equivocate. On the other hand, a tabular or graphic format may make data seem more authoritative than they actually are. Format is only as good as the data it presents.

Normative Data

Most behavioral data are gathered from experimental studies in which one or more variables were tested. One can also secure "normative" data—descriptive data about what humans do when they perform their jobs, and how well they do these jobs. Normative data differ from experimental data, in which one or more variables are being tested. In gathering normative data, the data collector may have hypotheses about the effects of certain variables on performance, but he or she usually cannot arrange conditions to vary these factors, as in an experimental design. The contrasting effects of variables in normative data are revealed in the pattern the analyst can tease out of variations over a mass of data. Normative data analysis therefore requires of the analyst even more ingenuity than is required of the creator of experimental designs. One can, of course, make use of experimentally derived data for normative data purposes, but most experimental data are not designed or used for this purpose.

In gathering normative data, one wants to know, for example, that task X under specified conditions is successfully performed 98 times out of 100 (human reliability of .98) and takes 4.57 minutes (on the average) to complete, whereas task Y under the same (or other) conditions is correctly performed only 87 times out of a 100 and takes 8.2 minutes to complete. To this might be added such contextual information as the operator's rating of task difficulty (easy), need to use manuals (no), and so on.

So that the largest practical sample can be gathered, normative data must be collected on a continuing basis. Lacking experimental controls, the specialist must look for repeated patterns in successive data instances. Variations in normative data can occur as a result of natural changes in performance conditions—for example, the use of novices as well as trained professionals. Data collectors take what they can get, and this makes it necessary for them to look for instances that may contrast with previously gathered data. Waiting long enough for naturally occurring variations to appear requires great patience of the researcher.

Normative data are ideally gathered under operational (real-world) conditions or conditions that simulate or approximate the real world—that is, experimental data are acceptable if the experimental situation resembles the operational situation to some extent. The emphasis in normative data is on tasks rather than on equipment components or task parameters; the latter require experimental manipulation to extract data associated with them.

It is possible to predict with normative data because it is assumed that past performance will be replicated in the future, except when the past performance was not representative—as, for example, when the personnel whose performance one is recording are merely learning their jobs and perform as novices.

In collecting normative data, as many as possible of the conditions surrounding task performance must be recorded, because—this not being an experiment one cannot be sure during data collection which variables are exercising an effect; only later examination of data patterns will reveal this, if it does at all. As an example of the information to be collected, the conditions for task X might be: highly trained technicians, $N = 12$, reasonably well motivated; no time stress; no other constraining conditions; small range of performance, 1.0 to 0.97. For task Y the conditions might be: well-motivated personnel, $N = 18$, only minimal experience in performing the task; moderate time stress; considerable variation in performance, range 0.95 to 0.76. The conditions described correspond to what we previously called "information," as distinguished from data. Performance conditions must be specified in some detail, because otherwise the normative data cannot be generalized accurately. The conditions qualifying or rather explaining the datum should ideally include task description, number of subjects, amount of their training, experience level, motivation, fatigue, stress level, important items of equipment involved, environment (if relevant), technical aids utilized (e.g., computer, technical manual)—in sum, anything that at the time the task is performed could, in the data collector's estimation, have affected that task. Naturally, for any one piece of data not all these items of information might be available, but repeated data collection could provide coverage for many relevant conditions. Some conditions might require judgment on the part of the data collector. Moreover, the effort of collecting so much relevant information about a task places a strain on the specialist.

Can normative data as described above be collected, or is this no more than a pipe dream? The likelihood is reduced if these data must be collected in the operational situation and over a period of some time. Theoretically, however, there seems to be no reason why, given sufficient resources and effort, such data could not be collected. It may depend on whether the will to collect it exists.

STANDARDS

A standard is a description of the qualities that are either required or desired as part of the design or performance of a system, a piece of equipment, or personnel. Standards should deal not only with software and hardware but also with technical data and procedures. The standard would be incomplete without such needed personnel characteristics as skills, as well as system features related to personnel performance. We are concerned only with personnel performance.

As a requirement, the standard is the minimum *performance* that will be acceptable to the customer for the system, or it may contain a listing of *characteristics* considered necessary for effective performance. The word "desired" in the preceding paragraph also applies to a standard, because behavioral standards may lack enforcement power. As pointed out in Chapter 1, the system demands standards because without standards we do not know if the system has been designed satisfactorily or has performed well. Without this information the system cannot make corrections that may be needed.

The importance of the standard is most clearly reflected in the relationship between what operations analysts call a measure of performance (MOP) and a measure of effectiveness (MOE) (Rau 1974). To evaluate a system or system element, the MOE—which is a measure of the worth of the system in performing its mission—is necessary. Any performance measure, such as the number of requests to access a data base, can be an MOP, but until that MOP is endowed with a value, a standard, it cannot be used to evaluate; it is purely descriptive. Only if one is able to specify that an effective system accesses its data base N times can one use access rate as an MOE. Evaluation is based on the concept of worth or value, which can be made concrete only by imposing a standard.

It is appropriate to discuss standards at this point because the standard is inextricably linked to data. For example, one can think of normative data as a form of standard—not in the sense of a requirement, but in the sense of what can reasonably be expected of personnel.

One can develop a standard with little or no data support, but such a standard would be almost a contradiction in terms. A largely verbal standard, as many human factors standards are, does not provide sufficiently precise feedback. Although standards do not inevitably derive from data, data in which one has confidence tend to suggest the development of standards. At the same time, standards are developed only when there is strong professional (political) support for them. Many engineers view standards as design constraints, and many specialists view behavioral standards as a way to get their interests and concerns implemented in design.

The standard guides design by specifying the characteristics and performance that must be incorporated in design. Behavioral standards do not, however, include a description of *how* the performance and the characteristics can be incorporated in design, perhaps because this is assumed to be part of general human factors knowledge, available to practitioners. Unfortunately, this necessary knowledge does not, to a large extent, exist—which is one of the main reasons for the research suggested in Chapter 4.

There are two types of standards. One standard is specific to an individual system or item of equipment and specifies a minimum level of behavioral performance and/or incorporation of certain characteristics in design. For example, the standard might say that in developing system X all critical tasks must be accomplished correctly 99 percent of the time and all noncritical tasks must be accomplished correctly 95 percent of the time, or that the system must be capable of being operated by personnel who lack a high school education. This type of standard, which establishes a requirement that is the end result of design, however that design is accomplished, is imposed (when it is imposed) by the customer for the system or equipment.

The link with data is as follows. If it has been discovered that personnel operating systems of class X, which possess certain qualities of complexity and demand certain personnel functions and capabilities, can operate class X systems with an overall success probability of .93, then in the development of a new system of the same class possessing many of the same attributes it would now be possible to insist that personnel in the new system perform at an average level of .93. If such a requirement were written into the development specification for the new system, and if one could prevent the contractor and the government (for weapon systems) from waiving the requirement, as they would undoubtedly prefer to do, human factors in this system development would receive far greater attention than it had in any previous development.

This first type of behavioral standard is rarely applied to the design specification of a new system, although it is common practice to do so for physical standards. One major reason for not applying such standards is that the data needed in order to be confident that personnel could function at, for example, a .93 level simply do not exist. No one in government, industry, or academia appears to be interested in collecting such data—not the government, because lack of precise knowledge is often an advantage in governmental operations, and not industry and academia, because they are preoccupied with other questions. The lack of supporting data results in a lack of confidence, and so even human factors specialists involved in developing governmental specifications for new systems would be reluctant to impose rigid requirements of this sort.

A second type of behavioral standard is general—it relates to systems and equipment, in general or to a particular type (e.g., aircraft). This standard contains design provisions that are related to personnel performance, dealing with the human-machine interface, and should be included during design. This standard, in contrast to the first, output-oriented one, is an in-process standard, meaning that it prescribes what should be done *during* design. It is written by a government agency or a particular industry (often an industry association) and is mandatory for all system or equipment types to which its provisions apply. It does not specify a required level of performance.

The major behavioral standard of this type is the Defense Department's MIL-STD 1472C (Department of Defense 1981). Certain engineering standards involving aspects of human factors (e.g., safety, maintainability) may include a few of the provisions of MIL-STD 1472C, but only 1472C is comprehensive. An example of a provision of that standard is the following section, which deals with displays.

5.2.1.4.11 *Maximum Viewing Distance.* The viewing distance from the eye reference point of the seated operator to displays located close to their associated controls shall not exceed 635 mm (25 in.). Otherwise, there is no maximum limit other than that imposed by legibility limitations, which shall be compensated for by proper design.

Note that the recommendation in the example above is phrased in very precise terms that enable the engineer to design to the recommendation easily. Unfortunately, many other 1472C statements lack this precision, and consequently designers do not know how to design to them. The statement "design shall reflect applicable system and personnel safety factors, including minimization of potential human error" is at best a pious hope.

Because it is an in-process design standard, MIL-STD 1472C serves to some extent also as a design guide, which means that it performs or can perform a tutorial function. Its contents describe topics that human factors engineering is concerned with, although not how it is implemented. A truly effective standard should describe how its provisions can actually be incorporated in design—for example, what the alternative options are, their positive and negative features, and the performance that should result from each option—but unfortunately 1472C does none of these things, perhaps because, as a governmental document, its format is rigidly restricted.

Much of MIL-STD 1472C is nonquantitative. For example, the sections on anthropometry and environmental factors are very solidly based on quantitative data, but many other sections are not. No section has any task performance data. In effect, this standard includes no statements at all (quantitative or qualitative) about the effects on task performance of incorporating a provision in design. In fact, there are no references to tasks at all, and few references to any study that provided the data on which the standard was based.

Much of the material in MIL-STD 1472C and in compilations of software standards (e.g., Smith and Mosier 1986; Williges and Williges 1984) has been produced by experientially based judgments of experts rather than by directly applicable research, because for many design parameters there is no relevant behavioral research. As a result, expert judgments vary widely. For example, standards from various countries about viewing distance from a computer terminal (Banks, Gertman, and Petersen 1982) vary widely.

Design standards are developed by subject matter experts who first decide that certain equipment components and parameters are important for human operation of equipment, and then examine the literature to determine what relevant behavioral data are available. Often they find few or no studies dealing with these topics, so they rely on their experience and a consensus judgment (which should, however, not be denigrated too quickly) for the provisions they include in the standard.

Whether because the standard lacks substantive data support or because human factors is generally viewed by engineers and developers as a constraint on their freedom to design, MIL-STD 1472C is honored as much in the breach as in the observance. My assumption, backed unfortunately by few empirical studies, is that this results in less than optimally effective equipment and systems. It seems logical to assume that the availability of the kind of data produced by the research program described in Chapter 4 would result in a more effective standard.

SUMMARY

Taxonomy, prediction, data, and standards are attempts to organize and control the multidimensionality of human factors.

Taxonomies underlie such analytic methods as task analysis and human-engineering checklists. The lack of accepted taxonomies makes it difficult to compare tasks and to combine the data from experiments with individual tasks. Taxonomies for equipment, systems, measures, and underlying processes are linked to one another because they act as modifiers for generic tasks, which are essentially only purposes; the modifiers give them individuality by permitting them to function meaningfully in various contexts. There are a number of taxonomic types, including those that are descriptive and others that are based on inferred properties. Data-base taxonomies are needed for predictive purposes. Taxonomic validity is determined by utility.

There are two forms of human performance prediction: prediction of system, equipment, and task features that will lead to superior performance, and prediction of the personnel performance that can be expected when the system is installed and operating. The capability of human factors to predict is poor, at least with regard to more complex systems and phenomena, because we lack data from the uncontrolled environment of real-world system operation.

Data are essential for prediction and for development of normative standards. The kinds of data needed are error and task/mission success completion data. Data that are inherent in task performance must be differentiated from task information, which is contextual. Application data are qualitatively different from research data; the effort to secure the former involves compilation, organization, refinement, and extrapolation of research data. Refinement of research data requires development of a data-base taxonomy, data selection criteria, data qualifying factors, and a common metric. Human performance data can be formatted in various ways. Normative data can be secured either from experimental sources or by passive observation of operational systems.

A standard is a description of the qualities that are either required or desired as part of the design or performance of a piece of equipment, a system, or personnel. Without standards, measures of performance cannot be transformed into measures of effectiveness. A standard without data is nonfunctional. The two types of standards are those specific to an individual system or equipment, which mandate a minimum level of performance and/or inclusion of certain characteristics in design, and those that are general, that is, those that relate to systems and equipment in general or to a class of systems or equipment. Lack of data hampers the development and use of these standards.

CHAPTER 6

Measurement Problems
in Human Factors

Human factors measurement problems are no different from those of behavioral science generally, but the special characteristics of human factors make these problems more difficult, particularly when one is attempting to generate the very precise data needed to make substantive performance predictions. In psychological research that emphasizes the experiment, data are important not for themselves but for hypothesis-testing. This chapter reviews the available measurement literature and examines the processes of human factors measurement and the methodological problems that complicate that measurement. The major technical problems in human factors system measurement (I shall not discuss nontechnical problems, such as lack of funding, tight schedules, and nonavailability of subjects) include:

1. The difficulty of achieving *experimental control* in operational situations and the consequences of that failure. The major question is: How does one achieve the equivalent of experimental control when conditions make this unlikely?

2. The *multidimensionality* of factors affecting human performance. This raises the question of how one isolates the effects of individual variables.

3. The special problems of *validating* research conclusions. What does validity mean for a system-oriented human factors?

4. The significance of *operational fidelity* and what must be done to achieve it. When measuring in other than the operational reference situation, of what does fidelity to that situation consist?

5. The relationship between *objective* data and *subjective* data and the uses that can be made of the latter.

6. The difficulty of selecting appropriate *criteria* and *measures*. How does one decide which criteria and measures are most meaningful?

7. The problem of *data obscurity*. What does it mean to say that data can be obscure and in which situations does this occur most frequently?

8. The relevance of *statistics* to system measurement. Does system measurement encounter any special problems with statistics?

9. The availability and suitability of *alternative paradigms* for conducting human factors system research. How can these be employed most effectively in human factors?

Although each of the above topics will be examined in individual subsections, all of them are interrelated, and it will be necessary to discuss some of these interrelationships in each subsection.

A GUIDE TO THE HUMAN FACTORS MEASUREMENT LITERATURE

Before considering methodological problems, it will be helpful to see what light the literature on system measurement can throw on these problems. The following review of the system measurement literature is more selective than an earlier review (Meister 1986) and emphasizes more theoretical writings. It therefore does not include reports that describe specific measurement techniques or reports of developmental tests. Moreover, space constraints make it impossible to discuss the studies cited in as much detail as they deserve, so this review merely points out what could be useful; the reader must refer to the originals for their content. This review does not emphasize computerized system literature because at the system level computer idiosyncrasies "wash out." Also, some of the material cited may be considered "old," but behavioral measurement methodology has not changed significantly over the past twenty-five years.

The most useful starting point is the annotated bibliography by Edwards et al. (1985a), who identified 244 books and papers as "potentially useful." Only 58 of these were considered by the authors to be "very" relevant, which suggests the bareness of the bibliographic cupboard. The most frequent concern of these papers seems to be how to determine appropriate criteria and measures.

The Edwards et al. bibliography and its companion studies (Edwards, Bloom, and Brainin 1985b; Bloom, Oates, and Hamilton 1985, the latter summarizing the system measurement research literature) are the culmination of a series of studies that began with Finley, Obermayer, et al. (1970) and was carried on by Finley, Muckler, et al. (1975) and Finley and Muckler (1976). Their orientation emphasizes something called the Systems Taxonomy Model (STM), an array of procedures for identifying variables that might be relevant to the individual system measurement problem. The model's major value is that it is a formal and systematic approach to measurement, but unfortunately it helps only slightly to solve the methodological problems discussed in this chapter.

The present author's previous work in system measurement (Meister 1977, 1978a, 1978b, 1980, 1985b, 1986) is also worth examining, as is his book on human factors evaluation in system development (Meister and Rabideau 1965), much of which is still valid. Erickson (1986) discusses measures of effectiveness in system analysis and human factors. Earlier, Rau (1974) developed a measures-of-effectiveness handbook. Havron (1961) described the establishment of criteria in terms of a duel between two military systems.

Perhaps the most important *experimental* work being performed in the study of human performance in systems is that of Rouse and his collaborators (Eekhout and Rouse 1981; Henneman and Rouse 1986; Knaeuper and Rouse 1985; Rouse 1978; Rouse and Rouse 1979). An important facet of Rouse's work (which is, unfortunately for those who are not so inclined, highly mathematical and system-engineering oriented) is that he demonstrates how system variables can be studied in the laboratory using symbolic analogues for the system. Moreover, Rouse is one of the few human factors specialists who even refer to the system as a behavioral variable.

Earlier (1951–67) laboratory work in behavioral system measurement is described in a now classic book by Parsons (1972), which provides in great detail a fascinating picture of the many American research centers engaged in this activity. Another early compilation is the review of the personnel subsystem (PSS) test and evaluation literature by Askren and Newton (1969), a record of much of the operational testing performed by the U.S. Air Force in the 1950s and 1960s. Somewhat dated but still useful is a summary by Keenan, Parker, and Lenzycki (1965) of the techniques used by the Air Force to assess personnel performance during system development.

A two-volume report from the same era (McKendry and Harrison 1964) attempts to explain how human factors effects are related to system performance through the use of existing field data. About the same time, Snyder, Kincaid, and Potempa (1969) published the proceedings of a conference on human factors testing, which despite its age has useful things to say. Along the same line is a hardbound set of proceedings edited by Singleton, Fox, and Whitfield (1971), which contains at least four papers worth reading. Of the same generation and still possessing some value is Smode, Gruber, and Ely (1962), which discusses measurement in general, selection of critical tasks and measures, and task taxonomies, among other topics.

The proceedings report of a symposium on applied models of system performance (Levy 1968) and the study by Markel (1965) on methods of system evaluation still have value. McGrath, Nordlie, and Vaughan (1959) published a systematic framework for comparing system research methods. The paper by Chapanis (1970) on physiological and psychological criteria in system research is as valuable now as it was when originally published.

Two papers by Hollnagel (1983) and Hollnagel and Woods (1983), which are interesting because they represent a nontraditional approach, view the human-machine system in cognitive and adaptive terms. The most recent work of the Rasmussen school (Goodstein, Andersen, and Olsen 1988) follows in this line. More conventional, perhaps because it is of an earlier time, is the classic study by Knowles, et al. (1969) on models, measures, and judgments in system design.

The system simulation work of Siegel and collaborators (e.g., Siegel, Leahy, and Wolf 1978) is also worth considering. Siegel was a pioneer in attempting to model human-machine systems and in applying psychological variables to the study of these systems.

The work of Bittner and collaborators (described in a summary report, Bittner, et al. 1986) deserves mention because it serves as a model of how performance research should be done systematically. Over a period of ten years, a program to evaluate the suitability of human performance tests for repeated measures application was developed and implemented. What is important is not that the research topic is of such overwhelming interest, but that the work was performed over a period of time long enough to secure meaningful results, that it involved a number of highly competent researchers working as a team, and that it addressed a single topic in depth. These are a few of the criteria of effective research, but very little human factors research has these characteristics.

Vreuls and Obermayer's (1985) prize-winning paper discusses fundamental performance measurement problems and research issues in the context of aircraft training simulators (although their work is relevant to performance measurement as a whole). In somewhat similar vein, Lane (1986) describes the history, development, and current practice of measuring operator performance in systems, with particular emphasis on military aviation.

Chiles and Alluisi (1979) compared five system output or performance measurement methods described in the literature as applied to operator or occupational workload specifications: laboratory, analytic, synthetic, simulation, and operational-system methods. DeGreene (1974) wrote a highly speculative "think piece" about models of man as these relate to systems. Such papers help push specialists beyond the concerns of their immediate research or immediate system problem.

On a more practical, "applied" level, the guide by Berson and Crooks (1976) is useful in painting a "concrete" picture of what must be done to collect and analyze human performance data in a system development project. The development of criteria and measures that make use of computer methodology has been explored by Connelly and his associates (Connelly et al. 1974; Connelly and Sloan 1976).

The behavioral measurement literature available to us is quite meager, and the works mentioned here are the best of the lot. The literature reflects the lack of governmental interest in sponsoring measurement research and unfortunately presents few suggestions about how to solve measurement problems. Therefore, in any forthcoming examination of these problems, readers must rely largely on their own resources, because the literature is not a very useful guide.

THE DIFFICULTY OF ACHIEVING CONTROL

Control of research is the ability to manipulate variables and to assign test subjects to treatment conditions. Control is desirable because it permits one to assay the individual contribution of the variables affecting performance. From that standpoint, the experimental situation is the ideal one because it affords the researcher the greatest amount of control. Complete control is not even theoretically possible; there are always some variables that cannot be controlled. Even under the most severe constraints, the test subject retains his or her ability to think and feel in ways that may affect measurement effectiveness. For example, the researcher may attempt to nullify subjects' training and experience by giving them tasks to perform that they have never worked on before, but one can never be sure that the experimental task is not similar to other tasks they have performed before. Control is therefore something the researcher can approximate but never completely achieve. If one asks what the irreducible minimum of control necessary is, the answer can be given only in terms of the individual questions asked in the individual study.

Experimental control requires the researcher to break up a unitary situation or phenomenon into its constituent parts, but the deliberate arrangement of treatment conditions is inherently artificial because the situation or the phenomenon being studied in its original natural form (i.e., within the operational system and environment) remains a whole. Every experiment is therefore to some degree artificial. This is especially important to a system-oriented behavioral discipline—human factors—whose reference situation by definition cannot be broken up.

In its natural state, as determined by its mission, the operational system is not under experimental control, and although the researcher can theoretically exercise some experimental control over that system (see, e.g., Schwartz and Sniffen 1980; Sniffen, Puckett, and Edmondo 1979; Army Research Institute 1977), as soon as that happens the operational system becomes less than completely natural and no longer serves fully as a reference situation. For example, in conducting battle exercises at sea, it is common practice to continue to fly aircraft that earlier have theoretically been shot down, a situation that makes the exercises highly artificial. Even passive observation can have some minimal effect on personnel.

Artificiality is defined by the lack of similarity of the controlled non-reference situation to the uncontrolled reference situation. Degrees of similarity are of course possible and will be discussed later in the context of operational fidelity. Lack of control means two things: the inability to arrange and assign subjects to treatment conditions in an experimental design, and the intrusion of unanticipated extraneous factors into the test situation. An example of such an intrusion might be, in the military, the abrupt substitution of one system mission for another—for example, the substition of reconnaisance for attack.

Lack of control is commonly associated with the operational system functioning in the operational environment, and there is a widespread impression that one cannot utilize controlled experimentation in the operational environment. That is not completely correct; it is possible with some difficulty to arrange conditions and variables in the operational system (e.g., the destroyer) or, more usually, in the subsystem (e.g., a fire control subsystem). This control cannot be as precise as it is in the laboratory, but it is often possible to compare situations with and without or with more or less of some object or some variable. Simple, single-factor comparisons are possible, but probably not more sophisticated designs, such as Latin square or multiple factorial analysis of variance. The sheer difficulty of working in the operational environment may put the researcher off, but if one is not inextricably wedded to complex experimental designs, it is possible to conduct some controlled research in the operational setting.

If control means the ability to contrast alternative conditions, these sometimes occur naturally even in the reference situation. The nature of the mission may produce contrasting treatments—day versus night operations, experienced personnel versus novices, flight at nap-of-the-earth versus flight at altitude, and so on. Detailed analysis of the system mission and operations is needed to reveal these alternatives. Most of these alternatives occur at a molar level; only fortuitously and over a longer time period do molecular contrasts occur naturally (e.g., different types of malfunctions or errors). The major alternatives can be anticipated because they are inherent in system operations, but because the minor variations (e.g., various levels of personnel experience) are not necessarily inherent in the system, they cannot be anticipated or controlled too easily. The researcher will record masses of data over long periods before being able to single out minor variations.

One can postulate an inherent conflict between the desirability of the experimental study (representing maximum control) and the need to reproduce in that study characteristics of the reference situation that may make control more difficult. Every researcher has a reference situation or model for each study he or she performs, and it may not be the same one for every study. For the system-oriented researcher, the model is a concept of how operational systems function; for the theoretically oriented researcher, the reference may be derived from a particular theory. Unless research is being performed directly with an operational system, the reference situation is almost always symbolic; it is reflected in the researcher's concept of what the test results would be if the study had been performed in the operational setting. With the reference situation as the criterion, the human factors researcher hopes that whatever comes out of the study will be meaningful—applicable—to that situation. For example, if the researcher performs a transfer of training study demonstrating that a simulator produces improved pilot performance in training, he or she expects and hopes that students training on the simulator will actually turn out to be better pilots in combat exercises (exercises that are as close as one can come to the combat reference situation).

In general terms, the reference situation for a human factors system study is always the concept of an operational system functioning in the operational environment, but the reference situation may also be more specific, depending perhaps on the intended generalizability of the study results. Before beginning the study, the researcher should decide what the reference situation for that study is, because that will aid the application of the results. The general reference situation—the operational setting—is a construct, but specific operational systems can also serve as models for a study. The studies by Kidd (1959) had as their reference situation air traffic control operations—a very specific reference. The studies by Chiles, Alluisi, and Adams (1968) had a more general reference, a prototypical work station in which personnel are presented with multiple competing stimuli and tasks.

Control is intimately related to questions of scale, complexity, and simulation. There are systems so large that one cannot install them in a laboratory (e.g., a complete ship). Typically the research solution for the problem of scale is to take the management aspects of these systems—represented by the work station interface (e.g., the ship's bridge)—and place them under control by simulating them. If one wants to study problems of pilot landings under low visibility conditions, for example, one does not place the entire aircraft under control, but merely the cockpit control and display devices and the electronic, hydraulic (and so forth) effects associated with activation of the controls and displays. This is the utility of the aircraft simulator.

Some compromise is needed to lessen the tension between the need to control and the artificiality that control generates. However, the kind of compromise in which the researcher ignores the artificiality is not the kind of compromise I mean. Truly sophisticated researchers will not ignore the existence of the reference situation but will attempt to introduce as many characteristics of that situation into their experiments as they can while still retaining substantive control. Pragmatically, the compromise is some form of operational simulation. This simulation has been aided by expanded computer capabilities in memory, processing speed, and graphics.

One must ask, however, whether exclusion from the simulation of all subsystems and subsystem effects other than the management effects taints the results of the simulator study. To this there can be no simple answer. It depends on how intimately interrelated all the subsystems are—the more they are, the more danger there is in isolating the management interface from the rest of the system. In the case of an aircraft the danger appears to be slight, but if one were to study a company by concentrating solely on its board of directors, the study results might be skewed.

Two types of simulation offer a way to exercise control over systems that in the operational environment might not be readily controlled. Physical simula-

148 / Conceptual Aspects of Human Factors

tion is the more popular way, but one can also simulate symbolically, conceptually, by developing a mathematical model of how the system functions. Mathematical model simulation is in fact more advantageous because it permits one to represent more of the system than a physical simulation does, and to introduce under experimental control such parameters as learning and motivation that might be difficult to control in the physical simulation. Because Siegel and collaborators (Siegel and Wolf 1969) have shown that it is possible to study personnel subsystem variables under control, the model is perhaps a partial substitute for working within the operational situation.

The mathematical model permits us to avoid the problems of physical, but not relational, scale. By relational scale is meant the relation between molecular and molar units of performance, between human performance at the individual work station and performance of the total system. For example, to include all levels of system performance in a model would require modeling individual switch activations as well as terminal system outputs such as system-to-system interactions in combat. Theoretically there is no reason that the same mathematical model cannot deal with all these levels, but the model will become quite complex.

However, any model, particularly one for a complex system, requires a great deal of data. The only way to procure those data is to conduct studies within the reference environment (the operational system) and the nonreference environment (e.g., the laboratory), specifically to secure these data. To the researcher this may appear to be another paradox, in the sense that to avoid working in the operational situation one must first collect data in that situation, a sort of down payment on the model. That is true enough, but once having collected the input data and developed one's model, it will be possible to exercise the control over the model that the operational situation would not permit. Moreover, the model can be a general one, applicable to more than one class of system, and it can be used as a general research tool. In this case the input data to be collected will be gathered with more than one operational system to avoid bias.

The mathematical model is more likely to be stochastic (e.g., SAINT; see Pritsker et al. 1974) rather than deterministic (e.g., the Human Operator Simulator; Strieb and Wherry 1979). Variables in the first type of model are governed by probability processes, and those in the second type by equations relating variables to performance. The major reason for suggesting that mathematical models are more likely to be stochastic than deterministic is that the amount of information needed to generate the deterministic equations required for complex systems is not present in great supply. Moreover, stochastic mechanisms presuppose a certain amount of uncertainty in the functioning of systems, which is in the spirit of modern physical concepts.

The act of exercising control over large, complex systems by simulating their inputs and outputs and the mechanisms that drive these adds an element of artificiality to the simulation, more so perhaps in the mathematical model than in the simulator. The question is, How much artificiality is bearable? To answer this question, studies of the operational situation(s) will be required.

From a reference system standpoint, control also has an effect on the research strategy adopted. It may seem logical to study the operational system first to discover which variables are important, and then to select the important variables to study in greater detail in a more controlled environment, such as the laboratory or simulator. But because the researcher lacks control over the operational system, it may be difficult to pick out which variables are most important, correlational analysis being somewhat imprecise. An alternative research strategy might be to study variables first under experimental control, because effects show up more boldly under control, and then to try to single out the effects of the same variables in the operational system—in effect a form of validation. The problem with this strategy is that without first preselecting variables on some basis as reasonable candidates for testing, one may have to test an excessive number of them. According to system theory, perhaps all variables should be tested experimentally if one is going to use an experimental methodology, but for practical reasons one must compromise. The solution may be to follow both paths—scan the operational system quickly to secure a "feeling" about variables, and then experiment. Consideration of the operational situation prior to an experimental study need not involve in-depth prior studies of that situation. For example, it may be sufficient to talk to subject matter experts who are familiar with a type of operational system or with systems in general.

Since the experimental study of variable X should have led to some understanding of its characteristics, one might then look in the operational situation for the same characteristics. Having found what appears to be a plausible trail, one might attempt to correlate data of what appears to be the effect of variable X with data from other variables. But because in the operational situation we use correlational statistics for data analysis, much more data must be gathered and examined than under controlled conditions to extract a discernible pattern for variable X. This makes operational research quite expensive.

Searching in the operational situation for effects derived from more controlled situations may be frustrating. The experimental methods used in the controlled situation cannot be applied in the operational one, at least not without major modifications. If the effects found experimentally depend too much on the methodology used, one may not find the same effects if the same experimental methods cannot be used operationally. This increases the difficulty of validation in the reference situation. In any event, when one begins an experimental study without first considering whether and in what way the variables being studied relate to those in the operational system, there is a risk that the effects found in the experiment will be irrelevant to that system.

All solutions to the problem of control are nonoptimal at best, but ignoring the problem does not dispose of it.

THE PROBLEM OF MULTIDIMENSIONALITY

When we say that human performance is multidimensional—and there seems to be general agreement among behavioral scientists on this point—we mean that a complex of forces both within and outside the system act on the system and its personnel. Personnel performance is determined at any one time by a number of variables that are either idiosyncratic (within the individuals) or system-linked (variables stemming from system characteristics).

Multidimensional effects are produced by or related to several things, particularly the type, number, and strength of factors impinging at any one time on the individual and the system. Swain and Guttmann (1983) called these "performance-shaping factors" (PSF). These are listed in Table 3.5. Other important factors are system complexity and sensitivity—the system's tendency to react differently to varying stimuli. With multiple effects occurring concurrently, it is often difficult to arrange operationally meaningful treatment conditions in an experiment. It also leads to problems with criteria and measures, because if one assumes that each system dimension requires a criterion for measurement and at least one measure, an excessive number of criteria and measures may result. The difficulty increases because the relative strengths of the variables involved are unknown. The extreme sensitivity of the human to even minor system factors tends to magnify whatever multidimensional effects there might be. For example, the placement of a single display at a work station may have a disproportionate effect on the operator's performance.

The number of PSFs influencing personnel is fortunately not infinite. They fall into various categories: some are in the operator (e.g., intelligence, skill, motivation), a few are in the physical environment in which the system functions (e.g., temperature, lighting), some are in the system itself (i.e., interface variables, which have traditionally been called human engineering factors), and still others derive from other systems in the operational environment or the suprasystem of which one's own system is only a part. These last are outside one's own immediate system; one might even call them contingent variables because they are not under our control. For example, if the system is an American naval vessel, a Russian submarine may accost it, or Naval headquarters may redirect its mission on an emergency basis. All variables inherent in the system (see Table 5.2) affect system output to some extent, but contextual variables are more uncertain in their influence on the system.

Every PSF has, it is assumed from system theory, an effect on human and system performance, but in many, perhaps most, cases the effect is so slight that measurement instruments may not be able to pick up their effects. For example, it is very difficult to sense an individual operator's motivational effect on a large system unless it is extreme; we may assume from interviews with personnel that there is some dissatisfaction, but except where the dissatisfaction exists throughout the system and a slowdown or strike erupts, the system maintains enough discipline that motivation does not distort the terminal output unduly. Other factors, such as procedures or technical data, are more directly related to system functioning and therefore may have greater effects on its output. It is assumed that the more directly related a factor is to the system's terminal output, in the sense of being involved in a task required to accomplish that output, the greater its effect on that output will be.

We are bothered by multidimensionality because it is not easy to interpret the variability we see in system outputs, whether these are intermediate or terminal, behavioral or physical. We view the system as functioning in a matrix of stimulus forces, some of which are strong, others of which are weak, in their effect on human performance and on the system as a whole. The relationship of these forces to one another and to the system varies in what appears to be, but may not actually be, an irregular manner. If these influences did not exist, the amount of variability in system performance would be much reduced, and system performance would be much more consistent. Thus it would more often accomplish its mission—or conversely, if it were poorly designed, fail to accomplish its mission. Because these influences exist, they determine the variance of the system output.

Sensitivity may be related to complexity. If a system is very complex, it may be more sensitive to both internal and external PSFs, and hence more multidimensional and variable in performance. If the hypothesis is correct, all other things being equal, simple systems are likely to be less sensitive than complex ones. Sensitivity may have an effect on control too. The more sensitive the system is to idiosyncratic and system factors, particularly the former, the more difficult it may be to achieve true control even under rigorous conditions.

At any one moment a number of behavioral and physical variables are influencing performance. These will not necessarily be all the variables that *could* influence performance. The problem of understanding multidimensionality is complicated by the fact that the strength of the individual variables influencing the performance will vary not only over time (the effects of learning, practice, fatigue, etc.) but also as a function of the relative strengths or weights of the other variables associated with it. It seems reasonable to suppose that individual variables have different effects on performance and on the system as a whole, that few variables exercise the same effect at all times, that the effect of a variable may vary from very great to nil, that the effect of one variable is influenced by that of other variables with which it is concurrently associated, and that consequently human performance has a variable effect on the system and conversely system variables have a variable effect on human performance.

If in the real, uncontrolled world all variables exercise their effects concurrently on one another and consequently on task performance, the experimental design paradigm that controls or limits the effects of all variables other than the independent (controlled) variable will produce performance results somewhat different from those that actually occur in the real world. How very different those results will be we do not know, because it is difficult to apply the experimental paradigm in the operational setting, and few have tried. The difference between the experimental-paradigm results and the real-world results may be of little consequence if one is trying to find out whether a particular variable is significantly important, especially because there are techniques for computing the proportion of the total variance accounted for by each component source of variance, including interactions. Unfortunately, many researchers stop with significance levels (.05, .01), but the significance levels do not tell us the proportion variance accounted for. The point is that while the experimental control *may* distort the picture we hope to achieve of real world performance, control is also necessary for certain problems, for example, to ascertain the relationships between interface parameters and operator performance, as described in Chapter 4.

If researchers take multidimensionality seriously, they would have to systematically vary and control every variable in every interactional configuration with other variables, so that they could examine the effect of a variable under all the important conditions under which it functions. One could then build up a picture of the range within which each variable functions. This would be a horrendous task that few would seriously suggest attempting. Multidimensionality is one aspect of the problem of relationship between the experimental study and the operational situation. It is an act of faith that we believe that the study mirrors reality at some degree of approximation, although we almost never know what that approximation actually is.

Multidimensionality is ubiquitous in operational reality. Take, for example, technical data as an independent variable: the performance of a novice using a technical manual will be significantly influenced—enhanced or degraded—depending on the nature of the task. If the same technical manual is used by a skilled engineer in performing the same task, the effects of the manual, positive or negative, will be much reduced, perhaps even nullified, because the engineer, being experienced, has less need of it. The specific influence of the technical data variable on performance is therefore dependent on the skill level of the subject and on the nature of the task.

In the traditional experiment the hypothesis would be "Performance with technical manuals is influenced by the user's skill level (e.g., skilled versus novice) and type of task," and would produce the same results. There is no practical difference between the experimental and the system orientation in this case, except that the latter would suggest that by controlling everything save the separate treatments (technical manuals, skill level, task) the researcher may be getting a somewhat artificial, and hence somewhat false, performance effect. Simon (1977) proposes techniques for including a large number of variables in a single experiment, but because these are still controlled the situation will still be somewhat artificial. Wherry (1986) suggested a technique he calls the "random sampling of domain variance" (RSDV), which has as one major objective "the providing of a methodology for the simultaneous investigation of multiple variables, each of which may have many different levels, in a controlled experiment" (p. 5–1). The RSDV also serves as a theoretical bridge for moving between laboratory and field studies.

Multidimensional effects can also be explored by using subject matter experts and policy-capturing techniques (Christal 1968). Subject matter experts presented with a variety of scenarios could be asked for their estimates of the effects of individual and combined variables on system outputs. Because these scenarios would be verbal and graphic, it should be possible almost to exhaust the ways in which system variables can function (although possibly exhausting the experts also). One or more theories of how variables influence task performance would significantly help our understanding of and ability to account for multidimensionality. Unfortunately, such a theory is not presently available.

Engineering limitations make it difficult for the designer to take more than one or two behavioral variables into account in his or her design. From that standpoint, human factors research might attempt to reduce multidimensionality by determining which factors in which situations have the *least* effect. Psychological research aims to discover variables that are statistically significant; human factors research could aim also at finding those that have the least effect so that they can be eliminated from consideration in system design. This may appear to be an effort to prove the null hypothesis, but whether one can do so or not, it is possible to build up a body of evidence to suggest the relative importance of variables.

VALIDATION

By casting the problem of multidimensionality in terms of the relationship between the experimental (nonreference) study and the operational (reference) system performance, it is necessary to examine that relationship. This is also the problem of validation. A system-oriented human factors has special problems of validity that more traditional behavioral science may not encounter. Because it is always possible that research conclusions may be erroneous, it is necessary to validate. This statement presumes that there is an inherent truth for which empirical data and conclusions are merely approximations—a very ancient notion, expressed by Plato, among others.

Brinberg and McGrath (1982) told us that "the term *validity* has many uses and many meanings." They suggest that there are many types of research validity linked to what they call the "validity network schema" (a three-stage theory of the research process (Brinberg and McGrath 1985). According to Brinberg and McGrath (1985), the type of validity one applies depends on the stage of research at which one is working. The various types of validity include construct validity, convergent validity, predictive validity, face validity, content validity, discriminant validity, internal and external validity, and something called statistical conclusions validity. Brinberg and McGrath even extend the concept of validity to concepts, as in the notion of "logical validity" or the correspondence between research methods and concepts or "instrument validity." According to these authors, "each is a useful concept, referring as it does to some particular aspect of the general problem of the validity of research information. Certain other terms as well, such as *reliability* and *generalizability* are part of the family of validity concepts" (Brinberg and McGrath, 1982, p. 5).

Underlying the various forms of validity are three concepts: (1) validity as correspondence between sets of things, constructs, observations or measures; (2) validity as generalizability or robustness, the degree to which a set of findings will hold up when extrapolated or extended to new materials, new environments, and new situations; and (3) validity as demonstrating the *truth* of a finding, in an epistemological sense of dealing with "real" phenomena. Validity is an abstraction, a construct; because research conclusions can never achieve the status of revealed truth, there is at most a probability that they are correct.

The three concepts are interrelated: correspondence between a set of conclusions and a set of phenomena in the real world would seem to reflect the "truth" of the conclusions. All the concepts enter into the human factors view of validity, with particular emphasis on the epistemological notion. Generalizability also suggests validity, although it does not demonstrate it; the more generalizable a conclusion, the more likely it is to be true. Most of the forms of validity suggested by Brinberg and McGrath are irrelevant to a system-oriented human factors because of the discipline's application-orientation. Whatever else these other validities may be, we reserve the term *validity* for the correspondence between effects produced by studies of variables in the nonreference situation and effects produced by studies of the same variables in the reference setting.

Truth for human factors is what has been termed the *reference situation,* defined as the performance of personnel within an operational system functioning in its operational environment. Even operational performance may, however, be invalid in the sense that special nonrepresentative circumstances may distort usual performance. Moreover, in any one mission operational performance will vary slightly from preceding and subsequent performances, which means that the "truth" of that performance can be ascertained only over multiple incidents. However, these variations should smooth out over time. By definition, "average performance" describes the way humans ordinarily perform, a performance that can be known only by collecting normative data. Operational performance is of course by no means "ideal" performance as system developers describe it in proposals—quick, errorless, highly efficient;

it may in fact be inefficient. Operational performance is ultimately whatever it actually is.

Given that performance in the reference situation is "true" performance, the only validity that is meaningful from the human factors standpoint is *predictive validity* (or what others would term "external validity"), which we define as the correspondence between findings derived from measurement performed outside the reference situation and findings derived from measurement within that situation. What we want to determine is whether our nonreference findings truly reflect the performance results we would get if the same variables were measured inside the reference situation.

The special validity problems derive from the difference in scale and in opportunities for control between the reference and the nonreference measurement situations. In the reference situation, systems are often large and complex. In the nonreference situation, results are often secured in small-scale or even molecular simulations of system components. For example, human performance in the laboratory may be measured with a representation of the system work station, such as the specially constructed control panel in the "synthetic" studies of Chiles, Alluisi, and Adams (1968). It is necessary to map into the reference situation the conclusions and data that were produced by more molecular performance units than one finds in the operational environment. Only occasionally does the researcher manage to simulate the operational system adequately. The phrase "map into" the reference situation means that nonreference findings must be related empirically to the elements and variables of the operational system. For example, do the equations relating personnel performance to design features (performed with highly controlled experiments, such as those described in Chapter 4) still hold when one studies these relationships in the operational system? Can one discern the effect of those relationships on the system output? Unless the answers to the preceding questions are yes, the relationships found in the nonreference situation are valid only for that specific situation and therefore have only restricted value.

Validation of research findings is necessary because these are almost always derived from the nonreference situation. But suppose that studies are performed in the "real world" of the operational system. Logically, then, should not the conclusions derived from such studies automatically be valid? If conclusions are derived from a study performed with an operational system, functioning under operational conditions, they are automatically valid, because any set of empirical results is valid *for the situation from which they are derived* (even if that situation is flawed). In making the previous statement, we assume that the operational study is not flawed and that the questions asked by the study are meaningful. If these conditions are met, the problem of validity disappears, because the operational study is automatically valid for all systems of the same type and conditions (e.g., trucks and truck driving), although not necessarily generalizable to other systems, such as aircraft and flying.

The validity of effects found in studies in the reference situation may not be in question, but their generalizability may be. Effects found with operational system X may not apply to operational system Y. This finding will limit the generalizability of the effect but not its validity. Few effects are so all-encompassing that they apply to the totality of the reference situation, which includes varying classes of systems, operational conditions, and so on.

Ideally one would hope to replicate results secured from, for example, simulator testing and the same set of tests conducted on the system that is the model for the simulator (e.g., landing the Boeing 757 simulator and the actual 757 aircraft). But even if the same tests were conducted in both situations, some differences between those results could be expected for two reasons: normal performance variability in both situations, and differences in test subjects and effects of uncontrolled contextual influences on the reference system (e.g., wind-shear conditions). One would expect to find even greater differences if the conclusions stem from a highly controlled test situation and are being validated against a situation that lacks experimental control. In this last case, one might find major differences, because a variable in an uncontrolled situation may well function differently from one that is controlled. Comparing results achieved in the nonreference and reference situations may be difficult because it may not be possible to repeat exactly in the operational system the measurement operations that were followed in the laboratory or simulator.

If the measurement requires control and that control cannot be achieved in the reference situation, one may have to look for validation in secondary ways. For example, assume that it has been found by using an eye camera that the pattern of foveal fixations predicts success in acquiring targets. It may not be possible to use an eye camera on personnel while they are performing their operational duties, but one could measure the foveal fixations of personnel in a laboratory (the nonreference environment) and then record their target acquisition performance at their air base while they were performing operational duties. If the fixations are important, those with more frequent (or less frequent) fixations in the nonreference laboratory test should acquire targets faster at farther ranges in the operational setting. Although this is a roundabout way of validating the original conclusion, it should produce desired answers. Unfortunately, the difficulty of attempting to replicate nonreference measurement operations in the reference environment discourages many researchers from working in that environment and validating their results.

There are a number of ways one can pursue validity, and in the discussion that follows these ways are ordered according to the degree of confidence they give us in the validity of our findings. One form of validation is to replicate findings from a nonreference situation by replicating those findings in the reference situation, or one can take a conclusion based on findings from a nonreference situation and make a prediction that a somewhat different finding will occur either in a different nonreference situation or in the reference situation.

The previous sentence focuses on several differences—the difference between replication and prediction, and the difference between findings and conclusions. I use "findings" rather than "data" because even when a study is replicated under identical conditions, one rarely gets identical numerical values for the data, considering normal subject variability. However, the trend of the data may be the same in both situations, which leads us to consider both sets of data as findings. *Findings* are equivalent to data, and *conclusions* are generalizations of the findings. One predicts from conclusions, not from findings; prediction from a conclusion may be assisted by a theory involving that conclusion. The point is that replication of findings is desirable but not as good as verification of a prediction resulting from a conclusion derived from findings. A *prediction,* as an extrapolation from the original situation, is more daring—and therefore deserves more plaudits—than simple replication. Replication and prediction in the same or a similar test situation is less desirable than replication and prediction in a test situation that is different from the one producing the original finding or conclusion. This may become clearer if we list each situation in a progression:

1. Findings from a nonreference situation can be replicated in the same nonreference situation—same tasks, same setting, although perhaps different subjects but of the same type. This is *reliability,* which is related to but is not validity because the operations performed in both cases may be flawed in the same way, or more likely could be irrelevant to the reference situation.

2. Findings from one nonreference situation are replicated in a different nonreference situation—for example, laboratory findings are repeated in a simulator or test site. This is also reliability, but one can have greater confidence in the findings because they have occurred in different settings.

3. Findings from a nonreference situation are replicated in the operational setting. This is reliability, but because the replication occurs in the reference situation, it is also validity.

4. Conclusions derived from findings gathered in a nonreference situation suggest a prediction based on those conclusions—that a somewhat different but related effect will be found in the reference situation. This prediction asserts that if x, y, and z are found in the nonreference situation, then in the reference situation x^1, y^1, and z^1 should occur. Predictive validity gives us even greater confidence because one would not have x^1, y^1 and z^1 if x, y and z were not "true."

5. The greatest confidence in predictive validity occurs where x, y, and z conclusions derived from one reference situation measurement are used to predict x^1, y^1, and z^1 effects in a different reference situation—that is, from one operational system to an operational system of a different type.

The literature suggests that there are few attempts at validation as it has been defined here. Most common is the attempt to replicate findings in the same or similar nonreference situation. It is necessary also to examine *invalidity,* the other face of validity. If variable x, determined to be significant in the non-reference environment, is found not to be significant when studied in the context of an operational system, a number of factors may have caused the discrepancy. For one, other variables in the operational system that were not operative in the original study may have reduced the effect of variable x; second, the original experiment may have been so artificial that variable x did not behave as it ordinarily does in the reference situation, so that the effect noted in the study was actually an artifact.

If an experimental effect is not verified operationally, it may be difficult to determine why, because the arrangement of treatment conditions needed for experimental control can be made only with difficulty within the operational setting. However, an effect discovered in an experimental nonreference situation can be examined in the operational setting by utilizing observational methods. Following the logic of the multitrait, multimethod manner of validation (convergent validity; see Campbell and Fiske 1959), if the same results were achieved with different methods—experimental versus observational—then one would have even greater confidence in the validity of the findings. Indeed, convergent validity requires two or more methods.

Another way of testing the robustness of a research finding (its endurance in the face of uncontrolled, apparently negative characteristics of the real world) might be to expose that finding to a degraded test situation assumed to be characteristic of operational system functioning. The degraded test situation might be created by one or more of the following: lesser skill or training in subjects, more stringent response requirements, the occurrence of random irrelevant events that compete for the subject's attention, or the nonavailability of a required system element, such as technical data. These degradations act to increase system demand and operator workload. An effect that persists under these conditions is likely to be important in determining system output. If under these circumstances a previous finding is replicated, it suggests, but does not prove, that the finding would hold up in the reference situation. While it does not obviate the necessity for ultimately replicating findings in the "real world," this approach to validation permits the researcher to approximate that validation.

Consider an experiment in two parts. The first part is performed with the most stringent controls, and an effect that represents the verification of a hypothesis is produced. We need not worry about a nonverified hypothesis; the second part of the experiment is performed only if one secures positive results in the first part. In the second part of the experiment, we take the same or similar subjects and expose them to the same or similar tasks with the same treatments, concurrently introducing all the characteristics that are supposed to represent the operational setting. The null hypothesis for the second part of the experiment is that we will *not* get the same results we got in the first part, so that the operational characteristics will have in fact canceled out our previously verified hypothesis. If that is the case, our initial experimental conclusions are valid only for the laboratory setting but cannot be generalized further.

Another form of validation, but a weak one, is application. If a conclusion not otherwise validated can be applied successfully, as in system development, one might say that the conclusion is informally validated. This proposition is likely to generate skepticism, but it is accepted informally by many specialists as a matter of pragmatics. Many human factors findings are *not* validated because validation is difficult and is not particularly exciting, because it means repeating studies (i.e., it may be viewed as lacking originality).

One may ask whether the reluctance to validate (in our terms, a failure to replicate in or predict to the operational setting) has had negative effects on the human factors profession as opposed to the human factors discipline. The answer to this question is unknown, but in a cynical vein one suspects that there is no effect on the profession but a great deal of negative effect on the scientific discipline. At least most professionals do not seem concerned about the widespread failure to validate.

It is only fair to say that there are those such as Campbell (1986), who consider the question of generalization from the nonreference situation (e.g., the laboratory) to the reference situation (the field) to be a false question. Campbell feels that the laboratory-field distinction is not useful and that there are more fundamental issues, such as what method best maximizes construct validity. Nonetheless, if we do not attempt to validate to the reference situation, how do we know whether there is a genuine need to validate? If we perform validation studies in the operational setting and *always* verify our nonreference results, perhaps validation is an unnecessary refinement. But how will we know if we do not try?

OPERATIONAL FIDELITY

Operational fidelity is the term applied to the relationship between the characteristics of the reference situation—previously defined as the operational system performing its assigned mission in its assigned environment—and the characteristics of studies performed in a nonreference environment. It is presumed that the aim of human factors measurement is to maximize the closeness of this relationship because human factors data, conclusions, and theory have meaning only in relation to the reference situation that represents their reality (see Chapter 1). Whatever is *not* representative of the reference situation can be understood only in relation to that situation.

The reference situation is a construct rather than a physical entity or set of phenomena and hence cannot be viewed directly. Even so, it has specific physical counterparts in the form of operational systems, so one would want to learn as much as possible about these systems. For this reason, in any human factors research program, studies of the operational system in its operational environment should have high priority.

Operational fidelity has a number of dimensions: *physical fidelity* (e.g., corresponding to physical elements, similarity of equipment, technical data, and communications), *task fidelity* (similarity of tasks to be performed), *organizational fidelity* (similarity of team and subsystem organization), and *personnel fidelity* (similarity of personnel background, training, skill). In computer simulations of the system there is also *symbolic fidelity,* which is the degree to which software accurately reproduces the operations of the system's physical and behavioral elements.

Operational fidelity also has a number of applications to simulator design and to research in general. Fidelity is not an all-or-nothing affair. There are degrees of operational fidelity, so a question that has exercised training researchers in particular is, How much fidelity is necessary in simulators?

A great deal of research focused on determining the value and necessity of creating training simulators that are as much like their operational systems as possible. Simulation fidelity research derives its motivation from the effort to reduce the expense and time resulting from the need to replicate in detail the physical operational system, or at least its management control aspects. If research could show that fidelity can be reduced and still result in transfer of training, the cost-effectiveness of simulators would be increased. Just how much simulation fidelity is necessary is unclear, despite the many studies performed, although it is clear that for some forms of training excessive fidelity is unecessary, particularly the early training stages, when students are learning general principles, nomenclature, and part-tasks.

The reference situation should not be thought of as ideal; it often contains elements that are inimical to effective performance, such as excessively long communications channels, a lack of tools, and poor technical data. In designing new systems, practitioners attempt to avoid such negative elements, but because they exist they should probably be included in measurement in order to secure valid data.

Most human factors research is performed in nonreference situations like laboratories, simulators, and test ranges, and much of it consists of stripping off the context of a task in an effort to get down to "fundamentals." (It is not clear what is meant by "fundamentals," except as an attempt to eliminate task context.) For example, someone will study military decision-making not at brigade headquarters but in the laboratory by giving officers (or even university students, as a substitute) paper-and-pencil analogues of the military problems. Presumably the situation can be controlled better in this way, but are the two task situations really the same even though the essential element is the same when abstracted from particulars—that is, solution of a problem?

Logically, measurements in nonreference environments should resemble as much as possible those of the reference situation, because this makes research results more valid in the sense of corresponding more to that situation. (Locke [1986] points out the same thing: "What is needed is the *identification of the essential features of field settings that need to be replicated in the lab*" [emphasis in the original]). If researchers could do this without at the same time losing more control than they want to, they would have the best of all worlds. However, the introduction of operational characteristics tends to break down that control.

Before introducing these characteristics into the measurement process, it is necessary to determine what they are. We do not know these with any certainty, because relatively few studies of operational situations have been performed. Nonetheless, one can hypothesize that complete physical identicalness of the nonreference and reference situations (e.g., identical equipment) is not necessary to achieve a reasonable degree of fidelity. If, for example, one wanted to test a general principle that might be applied to a number of systems and situations, obviously the test environment would not be identical to any single operational system or setting, but would represent systems and the operational environment in general. Beyond physical identity, it is hypothesized that certain characteristics are common to all operational systems, and it is these that one wants to include in research.

The variables that most distinguish the reference situation from the nonreference situation can also be contextual in nature—that is, the basic task that is to be performed by the human is the same in both situations, but in the less well controlled reference situation what can be termed "nonoptimalities" modify the task and impact performance. The original assumptions about the system under design (the desired "ideal" system) may not have been fulfilled, for example, personnel are less capable than was expected, their training is less adequate, or administrative tasks unrelated to system operation compete for personnel attention. Other nonoptimal conditions may exist too, such as lack of necessary information, tools, and technical data, and inadequate supervision, the impingement of other, perhaps inimical, systems, and inadequate organizational structure.

Another factor that may perturb the system is the influence of the macrosystem in which one's own system is nested; in industry, for example, after two companies have merged, the functioning of the individual departments is disturbed by reorganization and changes of assignment.

It is hypothesized that what characterizes the operational reference situation is, first, system and task variables that are nonoptimal or deleterious and, second, idiosyncratic (human) variables that reduce the operator's capability to adjust to system demands. All these variables tend to make the system "sloppy" in its performance. Why these nonoptimal elements surreptitiously enter into the operational system even though system developers, assuming they do their jobs properly, try to avoid them is unclear. In complex system development it is difficult for developers to do their job properly. After a system has become operational, only rarely is an audit performed to determine what caused the nonoptimal characteristics (Schwartz 1981), so that little is known about what went wrong. One reason might be that the system changes over time.

Both statistical and anecdotal evidence suggest that performance in the operational system is substantially less than in the ideal system. In one study (cited in Meister 1984) actual airborne sonar operator performance was significantly poorer, both statistically and practically, than theory predicted. If it is common for operational systems to lose a certain percentage of their anticipated efficiency as soon as they are deployed; it becomes necessary to find out why. Only by knowing why this condition occurs can one attempt to improve it.

Much research has been performed on fidelity of simulation, but almost exclusively in relation to the effect of fidelity on training. Thus, simulation fidelity research has been concerned with the question of whether the replication of system physical features in the training environment is necessary for effective training. This is only a special aspect of the more fundamental question of what factors cause operational personnel and systems to perform differently from their hoped for, "ideal" level.

System operations create a demand or load on system personnel, a demand they must respond to if the system is to perform adequately. It may be that the strength of the system demand is underestimated by developers, or that they do not know how to provide the resources needed to accommodate it. Although engineers probably do not conceptualize system demand as such in their design analysis, they may unwittingly trade off demand against anticipated personnel capability or training and the cost of design features. If demand is underestimated, as is likely, because it is not consciously and deliberately analyzed, design inadequacies may be permitted to remain in the system. Indeed, from a behavioral standpoint, the notion of what a design inadequacy is may be quite nebulous in the engineer's mind, and specialists do not seem able to enlighten the engineer. Perhaps a design inadequacy is some factor that causes a discrepancy between system demand and personnel resources. It thus becomes necessary to quantify that demand.

It is possible that the major result of the demand levied on personnel, and equipment too, added to whatever contextual factors affect the situation, is an increase in performance variability and thus in the probability of error and task failure. Specialists' anticipation of how personnel will function before the system is operationally deployed is very crude and inexact. The specialist learns very little about that performance in developmental testing, and the operational test presents only a relatively few instances of personnel behavior. The task analysis performed during development may analyze "characteristic errors," but this information is qualitative only.

The point is that no one knows very well either the characteristics of the reference system and its personnel or those of the newly developed system as it is handed over to the customer, so it is difficult to predict how well the new system will function. Specialists know much more about the *ideal system,* the system as represented by written procedures, the system as it is supposed to function but rarely does. The ideal system differs from the reference system and the system as designed because it assumes no error or inefficiency. More of our human factors knowledge relates to the ideal system than to the other, nonideal systems. One reason that it may be difficult to predict operational performance is that human factors attention is centered on helping design produce an optimal system. Measurement during system development is geared to finding deviations from the optimal functioning of the system so that these discrepancies can be remedied. Because normative research is required to determine how operational systems actually function, and because this type of research is not popular among sponsors and specialists, research results apply primarily to the ideal system.

One situation in which it is possible to measure personnel performance in something approximating the operational situation is the simulator. If one could have pilots or nuclear control operators replicate their simulator tasks with actual aircraft and power stations, it might be possible to determine how much—if any—performance changes between the reference system and the simulator. Although "complete" simulation fidelity may not be critical to training, it is required in measurement, because (as indicated previously) even minor equipment, task, or procedural features tend to have exaggerated effects.

One factor differentiating the operational system from even a highly realistic nonreference test situation may be the subject's perception that in the latter he or she is in a test condition. The consequences of an error or a failure in the test situation will differ from those in an operational system. The more subject interpretation or diagnosis of system inputs is required, the greater the perceived differences may be. We simply do not know. Anything so basic to human factors measurement should be investigated.

SUBJECTIVE AND OBJECTIVE DATA

Much of the problem that human factors, along with the other behavioral sciences, has with subjective data—the term is used loosely to denote any subjective response—is that the scientific ethic derived from the physical sciences looks down its nose at subjective data. And subjective data—information transformed through human interpretation—does indeed present problems of validity and reliability. Nevertheless, subjective data cannot be eliminated from the discipline. Such data is necessary, even when more objective data is available, and specialists will not give it up. For example, subjective data is used extensively by test and evaluation measurement specialists (Meister 1986), and our survey respondents (see Chapter 1) also find a use for it. The recent emphasis on expert computer systems, based on the human expert's knowledge and perceptions, has made subjective data more respectable.

Moreover, because subjective data *do* bear some relationship to reality, such data can be a meaningful, though crude, approximation of reality, which can be refined as more data are gathered. In addition, subjective data are necessary in order to *explain* objective data. Objective data have only one or at most two dimensions (e.g., time, speed, distance, frequency, number, deviation, or error) and therefore present comparatively little information on their own. In the relatively uncontrolled measurement environment of the operational system, objective data do not have experimental treatments to clarify their meaning, so it is contextual and often subjective information that is required to make the objective data understandable. As an example, suppose that certain aircraft ground handlers consistently have slower turnaround times at a particular time of day. These data might mean nothing to us until one of the handlers, when questioned, reports that at this time of day parking bays are clogged and time is lost while waiting for parking slots to become available.

Data get their meaning from context. In the controlled experiment the treatment arrangements give meaning to data. If, for example, an experimental group is given a special kind of training, and experimental subjects learn in twelve trials while the control group learns in eighteen, then the difference between them can be assigned to the special training, assuming the researcher has controlled everything else. Otherwise, the meaning of the numbers 12 and 18 would be difficult to interpret.

Subjective data have more dimensions than objective data do. These dimension include logic, knowledge, experience, correlation of events, data integration, and rationale (potential explanation). Derived from the human who possesses information, they cannot be compared directly with objective data dimensions, but they are no less valuable, assuming that the human being is indeed an expert in what he or she is reporting.

Experimentalists are understandably reluctant to accept subjective data, because their studies produce data whose meaning is supplied by the experimental treatments. In less well controlled nonexperimental measurement situations without such treatments, subjective data are needed to provide this meaning, and specialists are therefore unlikely to give them up. It is not a matter of a choice between objective and subjective data; one makes use of both for the value each has.

It would be more correct to talk about subjective information than about data, because much of what we get in subjective reports is information, not data. Subjective responses are data only when they presume to report a condition of the human subject for which only the human can be the measure of that condition—this is, his or her feelings, attitudes, understanding. The accuracy of these subjective data may of course be questioned—perhaps the subject has misled himself or herself?

Subjective responses can also be used as data if no objective data exist.

Otherwise responses are information—different from data but also useful. Subjective responses are information when, for example, the subject explains why he or she did something for which objective data are available—why the automobile turn was to the right rather than to the left (the observation of turning being objective data), for instance.

The question is not whether subjective data and information are desirable, but what their relationship to objective data is. For example, one can ask subjects for estimations of their fatigue, stress level, awareness, and so on, and they can even quantify this on a scale, all of which would be subjective data. One might perhaps be able to get at the same thing through physiological (objective) indices, but the physiological indices often do not correlate with the subjective ones, suggesting that distinctive aspects of a phenomenon are being measured.

I have suggested that we should treat the human being as a measurement instrument that needs to be calibrated and refined (Meister 1985b). An entity that senses, perceives, and interprets stimuli like the human does *is* a measuring instrument. The fact that it is an awkward, primitive instrument is beside the point—so were the first telescopes and the first electrical measurement instruments. When conditions are poor—as when the phenomenon occurs rapidly or in darkness, when there are many events, and so forth—the subject's responses are weak, as we see from the confusion among witnesses' reports.

But there is evidence (Comer et al. 1984) that under the proper conditions humans can make very precise estimates of the probability that certain phenomena will occur. Unfortunately, there have been few studies of subject responses as data items, so we know little about the conditions under which they can be efficiently elicited (but see Ericsson and Simon 1980). One can gather subjective responses under highly structured conditions (e.g., an experiment), unstructured normal conditions (e.g., events occurring during work), or emergency conditions (e.g., an accident, a robbery). Subjective responses may concern the subject's own feelings, events in which the subject played no part, or events in which the subject did play a part. It would be interesting to determine how well subjects would report if, for example, they were intensively trained and tested to do so. There have been studies of report veracity (see Meister 1985b), but these have involved subjects with no special training on reporting. The failure to investigate the subjective response from an evidentiary standpoint is all the more astonishing because subjective responses offer potentially the most available and the largest possible data source for human factors.

Is it possible to train personnel to be observers and reporters in the Sherlock Holmes tradition? Several hypotheses on reporting can be advanced and tested. (1) Humans will report more precisely and correctly when what they are reporting is something they are personally involved with, when the events they report are structured, when the events they report on are repetitive. (2) Subjective reports can be quite useful when subjects are not asked to report in precise detail; just how much precision is sufficient requires study. (3) How accurate subjective data and information can be may depend also on how precisely a question is phrased; broad, general questions may produce less accurate answers than questions that are precisely focused.

The use of subjective data and information is fostered by very practical considerations. Instrumentation costs money, and such subjective instruments as questionnaires, interviews, and rating scales cost comparatively little to develop. Subjective instruments are easy to develop because, other than the most punctilious researchers, few go through the tedious process of developing these instruments in a psychometrically acceptable way. Often the subjective response may be the only practical data source around. I have mentioned subjective estimates in connection with development of human performance data banks. In view of the difficulty of getting usable data from other potential data sources, subjective estimates may be the only practical alternative (Meister 1988).

Studies of subjective responses and the conditions affecting their accuracy and reliability are an example of what in a previous paper (Meister 1980) I termed macrobasic research—research that directly supports human factors methodology. The question is whether researchers and sponsors can be persuaded to become genuinely interested in the subjective response as a data source.

CRITERIA AND MEASURES

Before performing an experimental study, the researcher engages in an analysis, the central element of which is the determination (often on the basis of theory) and arrangement of the treatment conditions to be contrasted to conform to a specific statistical design. This section examines system and measurement analysis in human factors system research, but without comparing it in detail to traditional experimental design; the latter would require a book in itself. The product of this analysis is the development of criteria and measures.

System and Measurement Analysis

Effective performance measurement in system situations is always preceded by system analysis. This analysis includes the nature of the system and its mission scenario, functions, and tasks—essentially the same analyses performed in applying human factors to system development. This is a critical link between human factors research and practice. Not only should human factors research be applicable to behavioral design, but the starting points of both are the same. The analysis also includes the determination of where (with which tasks) data are to be recorded and of the means used to record those data. If the nature of the system permits a contrast in conditions, the specialist also devel-

Table 6.1 Human Factors System Measurement Analysis Questions

---

System Analysis
What are the specific measurement objectives? How do these relate to the system?
What are the equipment and human elements of the system, and how do they interact?
What is the system's mission, and what variables are involved?
How is the mission accomplished? (Leading to development of the mission scenario)
What are the functions and tasks to be accomplished?
Does the system contain conditions that can be contrasted?

Measurement Analysis
What criteria and measures should be utilized?
At what points in the system mission are data to be recorded?
What is the most effective means of recording performance data?

---

ops an experimental design for these conditions. Table 6.1 lists the questions around which measurement analysis is organized.

The major common element in both traditional research and system measurement is the determination of criteria and measures. In experimental research these are also derived from analysis of the measurement problem, although system measurement analysis is much more specific because it deals with actual systems and experimental research rarely does. The measurement literature with which this chapter began also focused on these two analytic products.

Table 6.1 breaks measurement analysis into two parts: system analysis and measurement analysis. Because the measurement objectives are derived from the system and what it is supposed to do, it is necessary to examine the details of system functioning to determine the most effective means of satisfying those objectives. Analysis of the nature of the system will determine in part the answers to subsequent measurement analysis questions and the development of criteria and measures.

The non-system-researcher has no need to analyze a system because he or she has no system. This researcher is free to specify the conditions under which test subjects will perform, constrained only by the necessity to think long and hard about variables and any theory related to those variables. The system measurement specialist must think first of the objectives of his or her measurement. These differ from theoretically derived research objectives. System measurement is often evaluative, which means that testing determines whether the system as a whole and the personnel subsystem in particular satisfy explicit or implicit performance requirements. The specific objectives that derive from the overall measurement goal usually include an explicit evaluation goal: to discover how well personnel perform. Implicit goals—of a research nature, if the specialist cares to attempt them—are (1) what variables affect that performance and how much performance variance is affected by those variables, and (2) the relationship between personnel performance and overall system effectiveness.

The reader will recall that multidimensionality makes the determination of criteria and measures a major methodological problem, because there may be many criteria and measures from which to select a more manageable few (e.g., Vreuls et al. [1973] found some 800 measures for a captive helicopter simulator). An even greater problem is the relative effectiveness of criteria and measures in describing performance and the obscurity of rules for selecting the most effective.

For the system researcher, the means of accomplishing the measurement (e.g., instrumentation, manual data recording, observations, interviews) is partially dependent on the nature of the system, which may prevent the use of some data recording methods—for example, the system response may be too quick for a human observer and some kind of instrumentation may be necessary. Experimental researchers have few such problems because they can almost always make up their own scenario and tasks.

Criteria

Without the criterion, no meaningful measurement is possible. Without it, one can collect descriptive performance data (what are personnel doing?), but the meaning of those data, whether personnel are performing adequately or not, cannot be determined.

Meister (1985b) differentiates among three distinct types of performance criteria: those describing the functioning of the system as an entity (e.g., reliability and maintainability), those describing how missions are performed (e.g., effectiveness in mission accomplishment, output quality, and accuracy), and those describing how personnel perform. Only the last two are of much interest to us. System-descriptive and mission-descriptive criteria include personnel elements that must be differentiated from nonpersonnel elements. However, personnel performance criteria describing operator and crew responses (e.g., reaction time, accuracy) lack meaning unless they are considered in relation to the system and mission.

Performance criteria may act as independent variables or as dependent variables. As independent variables—for example, the requirement to assemble N units—they serve as a forcing function for operator performance; this is what personnel must do. As dependent variables they describe what the operator has done—for example, the operator has assembled N units.

In evaluative performance measurement, the criterion requires a standard of performance. Criteria are also necessary in experimental research (as dependent variables), but they do not imply or require standards. In evaluative measurement a criterion (e.g., efficiency) is meaningless without a standard because it does not provide a means of determining whether personnel are performing well or poorly. It is not enough to have a general criterion like "efficiency" or "number of information requests." The criterion must also be precise and quantitative. A criterion like that occasionally found in system procurement descriptions, "The system shall be so designed that personnel can perform their duties with minimum difficulty," is meaningless because it is not defined quantitatively.

Not all criteria are equally relevant and valuable for performance measurement. The level of adrenalin in the blood of subjects performing a visual vigilance task may be related to sonar target detection, but adrenalin level is not the most desirable criterion for measuring sonar detection because it relates only indirectly to system output. The relevance and importance of a potential criterion can be determined by asking how seriously the achievement of or failure to achieve this criterion would affect system performance. If the relationship of the criterion to system output is indirect or weak, it is not a very satisfactory candidate. The criterion is derived from what is required of system personnel, and whatever affects them strongly represents a potentially usable criterion.

Criterion objectivity and specificity will determine how adequately one can measure, and by what methods. For qualitative criteria, one must call on an expert—the subjective measuring instrument—because only the expert has the requisite experience to identify the performance involved. Qualitative criteria can be utilized, but it is not acceptable to rely solely on such criteria when more precise, objective criteria are also available.

Complex systems may have multiple personnel criteria because operators must perform a variety of functions. If so, one must measure them all—assuming they are all substantially related to system output. Criteria interact with other variables, such as the organizational structure of the system. As the focus of performance shifts from individual operator to team or from subsystem to system, criteria may change. In measuring team performance, for example, one must consider member interactions, something that is irrelevant to a single operator.

Measures

Many specialists have difficulty differentiating criteria from measures. A simple way of looking at the two is to note that the measure is derived from the criterion, not vice versa, and that the criterion is general and the measure is specific. The measure is a means of collecting data to describe the criterion. Any general criterion can have a number of specific measures. If the criterion is effectiveness of troubleshooting, one measure almost always used is downtime—the time it takes a technician to restore a malfunctioning item of equipment to operating condition. Other potential troubleshooting measures are time to find the fault, number of diagnostic tests run, time elapsed until the first diagnostic test, and number of "good" components checked out falsely as malfunctioning. Measures vary in specificity and therefore in diagnosticity—the more specific they are, the more diagnostic they can be. Overall downtime is not as diagnostic as the other troubleshooting measures above. More molecular measures are more likely to be diagnostic because problems are almost always very specific.

In developing the set of potential measures, it is necessary to examine the activities performed. If the major task of a forklift operator is to transfer cartons from an unloading platform to a warehouse storage area, the number of cartons moved per unit of time would be an applicable measure. The speed with which the operator moved them would be another possible measure. How would one decide between the two? The number of cartons moved is clearly a preferable measure because it is what the warehouse management is most interested in and it subsumes speed, because the number of cartons moved depends in part on the speed of operator movement.

Linked with the measure is the unit of performance or behavior (job, function, task, subtask) that it describes, but the specialist must decide on that unit independently of the measure. It is possible to measure performance time both for a task and for a subtask nested in that task. For example, the speed with which a page in this book is read (the task) can be measured, as can the speed with which foveal fixations change during the reading of that material (the subtask). One measures in order to secure certain information, and that purpose determines the level of the measures selected. This is why it is necessary to understand the system and its mission in detail. Certain functions are likely to be much more important than others—in terms of their contributions to mission accomplishment—and it is these that most require measurement. In evaluating combat pilot performance, for example, it would be more important to measure the tightness of maneuvering turns than to measure the speed with which ground preflight check-out was accomplished. The level at which one measures will determine in part how data are collected. Foveal fixations will require a sophisticated eye-motion camera, while reading speed requires only a timer.

Measures may describe terminal performance (the task output, such as reading a book) or intermediate performance (operator behavior that leads to task output, such as foveal fixations). Intermediate measures are more likely to be molecular and diagnostic. Both measures are desired, but terminal measures are preferred because they are more closely linked to system outputs.

Selecting measures becomes more difficult when the system has complex task interrelationships, because measures of secondary tasks may be less relevant to system outputs. Some measures may not reflect performance variance very well. The measure selected must reflect critical task performance if it is to be descriptive of performance. For example, errors may be indicative of performance quality—but only if the errors made have a significant effect on performance. This makes it necessary to look for critical tasks in which performance, and its measures, do make a difference to system output. To determine task criticality, one must ask what the effect on mission accomplishment or system outputs would be if the task were not performed or were performed poorly.

In selecting measures one must ask what additional information a potential measure provides beyond what is already available, because each potential measure presumably provides some increment of information. If a potential measure supplies little or no new information, it has little value. This is particularly likely to be the case for very molecular measures. One must also anticipate how the information resulting from a measure will be used. There may well be measures in which the behavioral specialist is not interested; those of a logistical nature would not reflect human performance or would do so only indirectly. For example, the amount of fuel expended during an aircraft flight is more likely to reflect physical design than the pilot's performance.

This review of criteria and measures reveals how important system analysis is to their development. In general, the problem of developing measures is greater for the system measurement specialist than for the nonsystem researcher, because the latter is generally dealing with only one or two tasks which he or she has selected or created, while the former has an entire system from which to select. In addition, the experimental researcher has greater control over the tasks, particularly if they are synthetic. If a task requires an intractable measure (one that is difficult to record, for example, and provides only little information), the researcher can drop the task and substitute another one, something that may be impossible for the system specialist.

MEANINGFUL DATA

To be meaningful, data must point to "something" other than themselves; they must have an external referent. A temperature of 98.5° Fahrenheit means nothing to us until we know it refers to a human body. All data have inherent meaning, but that meaning may be obscure.

In experimental study, meaning is given by the treatment conditions. If the performance of an experimental group is x units superior to that of the control group, the meaning of that x differential is provided by the way in which the two groups have been made to differ—for example, training, performance requirements, or equipment operated. That is why the researcher must be concerned about the possible confounding of variables in a study; confounded variables lead to imprecise meaning.

The situation is more complex in operational system measurement, where the experimental control that permits the researcher to develop treatment conditions is largely lacking. Data obscurity is related both to multidimensionality and to lack of control. Most performance phenomena are multidetermined, and unless one experimentally restricts the number of variables producing an effect, the answer to the question of which variables had primary effect on performance may be ambiguous. Moreover, data may not have the same meaning in the real-world situation that they have in the experimental situation because in the latter variables are not free to function without constraint.

When we say that the meaning of data in a measurement situation may be obscure, we mean that the specialist has difficulty hypothesizing on the basis of these data how these variables function and which variables are associated with each other and with mission success and/or terminal outputs. The data may not be obviously related to specific variables. Data obscurity may occur when there is no normative performance standard for the segment of performance being examined, so that one cannot tell whether the data reflect performance within an expected range or are outside that range. This presents no problem for the experimental researcher who does not use standards. Data may also be obscure if the questions to be answered by the measurement are ambiguous or incorrect—if the measures that produce them are wrongly chosen, are pitched at too molar or too molecular a level of behavior for the questions to be answered, or are inadequate to the measurement questions asked.

For example, data on performance times, errors, or difficulties encountered by subjects may be unclear. Unless a maximum reaction time or a minimum duration is required—that is, unless there is a standard—or normative data concerning expected performance times are available, performance times are not very revealing without a reference to understand what they signify. For example, is a mean performance time of 5.8 minutes fast or slow? In relation to what? With regard to data on errors, unless some quantitative standard is available (and error standards almost never exist), how does one know how many errors are too many? Only in the situation in which *no* errors are permissible can one be sure about the significance of any error quantity. On the other hand, if the subject matter expert can say, even without benefit of a formal standard, that x number of errors is too many, he or she possesses a usable, although crude, error standard. Even without knowing how many errors make a problem, errors may be of diagnostic value; the manner in which an error is made may indicate a problem. For example, misreading a gauge value may indicate that the gauge is difficult to read and hence poorly designed. Difficulties encountered by subjects is another area where data can be unclear. Subjects should be asked to report difficulties, and personnel sometimes experience obvious difficulties during the measurement, but how many difficulties represent a serious problem? Subjects are prone to exaggerate and also have problems evaluating their difficulty. Like errors, difficulties are more useful for diagnosis of design or task faults. When personnel must crane their necks to read a meter, for example, the meter may be poorly located.

Under nonexperimental conditions, meaning may be given by correlation of factors, events, and variables with one another and by their correlation either with mission accomplishment and/or with system output. This is because we want to know which system factors or variables have had the greatest effect on mission accomplishment and output. But correlation may not help much in identifying the mechanisms that produce that effect on system performance and output. In either case, specialists may have to interpret data with the aid of theory and hypothesis, which are mechanisms for endowing data with meaning.

The mechanisms that cause a variable to have an effect may in a complex system be somewhat removed from that variable because of interdependencies; the mechanisms may be akin to an "intervening variable." If too few personnel are working a shift, the effect may be that the rate of system outputs is slowed. The variable producing the effect is the number of personnel, but the mechanism responsible for the effect may be personnel overloading.

The meaning of a datum may also be derived from the context that produced the datum. The ideal way of producing that context is the experimental method, because by varying and controlling variables, it excludes everything but the single (hence unambiguous) context. In systems that lack experimental control, that context is produced by interpretation or by correlation, which involves arrangement of data elements, thus doing conceptually what is done physically in an experiment by arranging treatment conditions.

The answers to six questions about the occurrence of a phenomenon help determine context in nonexperimental situations: *who* (with what characteristics) performed the activity under investigation; *what* (the nature of the performance) was done or not done; *where* (in the factory, in a physical location) was the deed done or not done; *when* (in the mission cycle) was it done or not done; *why* (according to the performer) was the act done or not done; and *how* was it done? Readers familiar with journalistic aphorisms may recognize the preceding as essential elements in a newspaper story. The answers to these questions often come from the performer's verbal report—subjective information. Also valuable is the assistance of a subject matter expert experienced in the operations of the system being studied or a system similar to it. Experts can suggest the variables that in their experience are most important in affecting personnel performance at each stage of the mission scenario. The system analysis described in Table 6.1 includes determination of these variables prior to data-gathering.

Data clarity can be enhanced in several ways: (1) by ensuring that test objectives are quite clear and precise and that criteria and measures are clearly related to those objectives; in other words, precise objectives help assign meaning to the measures and to the data resulting from these measures; (2) by developing performance standards for units of performance so that one can say unequivocally that test performance is or is not within accepted limits; (3) by exploring prior to measurement the dependencies among variables and the terminal output, thus enabling the specialist to predict effects that, if they occur, are explained by the dependencies; and (4) by enlisting expert opinion to consider the meaning of data and soliciting the subjective responses of test subjects about their performance.

Researchers never completely eliminate data obscurity—that is why they continue to need theory. One can view theory as a matrix, or pattern, of hypoth-esized relationships that permit the researcher to assign meaning to data items that would otherwise appear unrelated. Theory may also substitute for data when the latter are incomplete. Theory is particularly necessary when the system is complex. However, the purpose of the research is not to develop theories. Ideally, if one had all the data that bore on a problem, and if all those data were completely meaningful, there would be no need for theory—one would *know*. But hardly anyone expects to live to see this happy situation in human factors.

THE IMPORTANCE OF STATISTICS IN SYSTEM MEASUREMENT

It may appear that in human factors system studies, where the opportunity to control treatment conditions is lacking or severely restricted, the need for statistics would be less than in experimental design. This is quite untrue. The opportunity to arrange treatments in advance may be missing, but the need for correlational statistics is all the greater.

There are certain occasions in research on operational systems when it is possible to arrange treatments and to make use of such significance statistics as analysis of variance:

1. When contrasting conditions are inherent in system operation (e.g., night versus day operations). The hypothesis in testing such contrasts is that the conditions are sufficiently different from one another to affect human performance.

2. When a system configuration is to be changed in equipment, operating procedures, number of personnel, training of personnel, or mission events, one can perform a pre-change/post-change study to determine whether the change has significantly affected performance.

3. As the system ages in operational use, it is possible to measure system and personnel performance to see whether the system has changed significantly over time.

4. If a performance standard exists, either as a requirement or as normative (expected) performance, one can test to see whether actual performance significantly differs from standard performance.

5. When two systems are competing, as when two developers are designing systems to the same requirement and the systems are tested against each other, it is hypothesized that one system will be significantly more effective in performance than the other.

Only the first occasion in the above list occurs with any frequency.

In their discussion of correlational statistics that can be employed when significance or experimental statistics cannot, Cook and Campbell (1979) include regression analysis, path analysis, cross lagged panel correlations, and time series analysis. These highly sophisticated methods will not be discussed here because they are described in Cook and Campbell and in other statistics texts. Correlational analysis is weaker than significance statistics, because it reflects no experimental control.

A major difficulty in system measurement is the small number of test repetitions (N) characteristic of full-scale system operations. In extreme cases, N may be only one or two, because full-scale missions with slowly acting systems take a long time to complete. Some missions (e.g., air combat maneuvering) will last only minutes, but a single operating cycle of a nuclear power plant may take more than a day from cold start to cold finish. Individual subsystems within the system may cycle through an operation many times in the course of completing a mission, but as a general rule one can say that specialists rarely have as many test replications of the full mission as they would prefer.

Related to length of mission is the small number of test subjects. The personnel unit in many systems is the team, however many operators it contains, and the system may run three or four shifts, which means that the total team N will be 3 or 4. The small number of test replications and test subjects means that system specialists cannot have as much confidence in the representativeness of their data as they would if they performed a non-system-related laboratory study, which usually involves a relatively large number of subjects. It is no good to say that specialists should exert control over the system to increase N. Almost never do they have the authority to do this with actual operational systems, although they may have slightly more control over simulators.

Because of the small N available, it would be desirable for the system researcher to combine data from a number of instances of operational exercises and individual tests of the same or similar systems. However, this is almost never done, in part because we lack an agreed on taxonomy of system characteristics (see Chapter 5), which would enable the measurement specialist to categorize the various system functions and operations in term of their similarity. More important, perhaps, researchers feel no compelling interest in combining data. As far as I know, a catalog of operational systems describing their common and similar functions and tasks has never been attempted, although the military maintains lists of tasks in each system as well as task analysis documentation. We do not know if data from individual system tests could be combined, but the effort should be made. Even where systems differ in their external configurations, they may upon analysis be seen to perform common functions and tasks.

RESEARCH PARADIGMS

A research paradigm is a strategy for performing research. It is not the same as the experimental design for an individual study, but is rather a general method of collecting data. The most common research paradigm is the experimental study that involves the development of hypotheses, the assignment of subjects to treatment conditions, and the selection of a statistical design for the study. There are other paradigms, however, that may be used in human factors system research.

A second research paradigm is non-experimental, with no manipulation of variables or performance conditions. A third research paradigm, not quite as common as the two preceding, is subjective response, in which an individual—sometimes an expert, sometimes a subject or participant in the measurement—provides information and thus becomes his or her own measuring instrument. All three paradigms may be combined in the same research, although this is not common. A fourth paradigm that has some limited value is one in which the research is incidental to, a by-product of, other activities. For example, data on troubleshooting durations may be gathered as part of the collection of logistical information (e.g., parts usage), or clinical psychologists may collect case histories as part of their therapeutic work and then content-analyze these histories.

In examining research paradigms, one must begin by asking what research is for and how well these paradigms satisfy those purposes. It is necessary to exclude purposes expressed in the phrase "It's fun" because personal amusement is not particularly important for a discipline, although it may well be for the individual researcher. Also excluded is the stock phrase "Research is performed to increase knowledge," because this goal is impossibly general.

Human factors research may be performed to describe and predict what people do, to demonstrate that an effect can occur, to find out how an effect occurs, to discover why an effect occurs, to determine that a research conclusion is stable and generalizable over a number of test situations, and to determine that an effect, a finding, a principle, and so forth, can be applied in a nonresearch situation. Of course, no single study includes all these goals. The ultimate goal of all research is to describe and predict, but these terms are used in a human factors context in a more specific sense—as in the generation of normative data about such things as the frequency of operator errors and the development of tables for predicting errors as a function of specific variables.

Most experimental research demonstrates merely that an effect occurs—for example, variable X has a statistically significant effect on performance, or one training methodology is more effective than another—because it is much more difficult to determine *why* variable X is significant and *why* that training methodology is better than merely that they are. A few studies combine several purposes, but many researchers prefer merely to demonstrate an effect and then theorize about its causation in the discussion section of their research reports.

Research on how and why an effect occurs is often linked, although theoretically they are not the same. In the case of the more effective training technique, it might be hypothesized that the reason it was more effective was that performance feedback was given to students more often than in the competing technique. A study could then be performed in which the more effective method was employed in all treatments, but in one treatment feedback was given and in another it was not. If the method with feedback was found to be superior, it could be surmised that the reason for the superiority of the method was the feedback provision.

To study generalizability, one might utilize the new training method in various disciplines (e.g., target recognition training, troubleshooting training) to determine that the new method was uniformly effective. An example of applicability research would be the case of the researcher who, having determined that a training method worked in didactic, direct verbal presentation in classrooms, attempted to determine whether the method would be equally effective in the context of embedded training—for example, as part of a primary equipment used aboard ship or aircraft—or who applied the methodology in a standard curriculum for pilots and noted whether students given this training did in fact graduate as superior pilots (something like a transfer-of-training study).

Excluding incidental research, which cannot be considered in the same light as the others because it depends on other factors, the three methods—experimental, nonexperimental, and subjective response—are probably equally valuable, although not for every one of the purposes of the preceding research. Experimental hypothesis-testing does not do a good job of describing and predicting to the reference situation, because the laboratory (and the simulator less so) does not use that situation as a model and because experimental research does not include a very wide range of human performances. Hypothesis-testing does a good job of demonstrating an effect and a fair job of finding out how and why, but a less adequate one for generalizing and applying. The nonexperimental method would probably be more readily generalized and applied. The subjective method does well in describing and predicting, but not very well in demonstrating an effect or finding out how and why that effect occurs or in generalization, but it is probably excellent for application—in which subject matter expertise is necessary. This suggests not that the paradigms are alternatives to each other—they are different ways of getting at the same "truth"—but that they should be used in combination to supplement one another. Since most formal research has involved experimentation, additional attention should be given to nonexperimental and subjective methods.

The ideal research paradigm would be one that makes use of all methods as research questions warrant. Human factors texts often imply, if they do not specifically recommend, a four-part paradigm. One might begin by collecting descriptive data in the operational environment (nonexperimental method), discover by analyzing these data that certain variables and questions require more detailed study, investigate these in a laboratory or simulator (experimental method), and then return to the operational environment (nonexperimental method) to validate and generalize the conclusions derived from the more controlled environment. Only the experimental part of the paradigm is usually implemented. In all the phases above, subject matter experts familiar with the operational system and with subjective judgments might be useful. However, subjective responses are not usually considered as a distinctive paradigm, but rather as a minor method, as merely another way of collecting information when the other two methods are not feasible. If one cannot get objective data, one makes use of subjective estimates. Subject matter experts might, however, be used to test hypotheses relative to operational systems by presenting the experts with contrasting situations and asking for a quantitative judgment of the performance that would result in these situations. The percentage of experts judging that certain differences would result could be tested for statistical significance.

The same technique might be used to gather normative data, by presenting the experts with a hypothetical mission scenario and asking them to estimate quantitatively the probability of successful task completion, the frequency of error, and the relative effects of specified variables in accomplishing the task. None of this could be done, however, without much more knowledge of the validity and reliability of expert judgments and the parameters affecting these judgments.

TOWARD OVERCOMING MEASUREMENT PROBLEMS

The reader may feel that the problems addressed in this chapter are difficult, if not insuperable. What can be done about them? An obvious solution is to ignore them. One need not, for example, think of a relevant operational situation in planning to perform an experiment. But someone who is serious about responding to these methodological problems can do the following:

1. Consider using nonexperimental methods as an adjunct to any experimental research being performed

2. Deliberately introduce into the experiment, to the extent possible, conditions representative of the operational environment to see how robust the conclusions are

3. Try to validate study effects with an operational system

4. Collect data from subjects on every major variable that might have influenced their performance

5. Analyze the data to determine the amount of variance accounted for by each variable that was manipulated

6. In system research, analyze personnel performance data in terms of their relationship to system outputs and mission success

7. Make maximum use of subject matter experts and quantified subjective estimates

8. Support research on the factors that characterize the operational environment

9. In system research, analyze the system and its mission before deciding on appropriate criteria and measures

10. Encourage the development of normative data performance standards to determine the range within which performance can be expected to occur

11. In nonexperimental situations, determine the context (who, what, where, when, why, and how) in which data are gathered

Doing any or all of the above will not necessarily eliminate the difficulties, but the researcher will know that he or she has done what can be done to overcome them.

SUMMARY

The special methodological problems of human factors are experimental control, multidimensionality, validation, operational fidelity, types of data and data meaning, criteria and measures, the relevance of statistics, and the alternative paradigms available for human factors research.

Experimental control requires the researcher to break up a unitary situation into its constituent parts. This creates special problems for a system-oriented behavioral discipline, whose reference situation is by definition nondecomposable. However, the operational situation may contain inherent alternative conditions that can be contrasted. Simulation is a way of exercising control over systems that in the operational environment might not be readily controlled.

Human performance is multidimensional because of the complex of forces both within and outside the system that act on the system and its personnel. The number of such performance-shaping factors is not, however, infinite, and in most cases the effect of most of them is slight. How strongly an individual variable influences performance varies not only over time but also as a function of the relative strength of the other variables associated with it concurrently.

The only validity that is meaningful from a human factors standpoint is predictive validity. Validity problems result from differences in scale and in opportunities for control between the reference and the nonreference situations. Results secured from studies in the reference situation are inherently valid. Validity can be pursued in a number of ways, depending on whether one replicates or predicts. Experimental results can be tested for robustness by exposing them to operational conditions.

The goal of human factors measurement is to incorporate as many operational conditions into the test situation without losing control. Consequently, operational fidelity is closely tied to validation.

Subjective data are needed to explain objective data, because the latter have comparatively few dimensions. Often subjective data and information are the only practical data sources available.

Effective performance measurement in system situations is always preceded by system analysis. The common element in both traditional experimental research and in system measurement is the determination of criteria and measures. This is also the most critical problem addressed in the behavioral measurement literature. Not all criteria and measures are equally relevant and valuable. Measures vary in specificity and diagnosticity. In selecting measures, one must ask what additional information a potential measure provides.

Data obscurity as exemplified in performance times, errors, and difficulties encountered by subjects is related both to multidimensionality and to lack of control. Data meaning may be derived from the context that produced the data. The meaning of this context can be assisted by information about performance as related to who, what, where, when, why and how that performance occurred.

Correlational statistics play a critical role in nonexperimental methods. Alternative research paradigms—experimental, nonexperimental, and subjective—can be utilized in performing human factors research. Each paradigm has particular value in satisfying individual research needs.

CHAPTER 7

Behavioral Design in System Development

To this point we have been talking about human factors largely as a research discipline, but the problems that human factors faces cannot be understood without examining its *application* aspects and what practitioners actually do during system development. This chapter focuses on the methods available to practitioners, because one of the important themes of this book is the discrepancy between the practitioner's needs for knowledge and methodology, and how well research satisfies those needs. In examining practitioner activities, we shall answer the following questions as completely as our data allow: How do practitioners perform their analyses and evaluations? How should these be performed? How effective are they? What do practitioners need to know and be able to do in order to perform their functions? What are the research and practical implications of these needs?

Practitioners divide their activities into two parts, analysis and evaluation, which are not entirely distinct—a few activities involve both. The section on analysis discusses mission, function, and task analysis, including function allocation; operational sequence diagrams; link and time-line analysis; and workload prediction. These are not all the analyses the Defense Department's MIL-H-46855B (Department of Defense, 1979) asks the practioner to make, but they are among the most important ones. Evaluation includes analysis or evaluation of design drawings and software algorithms; mockup testing or its analogue in computer terms, rapid prototyping; walk-throughs; and developmental and operational testing. The extent to which practitioners actually perform all of the above on any individual development project depends on whether practitioners are part of the design team from its inception, whether the project is sufficiently complex to require all these activities, and whether funding is provided for their performance.

These analyses and evaluations are, or should be, an integral part of design; they are performed to aid design, and if performed apart from design they are useless. They are *not* performed, as some believe, for the practitioners' benefit, to help practitioners understand system functioning. These analyses and evaluations are performed to provide answers to questions that arise in the course of system development (see Chapter 2) and are performed only when this need arises. For example, one would be unlikely to do a time-line analysis unless the system under development were highly time-dependent.

Another point that must be emphasized is that these analyses and evaluations are just as important for the development of computerized systems as for more traditional ones. Most systems, even when heavily computerized, retain many aspects that are not computerized and must therefore be analyzed and evaluated as before. Software designers do utilize special techniques to deal with the user interface, such as drawing individual screens, writing lists of commands, or constructing a scenario of the user's anticipated interaction with the software (Penn 1988), but at a more molar level the general design/development pattern is taken over from hardware design. For example, Baker et al. (1988) describe three phases in the design of the user-computer interface: a requirements analysis essentially as described in this chapter, a design/development phase in which alternative designs are developed and tradeoff studies performed, and a test and integration phase involving rapid prototyping (mockup tests) and user acceptance tests.

MISSION ANALYSIS

Mission analysis has three functions, all of which are important and one of which is of overriding significance from the standpoint of behavioral design. The first function is to determine what the mission consists of, based on information from planning documents, the system specification, the request for proposal, and previous test results. The second is to determine from this information specific system missions or goals (e.g., to detect a submarine, to produce machine tools), any required inputs and outputs (e.g., to receive electronic signals on 2,250 Hz; 40 messages must be transmitted per unit time), system capabilities and performance requirements demanded by the mission (e.g., store enough fuel for 30 days), environmental factors that may affect system performance (e.g., the anticipated temperature in which the system must function is 10° F), and finally, constraints on system performance (e.g., repair of any equipment module must not take more than 1.5 hours).

The third function, and the one that is of greatest significance for behavioral design, is to examine what the mission requirement means for system personnel. This is the process of deriving behavioral implications from the preceding information. The practitioner's examination centers on the potential effects on personnel of a system or a job that has certain characteristics. For example, if the system must be operated outside a shelter in arctic conditions, what does this mean for system personnel—beyond the obvious need for cold-weather clothing? It will be useful here for the practitioner to know what the available research says about the effects of cold weather.

Demand Stimuli

Underlying the need for mission analysis is the concept of the system as a source of demand stimuli. Human-machine interaction assumes that, although the operator controls the machine, the machine affects the operator directly or indirectly. Machine stimuli create in the operator a state of arousal that demands a response. The stimuli may arise from the machine itself (e.g., its speed of operation, thus pacing the operator), from the information it provides during its functioning (e.g., sensor data) or from task requirements (e.g., to assemble ten toasters per hour). The most potent stimuli arise from system operations—for instance, displayed information. The response required of the operator is channeled and externalized by operating and maintenance procedures. The response requirements create a demand for personnel resources that may or may not be available, including any of the following: strength (not usually in a highly automated culture); memory, both long-term and short-term; speed and precision; integration of information from multiple sources; and diagnosis, evaluation, and decision-making.

The concept of a match or mismatch between system demands and personnel resources may not seem particularly novel to the reader, because the relationship seems to be inherent in the very idea of a human-machine system. What is important are the implications of the demand-resource relationship for required knowledge. The practitioner cannot determine the behavioral implications of the mission without knowing what human capabilities are—not in the general terms in which they are often phrased in the behavioral literature, but in a specific system or job context. That literature must be *directly*, not indirectly, related to system design. For example, Yeh and Wickens (1988) have developed an elegant theory to explain why performance and subjective measures of workload often disagree. The authors specify that "a model of workload is of the greatest importance . . . to predict which configuration will maximize performance efficiency" (p. 111). However, their theory is of little use to practitioners because it fails even to mention physical characteristics of design.

In their analyses practitioners must judge which demands are being exercised and how strong they are. Practitioners are concerned only about demands that are moderate to great, but to make this judgment requires the ability to scale system demands on a continuum of strength. Moreover, the demand cannot be evaluated except in terms of human capability—a requirement that 1,000 pounds must be lifted manually would not be a significant demand if humans had the strength of Superman. Hence, demands cannot be easily evaluated without the knowledge generated by relevant research. In some areas, such as strength (anthropometry), access spaces, toxicology, and perhaps psychomotor capabilities, some information is available, but there is very little information with regard to cognition or any other complex function. Consequently, practitioners often fall short in their calculations of demand. The analysis the practitioner performs is logical and deductive, but it depends heavily on data that may not be available.

The Mission Scenario

The term *mental model,* mentioned frequently in the most recent behavioral literature, describes the practitioner's analytic processes. Experienced practitioners do not think of the elements of the new system in static terms; instead, they create a picture of how that system will function operationally. The dynamic quality of the model raises questions of personnel performance that must be answered. At early design stages, there may be nothing more available as a guide for the model than a written system requirement. The predecessor system looms important here. It is tremendously helpful if the new system being analyzed has certain characteristics in common with a predecessor.

If the system under development is quite novel, the practitioner's mental model of the new system will probably be only a vague outline involving only a few gross functions. Such a model will be progressively elaborated during design. The physical representation of a mental model is a *mission scenario.* The scenario describes in chronological order the major tasks to be performed, the factors that could significantly influence system performance, starting and ending times, locations (if relevant), planned changes in system status, expected performance of other systems (if relevant), and important geographic or climatic features. The model will probably contain some inaccuracies, because subsequent design events may invalidate some of the model's assumptions, principally the allocation of functions between human and machine. The practitioner's mission scenario may assume a role for the human that ultimately may not be correct. This assumption precedes any formal function allocation as described below.

Development of a mental model of how the new system will operate requires that the practitioner gather technical information about the predecessor system before beginning a mission analysis. Although the predecessor system simplifies the analytic task, it also reduces the amount of freedom the practitioner has to draw behavioral implications, because certain human roles in the earlier system will probably already have been accepted by developers for the new system. Many mission aspects can be ignored as posing no demands on the human. The requirement that an aircraft travel a minimum of 300 miles an hour at no more than 10,000 feet altitude has little or no impact on the human, but the requirement to travel 100 miles an hour on a rough ground surface would have significant human effects resulting from acceleration and vibration. The analysis may suggest that specific knowledge is needed for which the literature may not be completely adequate. If a system must make use of infrared (IR) sensing, for example, how well can operators in general detect targets of a specified size using an IR display? Knowledge about the effects of continous operation on human functions (e.g., in terms of fatigue) is also important.

Mission analysis occurs in a series of steps that require answers to the following questions: First, at what points, if any, in system operation could the human be affected by a specific system characteristic, and what is the nature of the effect and how strong could it be? Second, what research or other information is available about how the human would react to the system characteristic in the first question? This is also a question of capability because it asks how sensitive the operator will be to the potential effect. For example, assuming that before an amphibious landing Marines must be transported for fifty miles in a small boat over a moderate sea state (Stinson 1979), what is their propensity to sea sickness and how incapacitating would that sickness be?

Physical and physiological demands are easier for the analyst to identify. Perceptual and cognitive demands are much more difficult and may require research before analysis can be initiated. For example, suppose the system requires a security guard to monitor continuously eight television screens to detect human movement on the periphery of a facility. Does this represent an excessive perceptual demand? There are studies, such as those of Thackray, Bailey, and Touchstone (1979), that will help in determining whether a demand exists that will produce unacceptable observer error or false reports. As systems become more computerized, more information will be needed about perceptual and cognitive capabilities because operators will become supervisors and monitors instead of performers. The determination of demand will also become more difficult, because the functions being considered will be more covert.

Mission analysis has levels of difficulty, depending on how precise the answers required must be. If one is asked merely to indicate potential human weak points in system operation, the analysis can be qualitative, backed up by whatever the available literature says. If the analyst is asked to answer specific questions—for instance, whether personnel will be able to perform a particular mission effectively over a forty-eight-hour period, and what decrement will there be—the analyst will have to provide a quantitative answer, in which case specific research in support of the answer may be necessary. Fortunately for practitioners, designers rarely ask questions this precise because the latter do not think in these terms and/or because their experience leads them to believe that they could not get such precise answers from practitioners. Their scientific training often makes practitioners want to provide answers that are more precise than the available research and methodology permit. Paradoxically, this often makes them feel more guilty than unsatisfied designer expectations would warrant.

The mission analysis is a major opportunity to utilize the system concept in practice, because the analysis usually involves the entire system. This becomes less possible as design becomes more detailed and more molecular. Moreover, if the behavioral mission analysis is required as part of a predesign brainstorming meeting, its utility will probably be much greater than an analysis that is presented as a document merely to satisfy a formal requirement. However, an informal analysis should not be any less sophisticated than a formal one, and it should be prepared just as carefully.

Further mission analysis steps are optional. Some analysts proceed immediately to determination of system functions, but where the system has a natural sequence or activity over time that can be readily broken down into distinct segments, it may be valuable to profile the performance of the mission. This is particularly useful for such transportation systems as aircraft, which have very distinct sequential phases in their operations, (e.g., takeoff and landing). A mission profile or scenario would be irrelevant for systems that do not change function very much over the course of a mission.

FUNCTION ANALYSIS

Function analysis should lead to two things: specification of the functions the system must implement, and, as a follow-up, assignment of responsibilities to human or machine—otherwise known as function allocation.

System Functions

The *function* is the purpose for which a behavioral activity or an equipment subsystem is included in the system. Functions may be implemented by machines alone, by personnel alone, or as in most cases, by some combination of personnel and machines. Unless the new system has a predecessor system, the practitioner theoretically begins analysis with no preconception about how a particular function will be implemented. Although some functions appear to belong exclusively to personnel or to machines, it is a mistake for the analyst to jump to conclusions. For example, although many functions can be automated, the unthinking automation of functions may ultimately have negative rather than positive effects for the system.

By transforming inputs into outputs, the function contributes to the accomplishment of some part of the mission. Subordinate, more molecular functions are derived from more molar functions by imagining the processes required to implement the molar function. This is the "if—then" logic, which says: if function X must be accomplished, then subfunctions Y and Z are prerequisites and must also be performed. The logical-deductive process partitions gross requirements into finer detail by asking at each step of the process, "To accomplish this requirement or this function, to satisfy this constraint, what is needed in the way of inputs and outputs and implementing mechanisms?" This permits the analyst to subdivide such molar functions as "to navigate the ship" into smaller ones, such as "to activate LORAN." Gross functions have limited usefulness because they include large behavior segments that must be subdivided into smaller ones if they are to be more manageable. These subfunctions also have behavioral implications in terms of the demands for capabilities and effort that they impose on both personnel and equipment. Thus, the function "to monitor a display" raises the question of what perceptual difficulties the operator may experience in the monitoring process.

Functions describe relatively molar behaviors—for example, to detect, to analyze, to repair. The individual tasks and behaviors needed to implement or carry out the function are much more detailed. Functions can be instantaneous (start engines) or prolonged (monitor radar scope), apparently simple (detect blip), or complex (analyze battle strategy). There are no clear-cut rules that determine whether the analyst should call a set of behaviors a function or a task. At a certain level of detail—which is difficult to specify—the function shades almost imperceptibly into a task.

Major system functions are often quite obvious from the nature of the system. If one is dealing with an aircraft, for example, it is obvious that two major functions are "takeoff" and "landing." By the time the analyst becomes involved in the system development process, such top-level functions may already have been specified; this is particularly the case if the system under development is an update of a previous one. However, the analyst is not much concerned about major functions. It is in the identification of subordinate-level functions, particularly as they require human implementation, that the analyst is more likely to contribute to system design, because these may have been overlooked by planners.

Function Allocation

Logically one assigns a function to human or machine—function alloca-tion—according to which can perform that function more effectively. This was the basis for what is known as the "Fitts list" (Fitts 1951), a summary of functions that indicates which is supposedly better suited to perform each function—human beings or machines. The human or the machine must be better, however, in terms of individual system effectiveness, which means that they cannot be considered independent of the specific design context. This means that function allocation is an integral part of design, even though many design engineers might not think of design as a process of allocating functions.

These comparisons between human and machine capabilities assume that the analyst knows a great deal about their relative capabilities—at least with regard to humans, for presumably engineers can specify machine strengths and weaknesses. The things one needs to know about humans include: the precision and consistency with which major human responses can be performed, the amount of skill required to perform effectively, reactions to fatigue and stress, expected error rate, and costs in terms of the amount of training required to achieve a particular level of skill. Some of this information is available, but most is not.

A basic problem with simply comparing human and machine outside the design context is that each is described in different terms. A behavioral function may require certain qualities—such as multilimb coordination, finger dexterity, and dynamic flexibility (Fleishman and Quaintance 1984)—but what are their equivalents in machine terms? Machine attributes include such qualities as power consumption, heat output, response speed, and memory storage—but what are the human equivalents? It is too simple to say that one can compare the two in terms of functional performance (i.e., an output measure), because function allocation is a trade-off of qualities. In almost all cases, if one considers only output, the machine might be the logical choice to perform the function, except that ultimately the machine might be too costly, too large, require too much power, and the like.

Once it is determined how functions will be implemented, the specific tasks to be performed can be determined. If, for example, navigating a ship by taking sun and star readings is the selected design alternative, then certain tasks are implied and must be identified. If navigation is accomplished using LORAN (Long-Range Radio Aid to Navigation) equipment, then other tasks are implied. Each set of task implications also imposes a set of demands on the system as a whole and on the operator or technician in particular. The task may make demands on the operator/technician, such as extremely acute hearing or pitch discrimination, as was the case with sonar operators in World War II. The introduction of human-computer dialogues imposes more complex cognitive demands. These demands can be ascertained only through analysis of the task, because the function is too gross a behavioral unit to be useful in determining demand.

Theoretically, in allocating functions the analyst should conceptualize all reasonably feasible ways in which the functions could be performed, determine the level of behavioral effectiveness (i.e., response precision, consistency) to expect with each alternative, and then select the most effective alternative. Such a procedure, described in Meister (1985b), is rarely possible, simply because the amount of effort involved is great. Perhaps it would not be excessive if function allocation were conducted independent of design, but as an integral part of a design that is almost always hurried and unsystematic, function allocation also may become hurried and less systematic than desirable.

A possible substitute for comparison of all possible ways of implementing a function might be a comprehensive catalog of human capabilities, together with the kind of performance that could be expected under the most common conditions in which the function would be exercised. Research might ultimately be able to give the analyst probabilities of correct performance for generic functions, such as driving an automobile. Of course, in producing such probabilities, one would have to take into account the general types of equipment used to perform the function and the common operating conditions. But even if it were not possible to include in the catalog all factors potentially influencing capability, data should be available to provide range estimates. The catalog referred to prevsiously would have to be updated periodically too.

Some specialists (e.g., Price 1985) reject the notion of allocating functions on the basis of performance estimates, and it is true that the prospect of securing enough data to support quantitative allocation judgments is daunting. The alternative, however, is the subjectivity of the Fitts list. Is it unreasonable to suppose that just as chemicals have specified properties that produce certain effects, so functions and tasks under specified conditions also have performance characteristics that can be documented? The objection sometimes raised that human performance is too variable to permit quantitative prediction of performance seems unjustifed, especially because there have been few such attempts at prediction. There is an implication in this objection that human performance cannot be described quantitatively, an implication specialists should emphatically reject.

Type of Research Needed

The research needed for the analyses described so far is predictive, not explanatory, research. The outputs of this research should be able to say: given a certain situation, one may expect such and such performance. Explanation—the description of the mechanisms responsible for the performance—while desirable, is unnecessary at the primitive stage of a discipline but will, one assumes, follow on the increasing accumulation of data. For engineering purposes the explanation is unnecessary, although desirable. What we have now in human factors research is a concentration on explanatory attempts while simple prediction is ignored. Explanation is certainly more sophisticated, more "scientific," than the mere accumulation of data, but the primitiveness of human factors as a discipline suggests that, at the present time, data accumulation is more useful. To paraphrase Sherlock Holmes, it is a capital mistake to theorize before one has sufficient data.

In soliciting the development of a catalog of capability data, we approach the beginning of a human performance data bank. The reader may feel that this theme has been overemphasized in preceding chapters, but without such data banks (or at least the effort to develop them), the engine directing the forward progress of the discipline will grind down to silence. In the absence of data the practitioner is largely blind.

Design Alternatives

To the extent that each design alternative considered by engineers represents a function allocation, it would be desirable if the practitioner could analyze each one in detail, but the opportunity rarely exists, because engineers concentrate on a small subset of all possible design alternatives (Meister 1971). In examining design alternatives the practitioner will ask the following questions: (1) How well will the operator perform in each alternative? Will the operator be able to satisfy system requirements? On what evidence is this judgment based? (2) What is the anticipated operator effectiveness (in terms of performance, reliability, fatigue, etc.) of each alternative against anticipated machine effectiveness? (3) What special provisions or facilities (e.g., special displays, increased working area) should one provide for personnel in each alternative? (4) What potential problems might the operator encounter in each alternative? (5) What special advantages or disadvantages will the operator add in each alternative?

The analyst must first determine whether any humans involved in an alternative can physically do the job. If they cannot, the function automatically passes to a machine alternative. Where a design alternative imposes requirements on the personnel that obviously exceed their physical, cognitive, or perceptual limitations, the alternative is not feasible and must be discarded or revised. Engineers are unlikely to make such gross design errors. It is much more likely that within some intermediate range of behavior one design alternative or the other creates a greater propensity to error or stress. It is this increased error or stress probability that the behavioral analyst should be able to point out. Unfortunately, the traditional experimental study that tests only the extremes of a distribution often provides little information about the intermediate behavior range.

TASK IDENTIFICATION

Functions shade almost imperceptibly into tasks; the unit of performance is smaller in tasks, so that tasks fit into functions, but not vice versa. Task identification and analysis are two separate activities: *task identification* is the listing and description of tasks to be performed; *task analysis* is the examination of task characteristics in terms of their behavioral implications. The dividing line between identification and analysis is unclear. Some specialists think of the two as being quite distinct; others ignore identification and proceed directly to analysis; others do not analyze the task at all. Task identification poses relatively few difficulties for the practitioner, which is perhaps why it is often ignored as a distinct phase of behavioral analysis.

But task identification is a critical part of behavioral design. If practitioners specify that a particular task must be performed, this essentially creates a design requirement. Again "if—then" logic, as it was used during function analysis, helps identify tasks. Given that (if) a particular function must be performed, it follows (then) that certain tasks must also be performed. For example, if the function is to taxi an aircraft, it is necessary to start engines; if one must start engines, then the pilot must move the throttle. The derivation of tasks is therefore not a very sophisticated process. Although it helps to have a behavioral orientation, engineers can and do identify tasks, although they might not use that terminology. Task analysis, on the other hand, is an extremely sophisticated and much more difficult process and is rarely if ever performed by engineers.

The task is defined in terms of an action to be taken (a verb in the task description) and the object acted upon (a noun). A very molecular task—actually a subtask—might be "throw switch"; the verb "throw" is the action and "switch" is the object of that action. The one who performs the task—the operator or maintenance person—is implied but rarely stated.

The action performed in the task produces a response in the equipment, and that response serves to initiate the next task in sequence. This has certain similarities to the stimulus-organism-response (S-O-R) paradigm in psychology, since the action of the equipment usually serves as a stimulus to the operator, who then acts again on the equipment (chained S-O-R). In S-O-R the stimulus acts directly on the organism that is the one emitting a response. In the task, the stimulus activates the operator, who does indeed emit a response, but now it is a response that energizes or modifies an item of equipment, which then produces a response (e.g., a computer message) that initiates the next sequence by stimulating the operator. The task then conforms to psychological principles, but it complicates these and subordinates the operator in a somewhat lesser role. S-O-R does not consider anything beyond the individual; the task raises the equipment and its responses, and thus the system, to the same level of importance as the operator.

Task identification and task description have several purposes. The listing of tasks permits the specialist to organize and group them on the basis of such criteria as purpose or function, a common equipment and location, performance by the same operator, and so forth. This helps organize tasks into groupings of jobs and positions. The task description also provides the basic source material for the task analysis, although this description rarely suffices for this purpose and is often supplemented by information from other sources.

Practitioners may encounter difficulty in deciding on the particular level of detail a task should describe. They must decide whether they want to describe the action (task) at a very molecular level, such as the individual control or display (e.g., reads meter), or at a somewhat more molar level (e.g., determines that temperature is within acceptable range). This is not merely a matter of semantics. In the first case, the task has been reduced to its behavioral fundamentals. In the second case, the task description subsumes but does not make explicit a number of more molecular subtasks inherent in the performance of the task, and it may be necessary eventually to break the task down into those subtasks. The consequence of describing the task at a more abstract level is that the analyst may overlook some hardware or software needed to implement the task and/or some behavioral implications of performing the task. There is also a relationship between task detail and the practitioner's mental model of the system—where the former is vague, so is the model.

TASK ANALYSIS

Task analysis is an essential part of the behavioral analysis of systems during development. The government agency document known as MIL-H-46855B (Department of Defense 1979) requires task analysis for all systems developed for the Defense Department. There are four major reasons for performing a task analysis: to assist in the design of the system, meaning the human-machine interface, the total job, construction of procedures, job aids, etc.; to assist in the manning of the system, meaning development of selection criteria and determination of the number and type of personnel needed; to assist in the development of an instructional system, meaning development of the curriculum, selection of critical tasks to be trained, etc.; and to assist in evaluation of the completed system by establishing performance criteria against which system personnel performance can be measured.

Task analysis as we know it today was first developed in the 1950s by Miller (1953), although the notion can be found even earlier in the work of Taylor (Taylor 1911) and of Gilbreth (Gilbreth 1911). Task analysis is the process of attempting to extract underlying attributes of the task by asking certain questions, listed below, of the task description.

Design questions. What tasks are to be performed? How critical is each task? In what sequence will tasks be performed? What information is required by the task performer? What control activations are required? What performance requirements are important? Is coordination with other tasks or personnel required? Are perceptual, cognitive, psychomotor, or physical demands imposed by the task excessive? What errors are possible, and how likely are they? Answers to these questions will indicate whether the demand imposed by the system is excessive or not.

Manning questions. How many people are needed to perform the task or job? What skill level is required?

Training questions. On what behavioral dimensions are the tasks based? How difficult or complex is the task or job? What information does the operator need to perform the task or job? How is the task related to other tasks? to the total job? How frequently is the task or job performed? Answers to the preceding determine the nature of the training curriculum.

Test and evaluation questions. What performance criteria indicate that the task has been correctly performed? What are the consequences if the task or job is not performed or is performed incorrectly?

The answers to some of these questions are very difficult. Some are relatively simple and concrete—for instance, the sequence in which tasks must be performed. Others are more complex and judgmental but still readily answered, such as: How critical is the task? These are not really attribute questions, which task analysis seeks to answer in order to characterize the fundamental qualities of the task. The primary attributes that interest the analyst are *task difficulty,* which is related to task demand, *workload* and *human reliability*, and the *skill* dimensions required by the task.

Task Difficulty

Difficulty should be differentiated from workload. Difficulty is an attribute of and inherent in the task and job, and this makes it more amenable to design modification. The feeling of being loaded is the individual's response to difficulty, along with other factors, but workload also depends on personnel and contextual variables, such as personnel capability and training, response requirements, the availability of time to respond, and the like. Workload is being extensively studied (see Hill et al. 1987), but there has been no corresponding effort to study difficulty perhaps because difficulty is linked to physical system and task characteristics and is therefore of less interest to behavioral specialists. An equipment or task can be difficult, but not a person; and an individual experiences workload, but not a system. Presently one can infer difficulty from task performance (for example, it takes longer, more errors are made), but lacking knowledge of the design factors that induce difficulty, there is little we can do about difficulty. Certain interface conditions are conducive to difficulty (see Table 7.1), but these are very gross and not performance-oriented.

Determining task difficulty on the basis of written task descriptions, especially if these are only one line long, is very arduous and probably unreliable. For this reason, practitioners have adopted the procedure of questioning subject matter experts when the tasks under examination are utilized in or resemble those of a predecessor system. The reliance on such experts as surrogates for observation of performance has become so common that they are asked to supply the analyst with judgments about task difficulty and skill requirements as well as about other task analytic parameters. Excessive reliance on these experts is objectionable, because until practitioners are forced to contemplate their own analytic inadequacies, they will do nothing to improve their ability to derive behavioral implications from tasks. Allowing lay experts to substitute their judgment for the analysts' observation and judgment assumes that the individual expert is capable of making judgments based on experience and observation that are at least as valid as those the analyst might make. No empirical evidence of the validity or reliability of expert outputs has been collected, and analysts who routinely make use of experts recommend using more than one because of possible inconsistency among their reports. One might well add to the list of necessary research projects in Chapter 4 an examination of task difficulty dimensions, a continuation of research on skill dimensions, and study of expert accuracy.

Methodology

Underlying task analysis methodology is the assumption that one can partition a unitary behavioral activity into its constituent elements and attributes.

Table 7.1 Interface Characteristics That May Lead to Operator Error

HARDWARE
Input Characteristics
1. Displays to be discriminated have many common characteristics.
2. Displays to be discriminated must be compared rapidly.
3. Events presented in displays change rapidly.
4. Inadequate visual feedback provided.
5. Low signal-to-noise ratio in detection displays.
6. Displays must be monitored over long periods.
7. Nature and/or timing of inputs cannot easily be anticipated.

Output Characteristics
1. Many controls must be operated in sequence or rapidly.
2. High degree of coordination with other operators required.
3. Decisions are based on inputs from multiple sources.
4. Decision-making time is short.
5. Responses must be very precise.

Physical Characteristics
1. Controls and displays are crowded together.
2. Controls and displays with differing functions are not correctly distinguished.
3. Where there are many controls and displays, these are not organized in modules.
4. Controls are not associated, or associated only indirectly, with corresponding displays.
5. Emergency, maintenance, and malfunction controls/displays are mixed with operating controls/displays.
6. Nomenclature of different controls/displays are too similar to one another.
7. Controls/displays are located outside optimal operating and viewing areas.
8. Critical controls are not safeguarded.

SOFTWARE
1. CRT display density is excessive.
2. Prompts, helps, and safeguards against catastrophic errors are insufficient.
3. Command instructions are obscure.
4. Feedback (error explanations) is missing.
5. Instruction manuals are inadequately descriptive.

Source: Modified from Meister 1985b.

What is distinctive about task analysis is that certain meanings (e.g., implications for design, manning, training) are assigned to those elements and attributes. Procedures for developing the deductions resulting from analysis of the information in the task description are indicated somewhat sketchily in reports describing analytic methodology, but for the most part they are left to the analyst's expertise.

Inputs for the task analysis can be secured from many sources other than the task description. System documentation includes any previous task analyses of a predecessor system, planning documents, test reports and specifications, procedural documents, operator manuals, and so forth. Interviews with predecessor system personnel are by far the most common method of securing information. Observation of predecessor or related system operations is yet another means, but this is infrequently utilized, greater reliance being placed on interviews, because analysts often do not know what to look for.

Before beginning the analysis, analysts must answer certain questions: (1) What is the purpose of the analysis? Purpose (e.g., training, determination of potential workload problems, design assistance) affects the nature of the analysis. (2) What questions does the analyst want the analysis to answer? (3) Should the analysis encompass all tasks or only certain ones? all subsystems or only certain ones? (4) What level of detail should the analysis include? down to the cues used to initiate the task? How many information categories should there be? (5) How are these questions to be answered? The last question is the essence of the analytic methodology. A review of the behavioral literature suggests that task analysis has been applied more for curriculum development than for any other purpose. It plays little or no role in the selection of design alternatives, because the practitioner does not know how to translate such task attributes as difficulty or required skill level into physical design equivalents.

The system characteristics to be examined in task analysis are those that increase the complexity of the operator's response, such as the need to integrate multiple data channels or the need to rely on long-term memory. The search for such task characteristics requires comparative research. For example, if the conventional wisdom is that the requirement to integrate multiple data channels will have a degrading effect on performance, one needs to be able to compare this effect with that of handling only a single channel (again, in terms of comparative *data;* being able to say only that handling two channels is more difficult than handling one channel is nothing more than common sense and has little substantive value). Human factors research has the responsibility to perform such comparative studies, which are more readily performed under controlled circumstances than in the system development setting.

To date, the analytic techniques in general and task analysis in particular have not been computerized. There have been attempts to use the computer for function allocation (Parks and Springer 1975) and for task descriptions (Wilson 1967), but these have not gone very far because the analytic methodology is not sufficiently proceduralized to be put into software format.

AUXILIARY ANALYTIC TECHNIQUES

Techniques have been developed to assist mission, function, and task analyses. For a complete description of these techniques, see Geer (1981). Graphic techniques used to develop computer programs are not included because they are not analytic or behavioral tools. The effort here is to give the reader the flavor of these tools, in particular their graphic qualities, and the major concepts on which they are built. The graphic quality of these techniques is derived from engineering, particularly from such industrial engineering techniques as time and motion methods (Barnes 1980). The graphic characteristic is assumed to illustrate more vividly relationships among equipment and task elements and personnel actions. A critical feature of some of these techniques, especially time-line analysis and workload prediction, is that they center around time, because time can be a significant requirement or constraint, leading to difficulty when tasks must be completed at a precise time or as quickly as possible.

Functional Flow Diagrams

A functional flow diagram is a chart that displays the sequence and arrangement of functions within the system. It enables analysts to examine the sequence, timing, and time relationships of system functions to see how much flexibility they have in organizing them. Using data derived from mission profiles and scenarios, the diagrams are developed iteratively for more detailed system requirements down to the level of specific tasks (at which point other techniques become more important). The concept of the diagram is based on schematic block diagrams derived from engineering that depict relationships between items of equipment in a system. The major difference between the functional flow and the schematic block diagram is that the block in the functional flow diagram represents a human function.

Functional flow diagrams are best suited to gross analysis at a very early stage in system analysis because the amount of information they contain is limited to function sequence and relationship. They are constructed by arranging in sequence all the functions of a particular subsystem or equipment. Each function is depicted within a rectangular block that is numbered for reference according to its sequence on the page (see Figure 7.1).

Decision-Action Diagrams

The decision-action diagram (see Figure 7.2), also referred to as an information flow chart, a decision-logic diagram, or operation-decision diagram, is a technique similar to the functional flow diagram. It shows the flow of system operations in terms of decisions and actions performed by personnel. Special symbology may also be used at a more detailed level to indicate allocation to human or machine (e.g., single-line symbols mean manual, double-line mean automatic).

Like functional flow diagrams, decision-action diagrams may be developed and used at various system development phases and levels of detail. Input data come from mission profiles and scenarios.

Decision-action diagrams are so similar to functional flow diagrams (and only slightly more complex) that one would not draw both for the same project. Because these diagrams are similar to the flow charts used by computer programmers, decision-action diagrams are generally used when the project is software-oriented.

Time-Line Analysis

Time-line analysis examines the temporal relationships among tasks and the duration of individual tasks. Time-line sheets are usually constructed with the

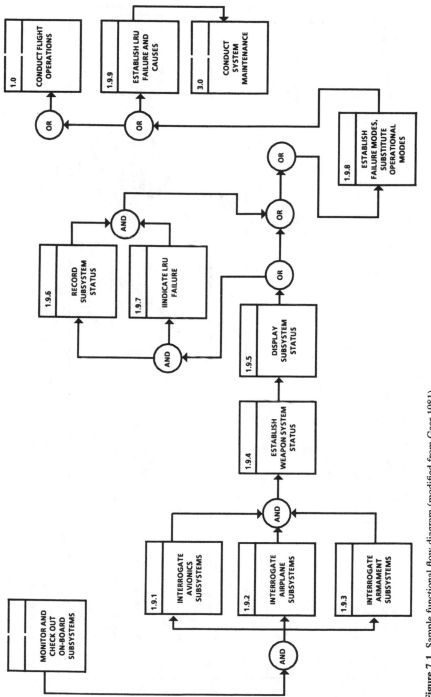

Figure 7.1. Sample functional flow diagram (modified from Geer 1981)

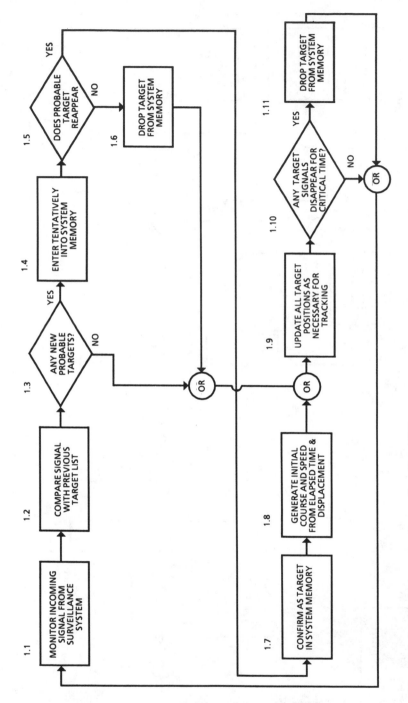

Figure 7.2. Sample decision-action diagram (from Geer 1981)

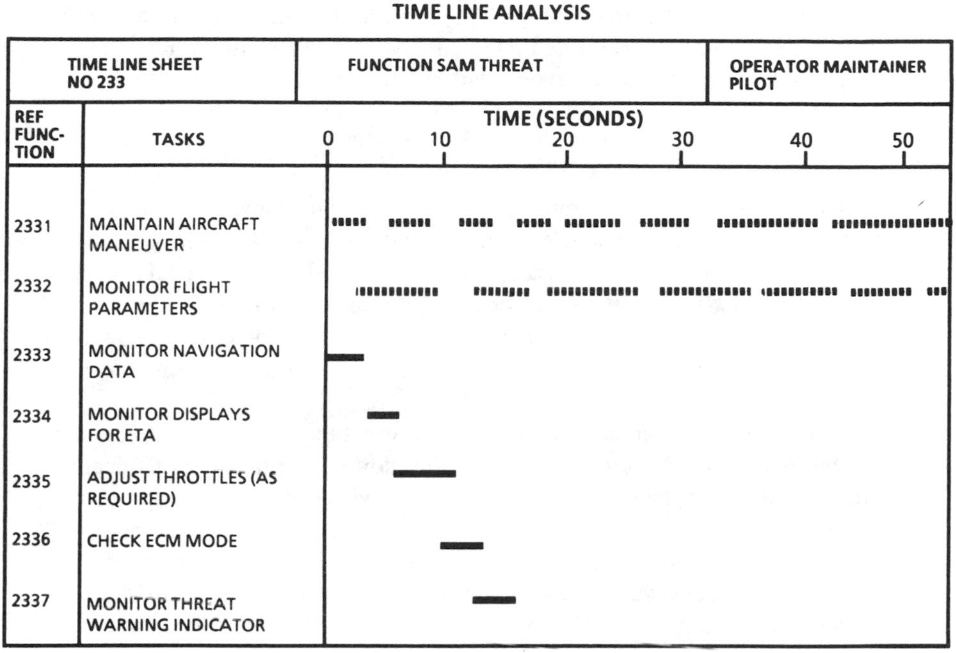

TIME LINE ANALYSIS

TIME LINE SHEET NO 233		FUNCTION SAM THREAT				OPERATOR MAINTAINER PILOT	
REF FUNC-TION	TASKS	0	10	TIME (SECONDS) 20	30	40	50
2331	MAINTAIN AIRCRAFT MANEUVER	▪▪▪▪▪ ▪▪▪▪▪▪ ▪▪▪▪▪ ▪▪▪▪ ▪▪▪▪▪▪▪ ▪▪▪▪▪▪▪		▪▪▪▪▪▪▪▪▪▪▪▪▪▪ ▪▪▪▪▪▪▪▪▪▪▪▪▪▪▪▪			
2332	MONITOR FLIGHT PARAMETERS	▪▪▪▪▪▪▪▪▪▪▪▪▪ ▪▪▪▪▪▪▪▪ ▪▪▪▪▪▪▪▪▪▪▪▪		▪▪▪▪▪▪▪▪▪▪▪▪▪▪ ▪▪▪▪▪▪▪▪▪▪▪ ▪▪▪▪▪▪▪▪ ▪▪▪			
2333	MONITOR NAVIGATION DATA	▬					
2334	MONITOR DISPLAYS FOR ETA	▬					
2335	ADJUST THROTTLES (AS REQUIRED)	▬					
2336	CHECK ECM MODE	▬					
2337	MONITOR THREAT WARNING INDICATOR	▬					

Figure 7.3. Part of a time-line sheet (from Geer 1981)

time on the horizontal axis and the listing of tasks on the vertical axis of a graph (see Figure 7.3). The time estimates associated with a task are indicated by bar graphs beginning at the start of the task and ending when the tasks are completed. The time reference in this analysis can be anything relevant to the task or mission—hours, minutes, seconds. Time-line sheets permit an appraisal of time-critical sequences to verify that necessary events can be performed and that there are no time-incompatible tasks. Time-line charts also serve as one of the inputs for workload evaluation and for determining the required number of personnel.

Time-line analysis can be approached in various ways. One can, for example, chart all tasks without considering who and how many personnel will perform the tasks. Such a time line would have value in determining required manning, because where there are overlaps of control or monitoring actions it is apparent that at least two operators will be needed. If the tasks are identified as to type, one could note whether the most frequent behavioral requirements are those of control activation, monitoring, cognitive functioning, and so on. This helps in understanding the overall job. One can determine whether personnel will be continuously loaded—where load is the absence of free time between tasks—and this might suggest the possible influence of fatigue.

The function of the time line is highly limited, because it illustrates only task-time relationships. Because it is relatively easy to prepare, a time line is usually cost-effective to develop, particularly if tasks are highly time-dependent.

Operational Sequence Diagrams

Operational sequence diagrams are supposed to have many uses: to develop operational procedures, evaluate interfaces and function allocations, identify critical mission areas, identify task under- and overload situations (Baker et al. 1979). This is almost certainly misleading; the diagrams illustrate the tasks performed, but the desired inferences about workload or interface evaluation must come either from cues that are as yet not specified or from special expertise.

The diagram plots the sequential flow of information, decisions, and actions through the performance of a mission. This flow is portrayed symbolically using a standardized symbology to represent the reception of information, decision-making, and control responses (Figures 7.4 and 7.5). The diagram can be drawn at a system level or a task level, and it can be utilized at any time in the system development cycle, *provided the necessary information is available*. It permits the comparison of actions involved in design alternatives. Its three significant attributes are its sequential flow, its classification of activity type, and its ability to describe interfaces. Because operational sequence diagrams are similar to decision-action diagrams, only more complex, where the latter are used the former are not. In complex systems, development of the diagram may become tremendously tedious and quite expensive in terms of analyst time.

Link Analysis

Link analysis is a very simple diagrammatic technique that represents the interactions among system components—usually the communications channels between personnel, the sensory or motor relationships among personnel and between personnel and machines, and connections among machines. Link analysis is most often used to plot the manipulations required in operating a control panel (for control panel layout) or on a larger scale the physical interactions among personnel and their machines in a working area (for work space layout). The diagram aids in minimizing traffic flow and is frequently used to verify the adequacy of design layouts.

Using paper and pencil, link analysis is performed to identify each required operation and operator (circle), identify related equipment (square), indicate the links between operators and between personnel and machines by the lines between them, evaluate each link for importance and frequency of use by applying scales, and redraw the diagram, reducing wherever possible link length and number of crossing lines (see Figure 7.6). The utility of this analysis

SECOND-LEVEL FUNCTION 2.4.1 PERFORM
PRESTAGING CHECKOUT

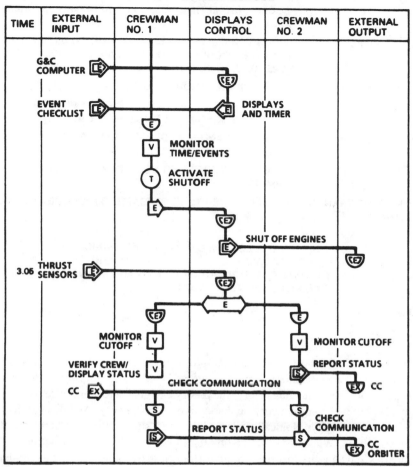

Figure 7.4. Sample operational sequence diagram (from Geer 1981)

is that it can contrast design alternatives. Numerous and crossing lines suggest busyness and confusion, so the reduction and simplification of these lines produces a cleaner design. Elaborate analytic deductions cannot be made.

Workload Analysis

In contrast to the previous techniques, which were essentially atheoretical, much theory is associated with workload methods (henceforth called "load"). This section does not, however, pretend to review that theory, because volumes have been written on these topics (e.g., AGARD 1978a, 1978b; Moray 1979;

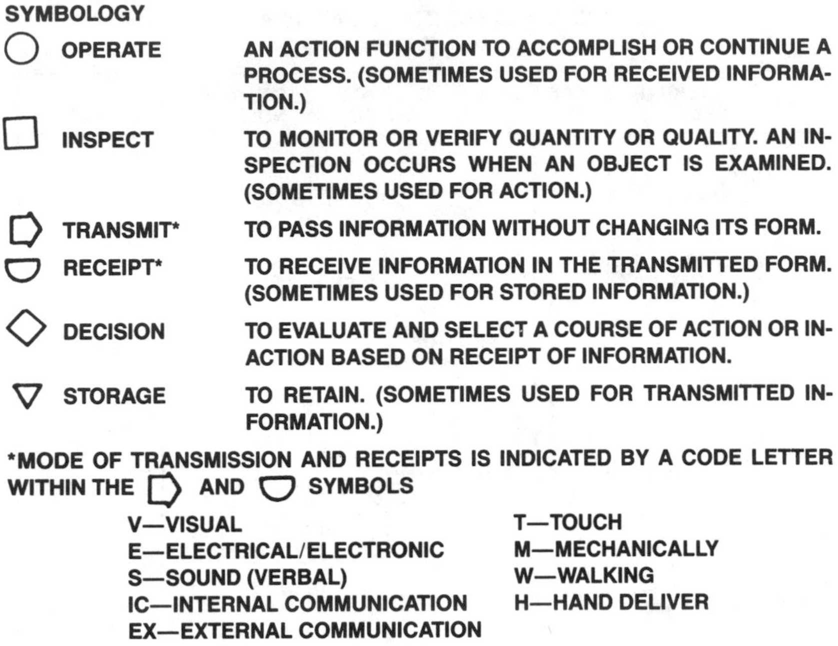

SYMBOLOGY

○ OPERATE — AN ACTION FUNCTION TO ACCOMPLISH OR CONTINUE A PROCESS. (SOMETIMES USED FOR RECEIVED INFORMATION.)

☐ INSPECT — TO MONITOR OR VERIFY QUANTITY OR QUALITY. AN INSPECTION OCCURS WHEN AN OBJECT IS EXAMINED. (SOMETIMES USED FOR ACTION.)

▷ TRANSMIT* — TO PASS INFORMATION WITHOUT CHANGING ITS FORM.

▽ RECEIPT* — TO RECEIVE INFORMATION IN THE TRANSMITTED FORM. (SOMETIMES USED FOR STORED INFORMATION.)

◇ DECISION — TO EVALUATE AND SELECT A COURSE OF ACTION OR INACTION BASED ON RECEIPT OF INFORMATION.

▽ STORAGE — TO RETAIN. (SOMETIMES USED FOR TRANSMITTED INFORMATION.)

*MODE OF TRANSMISSION AND RECEIPTS IS INDICATED BY A CODE LETTER WITHIN THE ▷ AND ▽ SYMBOLS

V—VISUAL
E—ELECTRICAL/ELECTRONIC
S—SOUND (VERBAL)
IC—INTERNAL COMMUNICATION
EX—EXTERNAL COMMUNICATION

T—TOUCH
M—MECHANICALLY
W—WALKING
H—HAND DELIVER

Figure 7.5. Operational sequence diagram symbols

Weiner 1982). Moray (1979), for example, in discussing load refers to random walk theory, accumulator theory, discrete and continuous information theory, supervisor theory, queuing theory, the theory of signal detection, linear control theory, optimal control theory, and adaptive control theory. And this list does not include the physiologically oriented theories, such as the arousal theory of Selye (1973). Wickens (1981) distinguishes between what he calls structural theories and capacity theories. In the former, it is hypothesized that a parallel system capable of processing separate and concurrent information channels "narrows" to a serial system that can handle only one input at a time. Capacity theories model the operator as possessing a pool of limited resources. Because a primary task demands more of these resources and therefore becomes more difficult, fewer resources are available for a concurrent secondary task, and performance of the latter degrades.

Because of the centrality of workload in personnel response to design, it is necessary to discuss it in greater detail than previous topics, but difficult to deal with the topic adequately. Not only is there no single, commonly accepted definition of load, but there are also many conflicting concepts of what it is, and the term is often used without any definition at all. There is also the maddening problem of differentiating load from stress; both have many features in com-

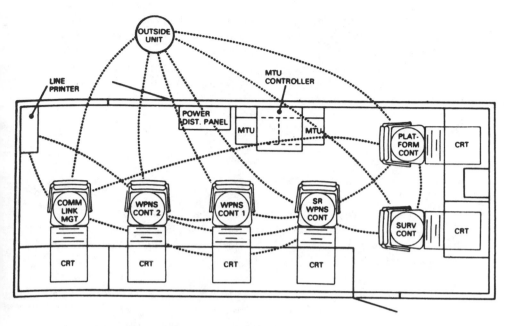

Figure 7.6. Sample link analysis for work-space layout (from Geer 1981)

mon. The practitioner's interest in predicting workload is to evaluate the demand imposed by the system, but the available methods are unlikely to be adequate until concepts are more adequately defined.

There are two problems of definition. Load is multidimensional and is also an intervening variable. It is multidimensional because it can be viewed in many ways (see Johannsen 1979; Rolfe and Lindsay 1973). As an input it is represented by difficulty stimuli that load operators in the sense of causing them to bear a burden. Load is also the operators' internal experience of difficulty and discomfort, their recognition that they are experiencing a load, and their strategy to overcome that load. Load not only affects human performance but has a negative impact on the system itself.

The stimuli initiating load can be either outside personnel or within them, can be physical or mental, can be expressed overtly or internally, and can be modified by the operator's intelligence, attitudes, and knowledge of consequences. Any stimulus can produce load, and almost any response can be the operator's response to that load. Other variables include: the consequences of failing to perform adequately in the situation, which may range from grave to minimal; the operator's recognition of a situation as being stressful or loaded, which determines in part the degree of loading—if the operator does not know the situation is loaded, it is per se not loaded *for that operator;* the operator's internal criteria as to what constitutes adequate performance, which determines how the operator evaluates his or her own performance; and external criteria, such as time, accuracy, or quality, which may direct performance and also serve as standards by which performance can be evaluated. All this makes it irrational to talk of load as a unitary phenomenon. It is more probable that there are different types of load, each type being described by a profile high on some dimensions and low on others.

Underlying the notion of load is the concept of *system demand* and the discrepancy between demand and the capability to respond to that demand. From the standpoint of the analyst, therefore, the essential questions are: What is the relationship of load to system design? and What are the design characteristics that increase or decrease load potential? Neither question can be answered adequately today.

A number of techniques for predicting load exist. Some have been part of the analytic inventory for years, others are presently under development (see, e.g., Bittner et al. 1987). What one might consider the "traditional" technique for load prediction is based on two concepts:

1. Tasks must be performed in a certain length of time; the degree of load is the percentage of that time which the operator actually has to perform those tasks.

2. The operator has only a limited attentional capacity. When the operator must perform multiple tasks in the same time period, there is competition among these for his or her attention. That competition "loads" the operator and results in a feeling of "effort" or "stress."

The predictive method described below (taken from Parks [1979] and Geer [1976, 1981]) applies to both concepts. In Concept 1, the operator's load is based on estimates of time required to perform a task in relation to the time allowed or available to perform that task. If, for example, operators have fifteen minutes to perform the task but it will take them only ten minutes, they have a load of 66 percent. However, if one has enough time to complete the task, where is the load? In Concept 2, load is the degree of loading in terms of attention-per-task-per-operator, during the time the task is performed. This load can fluctuate during the time of performance as attention requirements rise or fall. A degree of loading scale used to provide this rating is calibrated in terms of percent—0 to 100—of attention required by the task during its performance. Figure 7.7 is a graphic depiction of the load profile described by degree of loading. One may ask, however, whether attention alone is sufficient to define workload.

Among the factors that have been conceptualized as loading personnel are time pressure, perceptual load, display complexity, memory requirements, cognitive load in terms of having to analyze and evaluate stimuli, effort (concentration), response demands, emotional stress, overall task difficulty, and fatigue. When these were analyzed by multidimensional scaling techniques (Acton, Perez, and Reid 1986), the two orthogonal dimensions that resulted

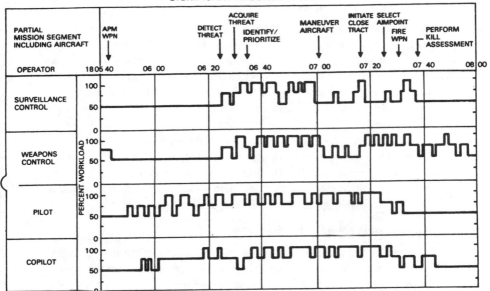

Figure 7.7. Sample attentional workload analysis profile (from Geer 1981)

were general task difficulty and another factor defined by central versus psycho-motor processing requirements. This result suggests the difficulty the practitioner has in deriving load from a task description that almost never refers to the factors listed above.

This discussion of auxiliary techniques has emphasized workload prediction, because load is a primary parameter the practitioner is concerned with in analyses. What the practitioner wants to know is what amount of load is associated with what equipment or task configuration. No technique presently available or under development even attempts to respond to this need.

The Subjective Workload Assessment Technique (SWAT; Reid 1985) has been under development for a number of years. In this technique, load is defined in terms of three factors: time, mental effort, and psychological stress. SWAT is an assessment technique that depends on operator ratings, which means we still do not have physical equivalents for these, and hence no way of applying the technique to design. However, if the technique proves valid and reliable—and there is some evidence for this—it might be refined to provide a prediction method.

Computer-Aided Techniques

One might suppose that the advent of computerization would provide powerful new tools to aid the practitioner's analysis, but so far this has been only a dream. This is not to say that it will never be so. Computer techniques are available to aid function allocation, workload assessment, and crew station and cockpit design as part of the overall CAFES model (Parks and Springer 1975), but this is merely mechanization of traditional techniques. In any event, CAFES is rarely used in actual system development.

Nor has there been any corresponding use of the man-machine models that have proliferated in the past twenty years (e.g., Siegel and Wolf 1969; Wortman et al. 1977; Pew et al. 1977). Before a computer can aid analysis, the software must contain the concepts and data to be applied to the problem; computerization merely speeds up an already existing process.

Inadequacies of Present Techniques

The preceding techniques illustrate the relative poverty of the analytic methodology available to the practitioner. They are descriptive, but not in terms of the system dimensions that actually influence performance. Some of the techniques, such as time-line and link analysis, are one-dimensional, focusing respectively on time and physical contiguity. Other techniques, such as function flow, decision-action, and operational sequence diagrams, are essentially sequence-oriented. Even the traditional workload analytic methods are time focused. More sophisticated techniques (the Display Evaluative Index and the Analytic Profile System of Siegel and his collaborators: Siegel, Miehle, and Federman 1964; Siegel and Fischl 1971) are almost never used by practitioners (see Meister 1986), either because the techniques require too much skill or effort on the part of the practitioner or because practitioners seem to resist the novel and sophisticated. All the techniques discussed permit some inferences about behavioral dimensions—but very weak ones, because the inferences do not stem directly from the techniques themselves.

EVALUATION

An integral part of the practitioner's activity is evaluation of system design throughout the development cycle, from initial design drawings to prototype production hardware and software. Evaluation is necessary for determining whether the system is being designed to specifications and standards. Evaluation methods can be categorized as experimental or nonexperimental, as formal or informal, as dealing with two-dimensional products (drawings and written procedures) and three-dimensional products (mockups, prototype equipment), and as being applied in a static (nonperformance) context or a performance context. The most significant dichotomy is the last one.

Formal evaluation methods are developed to accomplish certain functions, and they usually have well-defined, step-by-step procedures. Informal procedures do not have very clearly specified step-by-step procedures. When applied to drawings and procedures, the informal evaluation methods usually consist of questions about the attributes of these products. When applied to performance with mockups and equipment, informal methods usually consist of simple timing of operations, counting of errors, or interviews with operators.

The most commonly utilized evaluation techniques in system development are informal, being native to system development. Both formal and informal methods are useful; the informal ones become formalized over time, as, for example, when the questions an evaluator asks about control panel layout are written down and published as a checklist. Analytic techniques, such as those described in the preceding section, are almost all formal, while most evaluation techniques are informal. Why this is so is unclear, except that analytic techniques were specifically created to aid behavioral design, whereas the evaluation techniques, at least those involved in performance testing, may simply have been carried over from performance testing in psychology.

Like analytic techniques, the evaluation methods were developed to answer behavioral questions arising out of system development. The primary questions are: Which of two or more design alternatives is better from a behavioral standpoint? Does the design product contain the attributes of an effective product? Will system personnel be able to utilize the product or system without excessive difficulty? Will the overall system be able to accomplish its mission when it contains this product? How can the design product be improved? Some analytic techniques can also be used for evaluative purposes because they are based on implicit evaluation standards. For example, in link analysis an effective control panel or workplace is one that has the fewest links requiring physical movement. If one applies workload analysis to a product and derives a workload figure of merit for that product, it has obviously been evaluated in terms of its load potential.

To many researchers, an important criterion of methodological adequacy is that the technique should have some foundation in theory. In general, evaluation techniques are not based on theory unless one can say that the statistical designs sometimes employed in performance-testing originate in theory. On the other hand, operational testing does relate to the system concept because, theoretically at least, it is testing of the entire system functioning as a unitary whole. However, this connection with theory is only a weak one.

Static Evaluation

Static evaluation is as much analysis as it is evaluation, because it involves, first, an examination of the design drawing or software algorithm to determine its most important features, and second, a comparison of those features or attributes with a standard representing acceptability, and finally, determination of any discrepancies between the design and the standard. In connection with this last, software design evaluation may be at a disadvantage; the field is so new that software standards are only now being developed.

Static evaluation is based on the common-sense assumption that certain design characteristics have positive effects on operator and maintenance performance and others have negative effect. This is entirely reasonable, but difficulties arise because the nature of these design characteristics is unclear, particularly with regard to operator performance. Some characteristics are quite evident. For example, if two switches that have to be operated together rapidly are widely separated, the possibility that one or the other will not be thrown concurrently is quite high. However, this is merely one characteristic of many that operators are exposed to; they perform in a unitary work station, and their performance relates to the whole station, not to any single characteristic. This is clearly illustrated when the practitioner asks "What is the workload imposed on the operator by this station?" Single components (e.g., switches) and single design characteristics (e.g., functional arrangement of controls) do not have a workload index associated with them. As we shall see, there is presently no acceptable way of combining the presumed effects of single characteristics, so that total performance is difficult to predict.

For hardware design, a number of human-engineering rules of thumb are listed in MIL-STD 1472C (Department of Defense 1981), and it is possible to use this document as a guide in identifying discrepancies. Compilations of desirable software characteristics are found in, among others, Smith and Mosier (1986) and in Williges and Williges (1984). These are, however, rules of thumb for individual characteristics, and not attributes that are descriptors for the unitary equipment or software. Examples of attributes with which the practitioner would want to identify specific design configurations and the operator performance related to them are complexity, simplicity, determinacy, and dependency in internal relationships.

That one cannot properly evaluate without considering the total equipment is a practical demonstration of the validity of the system concept. Evaluation relates to the whole and has little significance relative to the individual components or modules, although one would expect to derive some information about the parts from the evaluation of the whole. This is not a reciprocal relationship; one can derive information about the parts from the whole, but not about the whole from the parts.

Presently the only way of evaluating individual characteristics is in terms of a deviation from a requirement specified in MIL-STD 1472C or from checklists based on similar documents. Checklist characteristics are phrased positively, but the analyst can utilize them only in a negative fashion. If the objective of behavioral design is to produce an optimal—that is, perfect—solution to the design problem, the practitioner automatically thinks in terms of nonoptimality, or that which is less than perfect. Perhaps as a result of this, human factors evaluations are commonly phrased in terms of negatives, which may contribute to the view held by some engineers that in system development human factors serves only to criticize design.

Attribute evaluation presumes a relationship between design characteristics, singly and in combination, and some operator performance effect. However, the relationship is almost never quantified during the evaluation, because, except for Munger et al. (1962) and Swain and Guttmann (1983), there are no normative data describing these relationships. Lacking such data, practitioners must assume that every design discrepancy is equal to every other in terms of performance, even though they know better. No summary evaluation, whether in terms of performance or even an arbitrary rating scheme, is possible because there are no design performance dimensional equivalents.

The process of evaluating design drawings and software algorithms is inferential because one cannot observe performance with them; moreover, the information available in drawings and print-outs is quite limited. For example, the fact that meters are shown in a drawing suggests a requirement for a monitoring function but does not describe the nature of what is being monitored or how the monitoring will be accomplished. Further contextual information is needed from procedures, test data, or task analyses, if these are available. The comparative lack of information in what is being evaluated makes the evaluation somewhat uncertain, which is not to say that static evaluation is without value.

As in the case of the analyses, the practitioner begins the evaluation either with a procedure describing how the human-machine interface is intended to be utilized and/or with a rough mental model of its operation. That is because behavioral design criteria are based on inferred relationships between the design and the operator's future performance with that design. For example, in reviewing a control panel layout the evaluator will think of the arrangement in terms of its possible effect on the ease with which the operating procedure will be learned and retained and the likelihood of error in operating the control panel as a result of the arrangement.

A complete listing of all the questions that can be asked about the human-machine interface would be lengthy and tedious at best. For each relevant equipment characteristic, an evaluation question can be generated. For practical reasons most practitioners scan the drawings to focus on their critical aspects, as suggested by the function of the equipment being designed.

There are also distinctive software characteristics that the practitioner should look for. These deal with the following topics (see Williges and Williges [1984] for detailed provisions): anthropometry of the video display terminal, control-display relationships, CRT screen characteristics (e.g., luminance, contrast), alphanumeric characteristics (e.g., character size, font), data organization (e.g., density, coding formats), dialogue modes (e.g., menu characteristics, command language characteristics, user control, query languages), user input devices (e.g., keyboards, data entry procedures), feedback and error management (e.g., status messages, error checks, helps).

In addition to the practitioner's mental model, which is actually a concept of the procedure for operating the human-machine interface, the evaluator also needs to know the important equipment and task characteristics that could negatively affect operator performance (see Table 7.1 for examples). This presumes some hypotheses about the potential effects of these characteristics on operator performance.

Only rarely does the practitioner evaluate operating or maintenance procedures, because of the large number that are produced during system development, but perhaps even more important, because of the lack of effective methods to perform procedure evaluation outside of performance tests. The analytic-evaluational process looks for design characteristics as the basis for evaluation, but these are largely lacking in a procedure which simply notes that the operator is supposed to turn controls on or off, monitor displays, and make decisions. Because data on procedure-performance relationships are lacking, the only characteristics the evaluator can focus on are second-order features—for example, whether sufficient information is presented to permit the operator to perform correctly (but what does "sufficient" mean?), whether safety precautions are emphasized, whether the sequence of operation is clear, how to respond to emergency events, and so forth. Procedures can be examined to see if they match the S-O-R paradigm, whether they indicate the time at which action is to be taken, the stimulus for action, the operator response required, the required communications, and the feedback displays (for example, see Brune and Weinstein 1980). Each procedural step should be capable of being broken down into the preceding elements.

Performance Evaluation

Performance evaluations include mockup testing (hardware) and rapid prototyping (software), walk-throughs, developmental tests, and operational testing. The essential characteristics of performance evaluation are that the operator is exposed to an item of equipment or its surrogate and that his or her performance is recorded and interpreted.

Mockup testing. There are several types of mockups, some of which are developed by engineers as an integral part of design, others of which are developed by practitioners as a means of collecting the information they need to do their job. The various types include: two-dimensional reduced and full-scale models, three-dimensional reduced-scale mockups; and three-dimensional static and functional full-scale mockups. (See Meister 1985b for additional details.)

The evaluations performed in static mockups can be either observational (using a human-engineering checklist to record judgments) or demonstrational.

In the demonstrational mode, subjects simulate the performance of tasks by pointing to controls they would activate and displays they would read. Reach envelope and component accessibility can be determined on a performance basis. The distance the subject must move from a fixed position to grasp a control can be measured exactly. If the full-scale static mockup (the most common type) contains actual equipment that maintenance personnel would ordinarily check, the evaluator can have a subject perform the check while watching for difficulty in finding various components of the equipment in response to instructions, connecting and disconnecting cables or tracing harnesses, climbing or descending to reach a component that must be checked or removed, reaching for and manipulating controls, removing and replacing cover plates, finding test points, removing or replacing circuit boards or other internal components, reading labels within the equipment with or without special lighting, performing visual inspection of components as in looking for cracks, holes, cuts, leaks, and so on.

Unless an actual task can be performed in the mockup and that performance can be measured in terms of such criteria as time and errors, the mockup simply makes the static evaluation a little more concrete. The goal of mockup testing is to discover whether the operator and the maintenance technician will be able to perform required actions. If the functional mockup is sophisticated enough that operating procedures can be performed in their entirety, the evaluator can approximate a true performance evaluation by determining whether operators can perform the functions assigned to them, how long it takes them to do these, the types of errors they make and the error rate, and the problems encountered. These data are of course only an approximation, because the functional mockup is not being exercised in the operational environment.

The mockup has obvious limitations. Corrective maintenance cannot be studied without actual equipment, and unless the mockup is also a sophisticated simulator, it is not possible to study personnel responses to emergencies. Mockup evaluations are, like the design-drawing evaluations, essentially determinations of discrepancies from desired performance, not true evaluations that make it possible to place the object being evaluated on some scale of adequacy.

Rapid prototyping. Rapid prototyping is a mockup test conducted with a computer terminal as the test vehicle and software as the object of evaluation (see Melkus and Jorres 1988). After software engineers write out their algorithms on paper, they quickly transform them into software and are able to observe their operation dynamically on the CRT screen. Because the CRT used for this test will also be used operationally, there is an irresistible tendency on the part of software engineers to "try out" their software as quickly as possible. In the hardware case, this has been termed the engineer's "flight to hardware" (Meister 1971). At the expense of thinking about the dimensions of the design problem, engineers prefer to try out various alternatives on the computer.

The evaluator exercises the software to see if anticipated effects are achieved and that no nonsensical results or breakdowns of the software occur. In the later stages of prototyping, problems requiring the use of the software will be devised, and another engineer assigned at a second CRT will try to solve those problems while the designer views the software and manipulates it in another room. This may be considered the start of developmental testing of software. A practitioner working closely with the software engineer might also look for undesirable software characteristics. Rapid prototyping is actually a developmental test designed to check that the software will perform; it is not an evaluation in the sense that subjects, other than software engineers themselves, are exposed to the software and testing is conducted under anticipated operational conditions. However, sophisticated engineers are beginning to use laymen as subjects.

Software design testing is as limited as its hardware equivalent, in the sense that in neither case are performance equivalents associated with design features. Whether there are characteristic or routinely utilized software procedures with which one could associate a performance value is unclear. Some computerized system aspects can be quantified. For example, the number of errors made with different types of entry devices (e.g., keyboards, light pen, mouse) or with form-filling formats versus a menu selection mode can be determined. However, there seems to be no effort to develop performance equivalents for software, just as there is no such effort for hardware features.

The Walk-through. The walk-through is a simulation of equipment operation, rather than an actual equipment operation. It can be performed with a static mockup or with prototype equipment that is not yet functioning. The purpose of the walk-through is to check the adequacy of design and procedures and to discover problems that need to be rectified. Like the other techniques described in this section, the walk-through is only partially an evaluation methodology. Its diagnostic aspect is perhaps even more important.

The walk-through can be performed mentally, so that the evaluator imagines or pretends that he or she is carrying through the procedural steps involved in operating the equipment, or the simulation can be partly realistic—for instance, the evaluator or a test operator points to or touches the mockup or actual control to be activated or display to be read. The walk-through begins with someone reading aloud an operating task to be performed. The operator in the walk-through—usually an experienced engineer, not a partially skilled operator—proceeds to carry out the task by pointing to, touching or explaining the displays to be read, the controls to be manipulated, the cues to be responded to, any decisions to be made, and problems or difficulties that are encountered. The goal is to determine that all actions required by the procedure can be performed correctly and in time. Problem areas hypothesized by the test operator (e.g., can't reach control in time) are noted as subjects for possible redesign.

The importance of the walk-through cannot be overestimated (see Francas, Goodman, and Dickinson 1985). I once participated in a verbal walk-through of the initial procedure for ground launch of the Atlas intercontinental ballistic missile engines, a walk-through that was aborted after the first six steps because the process revealed that essential connections between subsystems had not yet been designed.

Developmental tests. The Department of Defense (see Holshouser 1977) specifies that developmental tests will be conducted in all system acquisition programs. These are engineering tests designed in almost all cases to study equipment design functioning. They include tests of breadboards and pro-totypes, first production articles, qualification tests, and engineering mockup inspections. Because most developmental tests are specifically oriented to equipment purposes, their utility for human factors is limited. Many develop-mental tests have too narrow a focus, as, for example, tests of materials or nondestructive reliability tests. Nevertheless, it is sometimes possible for the practitioner to gather information of behavioral value from developmental tests. Any test that involves the human-machine interface, or one in which personnel take part by playing the role of operators, may provide useful data.

The methods used to secure behavioral data from developmental tests do not differ substantially from those used with mockups, such as the recording of performance time and errors, and use of checklists, observations, and inter-views. Software developmental testing involves exposing subjects to prototype software and asking them to solve some problem or perform a task (e.g., data entry, file-checking). Software developmental testing, like its hardware coun-terpart, is largely a search for design inadequacies, as reflected in a subject's inability to solve problems and difficulty in performing tasks. These may suggest behavioral inadequacies—for example, insufficient help aids or feedback.

Operational testing. Operational testing is performed to determine system adequacy for mission accomplishment. The information gained verifies that the system and its personnel can in fact do what they are supposed to do. Moreover, it unearths any serious deficiencies that need remedy. System evaluation infor-mation can also be used to design improvements in future systems or to modify training and selection programs. The data from such tests might serve as a source of quantitative predictive data, but this application has almost never been made.

The military regularly conduct battle exercises in the operational environ-ment to determine combat readiness. Comparable civilian exercises are held by Civil Defense, police, hospitals, and so on. Unfortunately, such evaluations are often subordinated to training purposes, so that complete realism and proper measurement are compromised.

As noted throughout this book, system evaluation can be performed in a number of ways. The ideal evaluation in terms of simulation fidelity is the operational system performing routinely in the operational environment—for example, a ship steaming at sea. However, one can also evaluate systems at a special test facility or in a simulator, where the simulator realistically represents the operational system, or a prototype system not yet fully debugged can be tested while performing in the operational environment—for instance, evaluation at sea of the first of a new ship class. All these situations, even the first, are simulations of the operational system to one extent or another. The question of simulation fidelity—how much is necessary, and how lack of fidelity will affect the performance evaluation—are questions that were discussed in Chapter 5.

Operational testing has certain characteristics (Johnson and Baker 1974) that differ markedly from traditional controlled experimental research. Operational testing is constrained by system characteristics, addresses real but messy problems, is time-limited and resource-limited, measures in macrounits (minutes) rather than microunits (seconds), evaluates both people and equipment, employs a system approach, has high face validity, has somewhat less control over the conduct of the test, has multiple objects and multiple criteria (intermediate as well as ultimate), and includes many levels of entry into the test and/or into the system. The literature on system testing is reviewed in Chapter 6.

If a system is to be tested in a truly operational mode, there are certain requirements, most of which center on operational fidelity. The system must be a complete entity—no missing modules. Personnel to operate the test system must be representative of or similar to those who will eventually operate the system and must have been trained to do so. Procedures to operate the system as it is designed to function operationally must have been written out. An environment representative of the environment(s) in which the system will routinely function—such as Alaska in winter for cold weather operations—must be prepared for testing.

The above requirements represent the optimal preconditions for operational testing, but in reality there are often deviations from the optimum, usually because of schedule speedups and financial deficits. The equipment may not be complete or totally integrated when operational testing begins; operational procedures may not be completely developed; the test subjects may resemble the ultimate users only partially, and their training may be less refined than that which the ultimate users will receive; and the test environment may include only certain aspects of the operational environment.

Operational testing is measurement, not research. There are research questions that can and should be addressed in an operational test, such as What is the relationship between personnel subsystem performance and system output? and What is the effect of system characteristics on personnel performance? But these questions are never asked. I make the admittedly perilous assumption that data relating to these questions can be secured in operational testing, albeit with difficulty, but these questions are not addressed because developers and customers are concerned only about the present status (deviations relative to explicit or implicit standards) of the equipment, procedures, and so on.

Explanations for personnel performance are required only if the system status appears unsatisfactory, and even then any explanation would probably be phrased in very discrete, simplistic terms—for instance, a mistake was made in anthropometric dimensions, or a procedure was developed in insufficient time.

There is no strong connection between research and operational testing, because evaluation questions are usually quite simple—for example, Does the system perform as expected? Is one type of equipment better than another in terms of personnel performance? Testing simply describes the system as it is. However, operational testing can be a significant behavioral data resource if it is exploited for this purpose.

The system concept, especially the part that emphasizes the need to include all factors that might affect performance in the test situation, does have a role to play in operational testing. The distinguishing characteristic of these tests is that the evaluator makes use of all available evaluational techniques. What makes operational testing distinctive is that it provides a formal framework in which these techniques can be applied and organizes and systematizes them. What further distinguishes operational testing, if it is performed correctly, is the attempt to measure under conditions of maximum fidelity to the operational environment.

Before operational testing can be planned, certain questions, which are prerequisites for testing, must be answered:

1. What type of testing are we planning for? The types of testing include *acceptance testing* of a new but not yet fully operational system (this requires an effectiveness standard); *testing of design modifications* (change in or addition of hardware or software procedures) to an operational system to determine that the modified system performs as well as or better than the preceding version (no standard is required, only comparison of conditions); *effectiveness testing* to determine how well an already operational system performs in order to provide feedback to management (this may include military exercises or reliability testing; also requires some sort of effectiveness standard).

2. What does the operational environment consist of? The effort to achieve maximum operational fidelity—a requirement for testing systems—drives much test planning. How much of the operational environment must be simulated? To answer this question, the evaluator must anticipate the effect of the environment on personnel performance.

3. How much control will the evaluator have over the test situation, and what constraints must be faced? This may determine the kinds of measures to be applied and the method of data collection. For example, if the evaluator cannot interview system personnel because the system occupies them fully, he or she must take this factor into account in test planning.

Planning for operational testing also requires development of specific test objectives, determination of whether any experimental comparisons can be made, determination of standards of comparison, development of criteria and measures, specification of data collection methods, subject characteristics, and methods of data analysis (see Meister 1985b for more detail). Although the purpose of this testing is quite different from that of experimental research, researchers will recognize many similarities to their own research planning, but also significant differences. The test objective is similar to the study hypothesis, and the determination of experimental comparisons is much the same as the study design, although much simpler. The use of standards is foreign to the researcher, but not the development of criteria and measures. The researcher usually pays less attention to subject characteristics than the evaluator does.

The great difficulty the evaluator faces is lack of a behavioral standard with which to compare test performance. Only this comparison will provide an answer to the question "Is system performance adequate?" This is not the evaluator's responsibility, but that of human factors research, because it has not provided the data on which a behavioral standard can be based.

In operational testing much more use is made of observation and subjective reports than is the case in experimental study. That is because no one is attempting to use only the most sophisticated methods; in fact, the developer's goal is to use the least costly method. Evaluators may use themselves and colleagues as subject matter experts, and the fact that test data may be based to some extent on intuitive judgments is just about irrelevant. The end result is what matters.

Because the operational test attempts merely to describe, not explain, it can afford to ignore sources of data contamination. The test is filled with contaminating inputs, but these are accepted perhaps as inevitable accompaniments of testing in an operational or quasi-operational setting.

One defect of operational testing as it is presently implemented is the inability or unwillingness of evaluators to relate personnel subsystem performance to total system output. It is possible to secure independent measures of each, but there is no effort to tie them together. Because of this, evaluation measurement is relatively crude and unsophisticated, compared with what it could be and perhaps eventually will be.

SUMMARY

The two major activities of the practitioner are analysis and evaluation. The analyses performed include mission, function, and task analysis, and function allocation. These analyses are aided by the use of mental models and mission scenarios. Additional analytic tools are functional-flow and decision-action diagrams, time-line charts, operational sequence diagrams, link analysis, and workload analysis. Evaluation includes analysis or evaluation of design drawings and software algorithms, mockup testing, rapid prototyping, walk-throughs, and developmental and operational testing.

CHAPTER 8

Nontechnical Influences on Human Factors Effectiveness

Previous chapters described the most important technical problems affecting human factors; this chapter examines the nontechnical problems. These problems stem from four sources, the first of which is the human factors community itself. This community is composed of four subgroups that distribute themselves on a continuum of application—academics on the nonapplication end of the continuum, and practitioners on the other end, with research contractors and government researchers tied closely to each other in the middle. The other sources of problems, related to these subgroups, are industry, government, and academia.

Textbooks describing human factors often inadvertently give the reader the false impression that specialists are insulated from any effects other than the technical influences inherent in the discipline. Like all other professionals, however, what the human factors specialist thinks and does is the product of many influences, some of them only remotely related to the discipline. Any serious examination of human factors at its present stage of development would be misleading if it did not include those influences, although how much can be done about them is unclear. The reader is warned that for some of the more sensitive material in this chapter there is no adequate documentation other than the author's informal observation. A more comprehensive discussion of some of the points raised can be found in Meister (1981).

Frankness in dealing with sensitive issues is often construed as negativism. Nevertheless, in the following description of nontechnical problems the goal is not to denigrate but to illuminate.

THE HUMAN FACTORS COMMUNITY

The role of the human factors community is to establish and implement the agenda for human factors research. The corresponding agenda for human factors application is set by engineering constraints.

Players in the Game

Human factors is defined in large part by the research issues it feels must be resolved. There are, however, nontechnical factors that influence these issues, in particular the influence exerted by key elements of the community. These elements include professional organizations such as the Human Factors Society (HFS) in the United States, the Ergonomics Society in Great Britain, the International Ergonomics Association worldwide; the journals in the discipline; the "influentials" referred to in Chapter 1; and the mainly governmental sponsors that fund human factors research.

The Human Factors Society provides a forum for discussion of issues through its senior organ, *Human Factors,* and its junior organ, the *Bulletin,* as well as through its annual meetings, at which papers are presented and published in *Proceedings* and at which specialists converse informally. The HFS itself does not attempt to raise epistemological issues, such as those presented in this book. The *Bulletin* occasionally presents short articles on methodological issues (e.g., the distinction between human factors and ergonomics; see Montmollin and Bainbridge, 1985), but *Human Factors* does not, except when issues are presented in the context of individual studies. (The same is true of the other behavioral journals, *Ergonomics, Applied Ergonomics,* the *International Journal of Man-Machine Studies,* and the *IEEE Transactions in Systems, Man, and Cybernetics.*) Papers presented at HFS annual meetings rarely deal with the topics addressed in this book, perhaps because although everyone is aware of these issues, they are "old hat" to most specialists even though they remain unsolved, or perhaps the problems are so difficult to solve and so depressing to contemplate that specialists would rather not think about them. In any event, the professional human factors societies influence these issues negatively by ignoring them.

The "influentials" play a role in bringing certain topics to the forefront of specialists' attention through the publication process, which will be discussed later. Influentials are more likely to be published because they do more research, present more papers, and have more contacts with other influentials—the "old boy" network. Influentials, too, rarely discuss epistemological issues.

Most "influentials" have had little or no application experience—that is, experience with applying human factors to system development or to operational system measurement. Many of them are academics, managers of research institutes, and the like, so that they are somewhat isolated from the rough-and-ready atmosphere of an engineering facility and the operational environment. As a result, the research they perform, sponsor, or manage is not often fertilized by a personal awareness of the problems that practitioners encounter in system development and operation, and they may lack a feel for what their research is supposed to do.

Perhaps most influence is exercised by funding sponsors, who for human factors are most likely to be government agencies. The agency that pays the piper calls the tune to which human factors professionals dance. Governmental funding sponsors are likely to be greatly influenced by nontechnical considerations, such as very specific operational military problems that need to be solved, and the amount of money available for research (which is almost always less than what is needed). Both directly and indirectly, government agencies set the human factors research agenda, although they may not view it in precisely these terms. Whatever the reason, the research supported by government does not seem to respond directly to the methodological problems we have discussed, although these problems are concealed in the research that is supported. Government research activity will be discussed in greater detail later.

The whole process is interactive. For example, funding sponsors are somewhat influenced by issues that influentials consider important, and influentials and the discipline as a whole are more likely to pursue topics that they believe will receive funding support. The process by which issues that define human factors are raised and discussed and by which a research agenda is adopted to solve them is both formal and informal. Occasionally a quasi-governmental agency like the Human Factors Committee of the National Research Council (Committee 1983) makes a deliberate effort to establish a research agenda, but such an agenda in large part merely summarizes a body of opinion that has already been developed informally. Thus, the National Research Council recommendation for more study of human-computer interaction merely reflects an already well-established belief among many specialists.

One can, of course, ask a very fundamental question: Should the process of issue selection and discussion and development of a research agenda be as informal, as uncontrolled, as it appears to be? Would it not be more valuable for a representative entity like the Human Factors Society to make a deliberate effort to develop a point of view on issues and to stimulate a research program that reflects a consensus on those issues? Would it stifle the initiative and creativity of individual researchers if their activities were recommended to them by others—although in an even more authoritarian fashion this is precisely what happens to research contractors and government researchers, and even academicians?

Publication

Central to the discussion of issues and decisions about which research should be done is publication. Publication is a goal indoctrinated in all researchers by their training, because without dissemination of information the research enterprise fails. Moreover, publication means recognition by peers, which may be worth more to researchers than even financial rewards.

Beyond this, there are very commercial forces that direct the researcher to publication. Many government laboratory managers urge their personnel to publish in the journals as partial evidence of professional competence. Contract researchers are interested in publication because it expands their resumes and makes them more attractive to potential customers in bidding on research proposals. Publication is a necessity for promotion and tenure in universities. A great deal of publication goes on in governmental reports, but these do not have as much cachet as publication in what are known as "refereed" journals, which rely on editorial reviewers to recommend or reject publication of the researchers' studies. In what many people believe is a highly applied discipline, academic standards of publication exercise extraordinary influence.

Because journal publication is the crown of the research edifice, and because publication depends on academic standards, these standards have a tendency to generalize to and direct actual research. This is one way the emphasis on experimental method is disseminated so widely. The journals are a primary mechanism by which the academic influence is channeled and maintained long after one graduates. Relatively little of the research described in government reports is published in scholarly journals, perhaps because much of this research does not fit the classic experimental design paradigm. Government research, although presented at conferences and published in conference proceedings, is often not considered important enough or sufficiently basic and scientific enough to warrant journal publication. On the other hand, the almost exclusive concentration in the journals on experimental hypothesis-testing studies tends to ignore worthwhile mission-oriented behavioral research.

There clearly are criteria and standards of research excellence, although it is almost impossible to formulate them operationally. It is not the business of this chapter to consider the value of the tremendous amount of published research, both behavioral and nonbehavioral studies, to what has been termed "knowledge," however one defines this term. But one cannot help wondering how much of this publication actually aids "knowledge," and how each study contributes its mite to the knowledge storehouse. Determination of research standards is a topic that needs wide and frank discussion, but this topic may be too sensitive for researchers. Much more important in research is the question of research relevance. A study may meet all criteria of research excellence and still be irrelevant to human factors objectives. The question of relevance is also rarely considered by journals.

One reason that there is little discussion of epistemological issues in human factors publications is that the orientation of the discipline's journals is heavily empirical and minimally theoretical. Concepts, when one finds them, are usually limited to a consideration of why the empirical results did or did not "come out" properly, as the researcher intended. One reason for this may be that the discipline's intellectual activity occurs mostly in its special interest areas, where methodological questions are highly technical and consequently narrower than the questions addressed in this book.

THE INDUSTRIAL COMMUNITY

Much has already been said here about the attitudes of managers and engineers toward human factors, so I offer only a brief discussion of this point. The industrial community is a potential source of questions and problems that can help stimulate human factors research, which is a positive nontechnical factor; it can also be viewed as a set of constraints on the application of human factors research results and a source of difficulty for practitioners. In fact it is both.

It has already been noted that most "influentials" lack system development experience. This has the unfortunate consequences that application problems and the need to solve them usually do not present a challenge that influences the researcher's choice of topic, and that the researcher's interaction with practitioners is also limited, so there is little cross-fertilization between research and application.

A number of things within the system development environment make that environment more difficult for practitioners. Although the Western world's preoccupation with technology is at least partly responsible for human factors, that preoccupation also tends to denigrate the importance of behavioral factors in technology. Although it is logical to want systems to function more effectively and more comfortably for their personnel, the means developers adopt to achieve this goal is usually increased automation, rather than enhancement of the human element in the system. There is also the notion that because everyone is human everyone is inherently competent to deal with behavioral factors. This syndrome contrasts with the layperson's awareness of medicine or physics, for which the populace has greater regard because it does not "understand" or empathize with nonbehavioral disciplines as well as it does with behavioral factors.

Another problem that human factors faces in industry is the inability to distinguish the human factors contribution to system development generally and to a specific design in particular from any other engineering contribution. Except for the simplest of products, design is a team effort in which inputs, successes, and failures are not totted up so that a score can be given at design completion to the individual inputs that produced the design (e.g., electrical, electronic, hydraulic). It would be highly desirable for human factors if one could do just that, but it is impossible. More about this later.

In the context of system development, human factors is not so much creative as it is analytic and evaluative. Engineers develop designs, or at least they have a much greater role in this than practitioners do. Because practitioners depend for their practice on these design products being available, they are often viewed by engineers as being critical and negative. The manner in which human factors is perceived by others tends to reduce funding in system development, elicits resistance to behavioral design by developers and engineers, and stimulates some designers' attempts to bypass the practitioner during the system development process.

As a defense against the preceding, the practitioner propagandizes for the "cause" of human factors. The "cause" is for greater engineering attention to the behavioral aspects of design. A scientific discipline—at least in its research mode—has no "cause" as such, but as an application, particularly a behavioral application in a physicalistic environment, there is definitely much to be done that resembles education and public relations. The practitioner has a major function to indoctrinate and tutor engineers to understand, and, one hopes, to appreciate, the role of human factors in system development. Sometimes this function is implemented formally as lectures to designers, more often it is performed informally, in personal contacts with them.

One response of the human factors community to the industrial situation is the notion that providing engineer-designers with reports and handbooks describing human factors principles and data will have a positive effect on their attitude toward behavioral inputs. As a result, reports and handbooks specifically written for engineers and designers proliferate (e.g., Woodson and Conover 1964; Van Cott and Kinkade 1972), each government agency developing its own, despite redundancy. Because most specialists are scientists by training—no matter what they do professionally—they are oriented toward communication in written form, and this generalizes into their relationship with engineers, although there is no evidence that handbooks, for example, enhance receptivity to human factors inputs (see Meister and Farr 1967).

The preoccupation with words as a means of argument and persuasion—which is a generalization of the training most professionals have had—is associated with an undesirable symptom or side effect: a lack of emphasis on quantitative performance data except in the context of the individual experiment. Studies performed by the author (Meister 1971) suggest that one criterion that engineers use to value inputs is whether the inputs include quantitative data, and this generalizes to the designer's viewpoint that human factors is essentially qualitative. Unfortunately, compilation of data for application purposes is viewed by many researchers as somehow less "worthy" or less scientifically justifiable than the production of data in individual "original" studies.

THE GOVERNMENTAL COMMUNITY

This section must be qualified by a statement that it is influenced by the author's experience as a research contractor for various government agencies (primarily the Department of Defense [DOD]), his years at the Army Research Institute (ARI), and most recently and up to the present at the Navy Personnel Research and Development Center (NPRDC). The NPRDC in particular is the model for many of the points made. There is unfortunately no documentation to support these points, because the problems considered in this section are never discussed in written form and/or published, and are spoken of only in private. It is necessary to examine them because the influence of government over human factors is all-pervasive. Any discussion of human factors that did not consider the effect of governmental influence would paint a wholly unrealistic picture of the discipline.

Government is important because it supplies almost all the funding for human factors research and system development through its acquisition of new systems, its research contracts with civilian contractors, and the government laboratories that either specialize in behavioral science or contain departments dedicated to human factors work.

The relationship between government and human factors has both positive and negative aspects. It is positive because human factors needs government, having no independent base of support; the physical, biological, and some of the behavioral sciences have such a support base in terms of their being recognized as scholarly sciences, to be funded at least partially in the university, in privately funded laboratories, and in institutes. The relationship is negative in the sense that human factors is too much the creature of government. The excessive influence of government is regrettable, because bureaucratic organizations encourage careerism, which inhibits rational scientific interests. Human factors lacks what every discipline needs—some corner in which it can feel even slightly free to theorize and conduct methodological research without being under the scrutiny of governmental onlookers. The logical inference from the preceding is that somehow human factors should build a foundation of support in an institution at least partially free of the government, preferably in the university. The onlookers referred to are the U.S. Congress, governmental agencies, the laboratories they control, and the contract researchers.

U.S. Congress

Of first importance is the U.S. Congress, because it appropriates the money that funds behavioral research and development (R&D). As a result, R&D agencies must be responsive to the desires, biases, and antipathies of Congress. Government agencies, such as the Department of Defense, make their financial requirements known to Congress through annual budget requests, but Congress often reduces, modifies, or eliminates what it does not like. The tendency in Congress, particularly in these straitened times, is to chop funding, and Congress comes down particularly hard on the behavioral sciences, although the percentage of behavioral research money relative to all other R&D money for science and engineering is very small (only about 6 percent; Kiesler 1977). However, the emphasis since 1980 on military buildup has probably aided funding for human factors.

Federal Government Agencies

Federal government agencies are the major executive departments and the Civil Service and (in the DOD) military personnel who run them. The most important agency, at least for human factors, is the Department of Defense. Some behavioral R&D is also conducted by other departments, most notably the Department of Health and Human Services, and the Education Department, but the latter two do not involve human factors.

The Defense Department does not perform R&D itself; R&D is conducted by the individual services—Army, Air Force, and Navy (which includes the Marine Corps). The DOD monitors what the individual services do through its Directorate of Defense Research and Engineering, although this agency does not seem to have much influence over what the individual services study. The individual services control laboratories that both perform behavioral research themselves and contract it out. Some of these laboratories, such as the Army Research Institute, specialize exclusively in the behavioral sciences; others, like the Naval Ocean Systems Center, are engineering laboratories with human factors personnel who support the engineering groups in their design and development of new systems.

Government agencies are important because many of the topics around which human factors research is organized stem from what the incumbents of these agencies perceive as problems. Government agencies are also important because R&D topics recommended by lower echelon agencies or laboratories must be approved by these offices and because funding is controlled and turned on and off by these offices. For example, funds approved by Congress for particular programs may be deferred or even confiscated by agencies for other purposes.

Government departments are not entirely free to select their own R&D emphases and to impose them on the laboratories; they must request money annually from Congress and justify these requests to an ever-skeptical Congress. For example, at one time, research to demonstrate that women in the military could perform as effectively as men was popular in behavioral research circles, until Congress mandated that no further studies of this topic were to be done. To help interpret behavioral R&D requirements coming from the laboratories, and to communicate them meaningfully to Congress, the departments may employ a few behavioral specialists. These liaison monitors do no behavioral research themselves, but ask the laboratories to perform it and interpret its progress and results to their superiors.

Most of the behavioral research sought by government agencies is mission-oriented; its purpose is to solve or help solve an operational problem of interest to the agency, and to help in the development of new systems. The consumers of that research are the research, planning, and evaluation organizations under an assistant secretary of a department. Some basic research may slip in, but not a great deal. In the past, government departments have emphasized research application and utility for payoff, for example, in terms of cost reductions. This has resulted in a certain degree of pushing and shoving between the agency and laboratory personnel, who are usually less utility-minded. The trend to increasing utility is found even in agencies whose charter is basic research.

The Government Laboratory

The mission-oriented laboratory is the R&D arm of the government agency. Some organizations such as the Office of Naval Research (ONR), that support fundamental research, do no research themselves, but merely serve as the channel for selecting and funding, by means of contract or grant, all the research over which they have cognizance. Most mission-oriented laboratories, however, both contract out research and perform research in-house. Each of the military services supports more than ten specialized laboratories, although most are not of a behavioral nature.

As agency arms, the government laboratories must be responsive to the desires of the agency. However, the relationship is interactive; agencies call their laboratories for consultation on research policy, for information, and for data support. They also ask the laboratories to use their behavioral competence to investigate problems. In return, the laboratories request financing, suggest topics for study, and lobby for support of certain R&D areas.

Some specific behavioral problems have always concerned the government. In the military these problems are how many people of what types will be needed, how one selects the most effective individuals for a particular service, how they can be assigned most correctly, what the cheapest way of training them is, how they can be retained in the service, and how systems can be designed so that personnel can utilize them easily. The last is the special problem of human factors. To the extent that these problems have been with the government for many years, their durability as questions for research is well established. Theories and variables to be studied—and hence methods of researching these questions—change over the years, but the problems are persistent because research has to date produced no final answers.

Laboratories may be organized along a number of lines. The mission-ented behavioral laboratory within the Defense Department has functional subgroups (e.g., training, human engineering, selection, organizational effectiveness). The hardware-oriented laboratory organization may reflect weapon system specialties (e.g., air, surface, subsurface, sensors, communications). Where the laboratory both performs in-house research and monitors contracts and grants, the organization is likely to be large. For example, the NPRDC has a professional staff of around 250, but the Psychological Division of the ONR, which performs no in-house research, has a staff of only a dozen or so, which is subdivided into groups or programs each with only two or three people.

One characteristic of the laboratory is the large number of projects being performed (both in-house and under contract) at any one time. For example, it is not unheard-of for a behavioral laboratory to have a hundred projects. The large number of projects makes it difficult for laboratory management to maintain quality control over the projects. Efforts to do so take various forms— semiannual or annual program reviews, R&D management plans, and monthly written progress reports—but these are less than entirely satisfactory. Moreover, technical quality must compete with political problems for attention from the higher levels of laboratory management.

Major competitors for attention include *justification* and *explanation*. With regard to justification, there are constant requests to supply data supporting the utility of the research being performed. One unfortunate consequence of the need to write justifications is a wild exaggeration of claims for research utility and value. For example, the laboratory may be asked how much cost savings will result from a given research effort. The implication of the question is that any project failing to anticipate large cost savings is unworthy and might be eliminated in any further competition for funding. The claims that are then made must themselves be justified by showing the logic or, better still, the data that led to the claim. Explanation is closely related to justification. Briefings to agency management describe what the R&D program should be, given that money is provided, or actually is, once established. Explanation inevitably shades into justification or is a necessary preliminary to justification. The dependency relationship between the laboratory and the agency that funds it, and the continuing need to justify, sometimes causes laboratory management to adopt a reactive stance in which the laboratory will study almost anything the agency wants it to study.

In actual dollars, funding for behavioral science research and development by the government is small, compared with the vast expenditures for new weapon systems. As an example, DOD funding for all services for human factors amounted to $24.6 million in 1979 (Meister 1981). This pittance, however, is important because of the control it gives the agencies. There is nothing extraordinary about that; it is probably just the same in government funding of medical research, high energy physics, and so forth. The effects of government control may be a bit more exaggerated for human factors because the latter lacks the clout that the better-established sciences possess.

Defense Department research is tied to the developmental cycle of new system acquisition. Category 6.1 is so-called basic research because it precedes system development; 6.2 is research in the exploratory phase of development; 6.3 is advanced engineering development; 6.4 is production/deployment. Presumably 6.2 research builds on 6.1, and so on, although in practice this is rarely true. Monies allocated to 6.2 and 6.3 categories must be tied to or support some developmental purpose. For example, if one could persuade the Defense Department to supply 6.3 monies for development of a human performance data bank, it would be in ostensible support of some specific system, such as ad-

Table 8.1 Human Factors Engineering Research Projects, Defense Department, Office of Naval Research, 1986

Basic Research Work Units (6.1)
Supervisory Control of Man-Machine Systems
User-Computer Interface for High-Resolution Image-Processing
The Structure of Information in Software Code and Data Bases
Goal and Plan Knowledge in Software Comprehension
Committee on Basic Research in Human Factors
The Integration of Spatial Information from Shading, Texture Gradients, and Surface Contours
Inferring 3-D Shape from Image Motion and Occluding Contours
Information-Processing in Primate Visual Cortex
Tests of a Multilevel Computational Theory of Stereoscopic Visual Image-Processing
Computation of Stereo and Visual Motion from Biophysics to Psychophysics
Image Representation
Inferences from Images
Study of Human Vision Using Cellular Automata
The Cortical Substrate of Haptic Representation
Object Exploration and Recognition by Touch
Recognition of Isolated Nonspeech Sounds
Effort and Accuracy in Decision-Making
Studies in Risk: Perception and Preferences
Probable Cause: A Decision-Making Framework
Decision and Judgment
Research in Distributed Decision-Making with Applications to C³ Systems Design
Mathematical Models and Theory of Distributed Tactical Decision-Making
Information and Schema Theory in Distributed Decision-Making
Models of Group Dynamics in Distributed Tactical Decision-Making
Distributed Robust Communication Control
Architectures for the Organization of Tactical Decision-Making
Acquisition and Representation of Knowledge for Distributed Command Decision-Aiding
Decentralized Resource Managmenet in Tactical Computer Executives

Source: Deputy Chief of Naval Operations 1986.

vanced sonar or laser sensor. The amount of money allocated to 6.1 purposes is comparatively small, and a large part of it goes to university researchers for studies that may appear to have only a remote connection with human factors. In this connection, see Table 8.1, which lists the basic research project titles for human factors in 1986, supported by the Office of Naval Research. Table 8.1 shows a certain degree of reductionism—as if, for example, the solution to problems of brain physiology will somehow solve problems of tactical decision-making.

Some professionals believe that the 6.1, 6.2, 6.3, 6.4 categorization of DOD research and development activities is incompatible with human factors research requirements because it is tied too closely to hardware engineering. Recall the discussion in Chapter 6 of the relationship between technology and human factors, particularly the question of research topics that transcend technology. The relationship can be so close in the Defense Department that the research performed becomes trivial.

Because of the 6.1, etc., schema, most DOD-supported research is developmental research. This means that much of the kind of "macrobasic" research needed (Meister 1980) to support human factors falls between the two categories of basic and exploratory development research. Basic research as conceptualized by the DOD is often too molecular to support human factors; exploratory development research is often too specific.

The competition for funds by and between laboratories and agencies involves a certain amount of marketing. Much attention is paid to efforts to secure funding. Clearly some choice must be made among research projects, and this requires "selling" to the funding sponsor. In more recent years, however, the pace of marketeering seems to have grown. The marketing would be justified if it led to wiser choices, but this is questionable from the standpoint of the discipline. The operational military insist on immediately applicable outputs. As customers, sponsors rightly insist on value for money, but this value is often extremely short-term. In consequence there is very little investment in human factors methodology, the one area that needs greatest attention if the discipline is to flourish.

The present one-year funding cycle for system acquisition and R&D, mandated by Congress, means that the government researcher can make few long-range plans. There are longer-term research programs, but funding beyond the initial year is only a promise and may be withdrawn at any time. The one-year restriction (it is possible that the DOD will in the future receive two-year funding) may be responsible for the relative absence of long-term research projects. Despite the continuing general behavioral problems noted previously, government quickly becomes bored with a specific research study unless it receives almost immediate reinforcement in the form of highly visible outputs. The effect is that research questions that cannot be solved quickly—usually the most important questions—do not receive sufficient funding.

Government support of human factors in system development as represented by the attitudes of project managers and monitors parallels the attitudes of industry. With the exception of occasional peaks of interest, such as the MAN-PRINT program (Elton 1986), the attitude appears to many practitioners to be lukewarm at best—in spite of periodic calls by investigative arms of government for greater attention to human factors in system development (General Accounting Office 1977). The bottom line for government project managers is bringing system development to a close without overruns and without serious deficiencies. Military project managers are concerned primarily about their efficiency reports during their three-year tours of duty.

Another potent factor influencing behavioral research and development in the government laboratory is its organization, including both its formal and informal operating procedures. This can best be illustrated by comparing the different ways in which contract researchers and government researchers perform. It is appropriate to talk about contract researchers in the context of government because the largest part of their work is done for the government.

Contract Researchers

The research contractor is a perhaps unique specimen in Western science—the researcher for hire. It has always been necessary to support scientists while they worked, but, despite the control theoretically exercised by the patron, it was usually the researchers who decided what they were going to study and how, largely because there were so few researchers and so few who could evaluate their work.

Research contractors were born in response to methods developed in World War II, when scientists and engineers were enlisted in war work. They are a unique phenomenon—unique at least in number in the United States because one does not find so many of them in Europe or elsewhere. Research contractors hire themselves out for profit to any government or industrial organization that seeks a research service. There are nonprofit research companies, of course, but all this means is that any profit that accrues is plowed back into the business to fund unsupported research, higher salaries, and the like. Their special characteristic is that, within limits governed by their special capabilities and interests, they will research anything the customer wants them to research. They do not apply their own standards of topic importance or scientific interest to the research requests they answer.

Theoretically contractors can pick and choose what they want to study, but actually they are under self-generated pressure to bid their services on whatever topic their customers want to study and whose requirements they consider themselves capable of satisfying. The pressure exists because almost all contractors support a staff of professionals plus support personnel. At least within the Defense Department, it is extremely difficult for individual researchers to win a contract because most contracts require more resources than are available to individuals. For example, a project may require access to laboratory facilities that an individual researcher does not possess. Individuals can be consultants to laboratories, but government regulations severely constrain the number of hours a year that they can work as consultants.

The importance of research contractors is that in many U.S. government laboratories a substantial proportion (e.g., 40 percent to 50 percent) of research projects will, as a result of congressional mandate, be let under contract. This means also that a substantial proportion of all human factors research is controlled by a very small number of government sponsors whose judgment about topics and methods, while theoretically not unquestionable, cannot be questioned by anyone who seeks a contract for that research. It is almost invariably fatal to one's chances of winning a contract to question the good sense of the Request for Proposal.

There are several types of research contractors. Independent contractors (e.g., Anacapa and the American Institutes for Research) are self-contained (not part of a larger industrial corporation), and their sole activity is research on personnel. Industrial research contractors are groups of behavioral researchers that are part of larger companies, often system developers (e.g., McDonnell-Douglas, Boeing, Westinghouse); they support that company on in-house system development but also actively seek contracts from the government for behavioral research. A third type is the university research institute, groups set up as part of universities to perform behavioral research in a business-like manner (e.g., the University of Michigan's Human Performance Institute). There are also "think tanks," dependencies of the government (e.g., RAND Corporation) whose behavioral work is likely to be less empirical and more theoretical than that of the other types of contractors. As one would expect, the last two are more choosy about what they do.

As entrepreneurs competing with other similar organizations, contractors face the problem of making themselves known to potential customers, of marketing their capabilities, of securing outstanding personnel who will make them more competitive—all this while maintaining their payroll. If there is any distinguishing characteristic among research organizations, it should be in the quality of the researchers they employ. However, it is unlikely that there are significant differences between the quality of the personnel employed by government research laboratories, industrial corporations, universities, and independent contractors. Background training is largely the same; the proportion of Ph.D.'s to lesser academic degrees is roughly the same. Areas of interest differ, of course, university researchers being more theoretically oriented than the others. Another difference is that the contractors' spectrum of research *experience* is probably broader than that of government or university researchers, because to survive the former must bid on and perform a greater variety of research projects, whereas government and university researchers tend to specialize more quickly. In addition, the bureaucratic rigidity of Civil Service tends to induce a comparable intellectual rigidity in long-term employees.

The conditions under which research contractors and government/university researchers work are somewhat different. Contract research is apt to be highly frenetic because of the need to market one's wares by visiting customer offices, writing proposals, and meeting deadlines. The government and the university exert somewhat less pressure on their researchers. Government researchers may take a broader view of things because they are in charge of an entire project, whereas contractors are usually responsible for only a piece of that project.

Unlike government researchers, contractors do not have freedom to explore new research avenues in a given study, but must be closely responsive to the Statement of Work that directs their efforts. They can be aggressive in undertaking new work only if they can persuade the customer that the new channel they suggest will be technically profitable, and the mechanism they have for making such suggestions (the unsolicited proposal or grant) must fit within the government agency's plans. Consequently, research contractors have little influence over the selection of research topics.

Government and Contract Research Compared

In comparing government researchers with contractor researchers, we are dealing with people of comparable capability. However, the longer government researchers remain in their Civil Service laboratories, the more they tend to deviate from their contractor colleagues, because their experiences are different. Contract researchers generally have a wider perspective on the discipline as a whole for two reasons: they may be involved in system development practice more often, and they are exposed to many more types of research situations, often as a member of a team.

Because contractors must sell their expertise where they can, they may work for the Army one year, the Navy the next, and so on—each time encountering new systems and situations. Government researchers tend to specialize more and are more likely to be singletons in their research because government seems to foster individual activity.

Government researchers allocate the tasks to be performed in-house and under contract and the monies to be paid for the contract research. They monitor and evaluate the research contractor's performance. To that extent they control what the research contractor does. Money plays an overwhelming role in all this. Ordinarily, once a contract is signed the money is "fixed" for the contractor, because there is a financial penalty if the government breaks the contract. The monies allocated to the government's research program are usually stable after they reach the laboratory, but until this happens it is not unusual for those monies to be reduced or even eliminated by the government agency providing them. For example, a new project that is more attractive than one already on the books may draw funds from the latter. Congressional funding reductions may require that all projects be "taxed" accordingly.

Contractor research is a contractual obligation, so it must be structured much more narrowly than in-house research. The government researcher is responsible for writing the Statement of Work, which is a legal document that states what the contractor is legally obligated to do and that must be as precise as possible. The SOW cannot be changed without incurring additional cost to the government. This tends to focus the contract research effort much more precisely than the in-house research. Such tightness means that contractor researchers can often do more sophisticated work because the research must be more completely thought through. It is possible to control the quality of contract research more precisely because each contract output is specified in detail. Although the criteria for what constitutes effective research are the same in both cases, scrutiny of contract research may be more intense because the government is monitoring an entity other than itself.

Because the government is a complex bureaucratic organization, it is much more difficult for the researcher to procure needed personnel and equipment on a timely basis to perform research tasks. For example, it is not unheard of for a government researcher with money allocated to hire personnel and equipment to be told that because of local policy the researcher cannot do so. If the researcher wants to contract out a task, he or she will find that getting a contract through channels will set the project back six months to a year. All this is much simpler outside government—personnel can be hired and equipment can be bought in a matter of days or a few weeks.

A need to support their staffs drives some laboratories to compete actively with contract researchers for business with other government agencies. A government laboratory other than one's own may decide to have its research performed not by an outside contractor but by another government laboratory that presumably has the same capability. Some governmental agencies are critical of this, because the laboratory is not doing what it was set up to do—that is, to do what contractors cannot do and to guide research efforts.

Human factors contract research may seem to be more effective than that conducted by in-house (government) researchers. Although there are no data to verify this, contractors can perform research more efficiently, meaning faster and more economically, because once a contract is signed they have fewer organizational barriers to leap.

Periodically the government asks how useful its behavioral research is. The answer cannot be given in terms of the accumulation of knowledge, because this criterion is too gross and too long-term. It can, however, be given partly in terms of the extent to which human factors knowledge is applied to system development. On at least one occasion, the General Accounting Office asked the question and recommended, after investigation, that because little use was made of human factors products during development its research efforts should be shut down. The uproar produced by this recommendation, made in the initial draft of the report, resulted in a revised final report that merely recommended greater use of behavioral research (General Accounting Office 1977). However, the question has never been satisfactorily answered and may never be answered, although it would be useful if the Defense Department supported some research to find out how to make its research investment more profitable.

THE ACADEMIC COMMUNITY

Universities play an important role in human factors by training specialists and performing their own behavioral research (Sanders 1985). They train specialists to do research using strategies that the specialists continue to employ after graduation. The experimental method, use of control groups, and sophisticated statistical designs become the standard that researchers seek to maintain. That standard is also utilized in other contexts—for example, in criteria used for acceptance of articles submitted to journals. Journal publication is the universally accepted standard of scholarship among researchers, and almost all journals have an academic tinge because their editors are very frequently affiliated with the university.

The relatively few academic programs specifically designed for human factors students are mostly attached to the industrial engineering and psychology faculties. Most human factors professionals have received their basic training in psychology, a few in industrial engineering, still fewer in one of the other engineering specialities. This is entirely understandable, given the very close historical connection between the interests of human factors and those of psychology (see Chapter 2), although one might desire a broader background.

The academic community competes for scarce government research dollars. Organizations like the Office of Naval Research and the Air Force Office of Scientific Research consider that their responsibility in dispensing basic research money is in part to help support the university, although again the amount of money they dispense is relatively modest.

The common assumption in scientific circles is that mission-oriented or developmental research can contribute nothing valuable unless it is supported by a strong basic research effort conducted primarily in and by the universities. This at least is the traditional claim made by the physical and biological sciences, and it may well be valid for those sciences, although Project Hindsight (see Kreilkamp 1971) suggested that basic research contributed less than one percent to the development of several large-scale defense systems. Behavioral researchers, assuming that a parallel exists between the behavioral and the physical/biological sciences, make a comparable distinction between basic research and applied research. Unfortunately, the level of description of university basic research parameters may not be completely appropriate to the parameters implicit in the questions posed for mission-oriented research. Basic behavioral research as performed in universities usually deals with molecular variables and even when the variables studied are molar they are usually so purified by elimination of nonbehavioral variables that basic study results cannot readily be translated into real-world terms (see, e.g., Mackie and Christensen 1967).

Despite these caveats, the influence of the university is demonstrated by the fact that academics are heavily represented on the committees advising government agencies, even those of the Defense Department. For example, most of the behavioral members of the Navy's Research Advisory Council (NRAC) and the Army Research and Development Advisory Group (ARDAG) have been academics.

If the university controls the training of future human factors specialists, one must ask whether that training is adequate for the future needs of these specialists. That training should be responsive to the similarities and differences between human factors and its related disciplines, particularly psychology and engineering. It is necessary to remember also the differences between human factors research and human factors application, or behavioral design. The distinction between research and application is important because at least half the human factors professionals in the United States and elsewhere work in some aspect of application. It is possible that because most practitioners do little if any research, the training appropriate for researchers will be only partially appropriate for practitioners.

The training that specialists receive in psychology departments emphasizes experimental method, statistical analysis and computer processes, plus purely psychological courses focusing on topics such as sensation, perception, learning and motivation. Human factors courses are also provided. All the courses offered emphasize a research orientation.

Experimental psychology is based on hypothesis-testing in a tightly controlled environment, which for the academician is usually the laboratory. Although much human factors research also involves hypothesis-testing in the laboratory or other controlled environments, research may also be required in less well controlled situations, such as at test sites or occasionally in the real world of operational systems. In any event, whatever is taught in the university involving classic experimental design is appropriate when the human factors specialist does the same kind of research. There will be occasions when the specialist must do research in the field, where stringent control may not be possible, and for this situation it is likely that the university will teach the quasi-experimental methods of Cook and Campbell (1979). But the difference between the university laboratory context and the human factors context is difficult for the student to experience as a student, because the field environment involves lessened control, an insufficient number of subjects, time constraints, inadequate or no instrumentation, and intrusions from an irrelevant world into the study. Nevertheless, within these constraints the classic rules of experimental method should apply.

If human factors research has been strongly influenced by experimental psychology, behavioral design has been just as strongly influenced by engineering. The outstanding characteristics of the system development environment have been described previously, but the important point is that the methods used in this environment are not experimental, but analytic and evaluational (see Chapter 7).

Human factors analyses are different from experimental methods; the former require a different kind of intellectual activity because, although they are procedural in nature, they are still much less constrained and less formal than those involved in statistical design and analysis. Above all, human factors analyses are subjective and creative. These analyses must be performed in a problem-solving environment with many unknowns, which differ in quality from the unknowns found in experimental research. Hence, from an analytic standpoint the experimental research orientation taught at the university is only partially relevant.

For the other part of human factors application—known as test and evaluation—much of what is learned in the university setting is relevant, because test and evaluation is measurement. Considerations of test objectives, criteria, measures, subject selection, data collection, and statistical analysis are appropriate, but test and evaluation is not research, and the setting in which it is performed is different from that of the controlled study. Even the scope is different; experimental research generally involves small, discrete units of performance, whereas test and evaluation may involve masses of equipment and personnel and a complex mission.

Although the research methodology taught in the university is reasonably relevant to human factors research, its conceptual orientation is not. The differences in conceptual orientation between human factors and psychology have already been addressed in Chapter 2. Human factors is (or should be) a system-oriented discipline, and psychology is an individual/group-centered discipline, but the orientation disseminated in departments of psychology breeds human factors researchers who too often study individual rather than system performance. The distinctive characteristics of human factors application require a type of training that is not taught too easily in schools.

It would be possible to prepare students for human factors applications by providing them with material that presents design problems and takes them through the solution process, perhaps something like the case history approach of the Harvard Business School, but with better results, one hopes. The practitioners' ability to communicate with engineers would also be much facilitated by requiring practitioners to take a special engineering course that would not of course qualify them as engineers but would give them a basic knowledge of the field so that they will be familiar with designers' concerns.

The strength of the present university human factors curriculum is in its research; its weakness is in analysis and behavioral design, which probably do not receive sufficient emphasis. Because jobs for psychology graduates are in short supply, some departments attempt to convert their students into human factors specialists. However, Howell and colleagues (1987) warn that this cannot be done merely by adding a few "applications" courses to the standard curriculum. A curriculum for prospective specialists should include—in addition to core psychology courses—courses in human factors methods, behavioral design, the conceptual foundations of human factors, the application of experimental methodology to human factors research, and basic engineering for behavioral students. Perhaps a partial solution to the problem of training the specialist would be to require, as some schools do, a year's internship away from the university setting.

THE WORTH OF HUMAN FACTORS

What value does human factors have as a discipline? This is not a question one ordinarily asks of a scientific discipline, but it deserves consideration because the concept of worth is a factor when sponsors decide whether or not to supply funds for research and development, without which a discipline stagnates. The following discussion is based largely on a recent study by Lane (1987), which summarized what little work has been done to determine the cost-effectiveness of human factors.

Worth in relation to science is measured not in terms of cost-effectiveness but in terms of relative importance. For example, physics receives much more attention and financial aid than psychology or human factors because it is viewed as being a more "fundamental", and hence more worthy, discipline. The worth of competing research and development proposals *within* even such favored disciplines as physics or chemistry is, however, viewed in cost-effectiveness terms. Worth is therefore not solely a question for human factors, although it hits this discipline harder than most.

The Measurement of Worth

Worth as measured in terms of cost-effectiveness is much more pertinent with regard to behavioral design, because behavioral design is not viewed by managers and engineers as inherently part of the design process and hence requires an investment of money, effort, and time. No one would ask about the cost-effectiveness of electronic engineering. For financial investments the question of cost-effectiveness is quite meaningful.

Human factors cost-effectiveness is merely one aspect of the more general problem of determining its relationship to, and the impact of human performance on, system operations. This is because that relationship, that impact, determines cost-effectiveness. If one cannot measure that impact, one cannot measure cost-effectiveness, and the whole question becomes pointless. The ideal method of determining the cost-effectiveness of behavioral design would be to build two systems that are identical except for the inclusion of "good" human engineering characteristics in one and poor human engineering characteristics in the other, and then to compare system performance. With the exception of a single study that Lane (1987) cited (Gartner et al. 1958), this comparison has not been made and is impractical for systems on a cost basis. (It is perhaps possible for simple pieces of equipment.)

The only other feasible alternative is to develop methods of measuring human performance in relation to discrete behavioral design characteristics and system performance, and then to examine a large number of systems that differ in these characteristics to see if there is any relationship between human-engineering variations and human plus system performance. If "good" behavioral design characteristics equaled high human performance equaled superior system performance, the case for human factors would be proven. Unfortunately, experiments to establish performance relationships between design characteristics and personnel performance, as described in Chapter 4, have not yet been conducted, and there has been no prolonged effort (which is what it would take) to gather data on system personnel performance together with data on overall system (mission) performance.

There are two ways of looking at cost-effectiveness—in performance terms or in cost terms. With the first we get superior performance; with the second, the overall cost of the system, particularly life cycle costs, are reduced. Human factors has the potential to achieve both effects. But quantitative evidence about human factors value is scarce. Only a few studies have provided quantitative data on either the impact of human factors on system performance or on the cost savings, and virtually none on both. Lane (1987) pointed out that the available data suggest that allocation of resources to human factors during design is likely to be a good investment, primarily because behavioral design is relatively inexpensive, compared with costs per equipment design.

Forecasting the Impact of Human Factors

Human factors has only a limited ability to document or predict its contributions as a design discipline. The greatest amount of attention has been paid to incorporating inputs into design, with evaluation of the effects of those inputs receiving much less attention. Lane suggests that the reason is a lack of attention to value issues within the profession and a shortage of dollars and people to investigate value. This is true, but there are serious methodological problems to overcome. Technical constraints on what can be said about the impact of human factors also exist; it is difficult to isolate specific human factors contributions to design from every other influence on that design, and estimates of such effects are inherently less precise than those of other disciplines because of greater human variability. The effectiveness of human factors in system development must be assessed against system objectives that are cast in equipment terms, which makes it more difficult to determine how these objectives have been satisfied by human performance. There are also almost no quantitative data on the performance of people working in existing systems to serve as a baseline for evaluating new development. The methodology needed to make the desired estimates does not exist.

The limited ability to make forecasts of the impact of human factors within specific design contexts has without question held back the growth and refinement of the discipline. Estimates of effectiveness, together with associated costs, would permit one to differentiate among alternative behavioral solutions to a design problem. This in turn would enable the discipline to make credible statements about payoff from human factors application programs and enhance the likelihood of acquiring funding support for behavioral design. The literature dealing directly with the value of human factors, particularly in quantitative terms, is very limited. Only three studies have focused on the question in any significant way. These include the efforts of Price and colleagues (1980a, 1980b) and Sawyer and colleagues (1981). Cost and value concerns are addressed as part of broader human resource issues in Goclowski et al. (1978) and in King and Askren (1980). There is also the work of Nelson, Schmitz, and Promisel (1984) and Promisel and colleagues (1985) as part of manpower, personnel, and training studies.

Past Interest in the Question of Value

Although questions about *quantified* human factors cost-effectiveness have been raised only recently, the issue of whether human factors has any value can be seen in the very early years of the discipline (Yarnold and Channell 1952). Throughout the 1950s and 1960s, most direct examinations of the value of human factors seem to have focused on the importance of human factors in reducing operator error instead of on its contribution to larger issues of system effectiveness (e.g., Meister and Rabideau 1965). Lane (1987) suggested that this emphasis resulted from a lack of concern for human roles in systems that was characteristic of design at that time. Practitioners were more preoccupied with "prevention of disaster" notions than with the systematic "top down" integration of people into systems. In such a context, the practitioner spent most of the time attempting to remove the obvious error-inducing traps for the operator. Practitioners still focus much of their effort on this aspect.

Only in the late 1960s, and only infrequently, did current concepts of human factors as a component of total system performance begin to appear (e.g., Meister, Sullivan, and Askren 1968). Little or no explicit attention to more global issues of human factors impact is seen in the literature until the early 1970s (e.g., Bernberg 1972; Coburn 1973). Although the system-wide nature of human factors contributions was recognized, a focus on specific value-related data had not yet emerged as a priority concern.

From the mid 1970s on, there has been a steady increase of interest in examining the impact of human factors in terms of the costs of investment. Some of these concerns for justification arose from within the discipline itself, but most were the result of external pressures or of the pull exerted by heightened awareness of cost-effectiveness issues in related areas, such as education and training. For example, the General Accounting Office (1977) indicated an apparent lack of utilization of work in personnel-related (human resources) disciplines and, by implication, questioned the value of investing development and design resources in those areas. These criticisms triggered direct interest in acquiring more precise estimates of human factors contributions.

Points of Agreement

Specialists appear to be in agreement on the following three points: (1) Determining the value of human factors is a most complex problem because it depends for solution on other methodologies, such as workload, performance measurement, and operator modeling, which are themselves not yet very mature. (2) Effectiveness means different things to different people. It can mean higher performance (more kills per unit time, rounds on target), reduced manning requirements, or increased system availability, depending on what is most likely to help sell the program or the system. Because all these criteria are potentially important, there should be (but is not) some explicit priority among them for a particular application. (3) Human factors effectiveness is not always linearly related to the perceived seriousness of discrepancies in design. Very minor problems can have a massive impact on a system, sometimes invalidating its use.

Components of Human Factors Cost-Effectiveness

There are two distinct components to human factors cost-effectiveness. One involves bringing about improvements in routine operation of the system, and the second involves preventing disaster that would result from inappropriate reactions to low-probability, highly critical events. Because determining impact on the former class of events is much simpler than for the latter class, so much of the human factors contribution is hidden.

Data on personnel performance in existing operational systems are essential for baseline purposes in determining the human factors cost-effectiveness of new systems. Performance data should be available in archival form for feedback on the effectiveness of methods, for decisions about resource allocation, and for estimation or documentation of human factors contributions. Few such data exist, and many specialists are skeptical about the likelihood of acquiring such data, which are almost never routinely collected; on some occasions system performance data have even been "deliberately suppressed."

The most significant contribution of behavioral design is in the area of prevention of later problems (cost-avoidance); its effectiveness lies in elimination during design of difficulties that ordinarily emerge only after fixes are impractical or extremely expensive. This value is "invisible" and may be unknowable, because it can be observed only by the absence of operational problems. Poor behavioral design is detectable but good design is not.

Factors Affecting Determination of Value

It is necessary to distinguish between the formal and the informal design process in which behavioral design functions. There are formal processes in which behavioral design contributions are required (e.g., participation in design reviews); parallel to this is an informal process (e.g, continuing verbal contact with designers), which is even more important in terms of design impact. Specialists report continuing difficulties in gaining acceptance of human factors within the informal process (Meister 1979; Rouse 1986). Most practitioners believe that they can eventually become effective within the design team for an individual system, but there is an absence of carry-over; in each new system it is necessary almost to start from scratch in building credibility.

The attitudes of the program manager and his or her concept of human factors are the main elements in success or failure of the behavioral design effort. These attitudes control human factors involvement in system development despite formal policy directives and are not always affected or modified by evidence of human factors value. Horror stories, the outcomes of ignoring or neglecting human factors in previous system development, are mostly discounted as leverage in gaining resources or drawing attention to human factors needs. Program managers do not consider that such "stupidities" could be committed on their systems. Program manager disinterest may be attributable to different, sometimes opposing, goals for the manager and for human factors. Many human factors contributions are long-term in nature, seen primarily in increased system operability and reduction in life cycle costs. On the other hand, the program manager is judged not on operability and long-term savings but on two main concerns—cost and schedule. In the short term, managers see human factors as likely to increase development cost and to delay schedule, creating an inherent conflict between human factors requirements and program manager accountability.

There have, as a result, been few adequately supported human factors programs in the last two decades. As drawdowns on development funding occurred, the human factors support programs on most acquisitions were historically the first to feel the impact.

Behavioral design objectives employ such terms as *optimum* or *optimal* (as in optimizing the human-machine interface). The view of human factors as an optimizing discipline in search of a single best solution is in sharp contrast to the usual engineering approach of simply finding any solution that satisfies requirements. In this engineering context, the behavioral approach may appear to be unproductive.

Among system-related disciplines, human factors is the only discipline that has no direct advocate, no statutory "constituency" in the decision-making power structure. Within each military service, there is management specifically charged with advocacy of engineering concerns and control of resources. As Council (1986) points out, the fields of manpower, personnel, and training (i.e., concerns for acquisition, selection, and training of personnel), which are historically weak in the design process, now have formal focal points that control identified resources. Because human factors lacks both formal advocacy and dedicated resources, it has had and will continue to have difficulty achieving recognition of its importance in system development.

Perhaps the most characteristic feature of human factors is its presumption that human competence in system operation depends on compatibility—matching what the system requires the human to do against the human's skill and resources. Human factors effectiveness should therefore be manifested most readily in metrics that are sensitive to the presence or absence of this compatibility, metrics that are performance-based and relate in some direct way to the purposes for which the system exists. Unfortunately, the metrics customarily used by developers and sponsors for evaluating system performance and effectiveness are typically insensitive to human contributions. They tend to be either equipment-specific or so global that good or bad human performance makes little difference in metric values.

The need to key evaluation to objectives is present for all disciplines involved in system development. However, because of its unique standing among the design disciplines, human factors may have more difficulty mapping its contributions into the usual form of system objectives. This results in part from the nature of these objectives and in part from the behavioral nature of human factors. Objectives at upper levels in the system hierarchy are broadly defined, and substantial differences in operator and maintainer performance may not be separately visible as sources of system performance variation. Meaningful objectives should be couched in realistic metrics of system performance of the type that human factors can influence, such as time to perform a correct intercept, the rate at which the target is detected and identified by an operator, or time to diagnose and fix a malfunction. Objectives at lower levels are likely to be cast in engineering performance terms (e.g., probability of detecting a submarine in terms of sound propagation contours), as if there were no operator in the system. Further, human factors has no individual system or subsystem whose effectiveness can be separately evaluated—from a hardware or software standpoint. Its impact is by its nature system-wide and embedded; operator performance has no inherent meaning independent of system context.

Levels of Effectiveness Management

Erickson (1986) has made the most complete examination of effectiveness measurement as related to human factors. His presentation is organized around the concept of the impact of performance as a function of hierarchical level and the visibility of that performance. Different measures of effectiveness (MOEs) are needed to represent the progressively more global concerns involved at higher levels. Erickson identifies seven levels of system and/or operator performance at which measures can be taken that show how good the design is.

1. *Subsystem component* (e.g., a single display). At this level, the effectiveness of the component itself and of the operator at using the component can usually be distinguished, and the impact of good or poor behavioral design can be isolated.

2. *Subsystem* (e.g., an avionics suite). The ability of the operator to use the subsystem is still a key component of effectiveness and can often be isolated by controlled studies.

3. *Mission segment* (e.g., submarine localization). This level may involve the combined effectiveness of several subsystems. Effectiveness may be driven

largely by equipment properties and the success of subsystem integration. The operator contribution, while still visible, may or may not be the prime determinant.

4. *Full-mission, single system* (e.g., a ship carrying out all aspects of a single, specific mission—such as for antisubmarine warfare, navigation, enroute steaming, target detection, localization, classification, or attack). Performance in this situation is heavily influenced by equipment and environment. It is rarely possible to isolate the contribution of the operator component. The best one can do is perhaps correlate effects.

5. *Multiple-element mission, single system* (e.g., one platform, such as a ship, engaged in antisubmarine warfare with the addition of, for example, surveillance and/or electronics countermeasures). Operator influence is essentially eliminated.

6. *Tactical employment of multiple systems* (e.g., a naval task force, a brigade). MOEs are most heavily affected by system reliability and the type and effectiveness of tactics. Erickson feels that the operator component contributes no visible variation to performance.

7. *Force level employment of multiple systems* (e.g., several aircraft carriers). Effectiveness is determined largely by variables independent of the individual system.

Effectiveness measures employed at the higher levels of the hierarchy are concerned primarily with the overall military worth of the system and its place in service, Defense Department, and national security policies. Erickson suggests that beyond level 3, above, there is little discernible effect of operator performance and thus no visible evidence for the adequacy of behavioral design. According to Erickson, the human factors impact can be traced at best only to the lower three levels, whereas program managers and other decision makers are most concerned about effectiveness at level 4 and above, in part because system objectives are frequently written to those levels. I suggest that, if the proper measures are taken, one can discern an effect at level 4, and that this is necessary because in order to evaluate personnel subsystem performance properly one must relate it to the total mission. However, it may be possible to do so only over several missions and only by correlation.

By virtue of its subject matter, human factors has inherently greater influence on some system characteristics than on others. Good behavioral design may have little impact on mean-time-between-failures (MTBF) barring maintenance error because that is predominantly an equipment metric, but it may have a substantial impact on mean-time-to-repair (MTTR) because that is driven primarily by human performance. If the first characteristic (MTBF) is specifically addressed in the system requirement but the second (MTTR) is not, human factors is at a relative disadvantage in showing its contributions.

The return on investment in human factors—its impact on cost-effectiveness—appears to be a very high multiple of costs. While operators and maintainers are individually cheaper than hardware and software, they are found throughout the system, and their collective care and feeding constitute the majority of life cycle costs (60 percent or more by most estimates). Thus, whatever human factors can do to, for example, reduce manning or required skill levels without compromising performance has an immediate multiplicative effect on life cycle costs that cascades throughout the operational life of the system.

Needed Research

Data important for estimating effectiveness are lacking in four areas. First, despite decades of basic research the characteristics, capabilities, and limitations of human beings that are important in a system context are not well defined. Second, there is little or no systematic feedback on operational performance to indicate how well previous behavioral design approaches worked in system settings (a lack of system baselines). Third, there are no good frameworks for linking the structure of human capabilities to how those capabilities (skills, abilities) are manifested in the performance of real-world tasks. Fourth, managers of operational systems are reluctant to support measurement of their operations, perhaps because a negative evaluation may result.

Recommendations for overcoming the problems of estimating human factors cost-effectiveness are difficult to develop. It is all very well to recommend, as Lane (1987) does, that human factors professionals need greater awareness of the need to estimate worth, but awareness alone is unlikely to improve the situation. The one concrete recommendation that Lane makes that might aid the situation, because it is fundamental to the discipline, is to develop a human performance data base. This recommendation has been made many times in the past but has never been acted on. It is unlikely to be implemented in the new context of human factors cost-effectiveness.

Where Do We Go from Here?

The percipient reader will now ask, Where do we go from here? So much of this book has emphasized the problems the discipline must overcome that the reader may wonder whether things are really that bad and, if they are, what can be done to remedy the situation. The problems are indeed serious, but only if the reader considers that human factors is a fundamental discipline. If one is not serious about one's profession, then the problems raised are only bogeymen with which to frighten children. These are problems only if one has a concept of human factors in terms of what it should be able to do—describe incisively, predict with precision, control with strength. If the reader is satisfied with the human factors status quo, he or she has been reading the wrong book.

To determine whether the problems raised in this book are genuine, it is necessary to distinguish between the human factors profession and the human factors discipline, however close they may appear to be. The profession is made up of *people,* most of whom may be experiencing career and professional growth, in which case the problems presented may not appear so serious. Professional growth in terms of such indices as number of Human Factors Society members and number of job opportunities seems to be increasing, which suggests that developers are more accepting of the discipline. However, the discipline is a state of knowledge, an inventory of concepts and methods, to which one must apply certain standards befitting a discipline. From the latter standpoint, I believe we are treading water at best.

The unknown person who reviewed the initial draft of this book called for a program of research to overcome the problems described. A specific program of research—one that requires extensive resources to implement, and resources that may not be available, considering the difficulties in securing funding from governmental sponsors—is recommended in Chapter 4. Whether or not that research can be funded, and because almost everything depends on government and academia, I recommend what I call a minimalist program: what is the absolute minimum the discipline can do with reference to its problems?

1. We in the discipline can discuss these problems on a continuing basis. As it is said, talk is cheap—that is, it may not be necessary to get a grant for it. The aim of this discussion would be to develop a consensus in the discipline about whether the problems noted are real and serious, and if all of them are not, which ones are real and serious—and what can be done about them. A prerequisite for such a discussion is the acquiescence of the learned societies—the Human Factors Society, the International Ergonomics Association—the journals they publish, and government agencies that support the discipline, such as the Human Factors Committee of the National Research Council. These should be willing to devote some of their resources to an ongoing debate. The sponsors of the debate should enlist some of the "influentials" to participate in small seminars and workshops in an attempt to find answers.

2. The societies mentioned, together with sympathetic government agencies, should fund efforts to discover what the state of human factors knowledge and capability is, and what is needed to move beyond the present status. Some of the financial resources available to the discipline should be used to compile the available data in various interest areas in order to determine more precisely what we do know and do not know. Because of the discipline's emphasis on original empirical studies, professionals have a curious reluctance to examine and evaluate what has been learned from past work. The determination of what we *should* know can serve as a goal toward which to work and as a measure of the effectiveness of our progress toward that goal.

3. Ideally, the learned societies, the journals, and the funding sources will sponsor the writing of position papers on the questions raised, and then publicize these extensively. Few such papers have been written.

The consensus that might result from this minimalist program might differ wholly or in part from the viewpoints expressed in this book, but at least the questions would be asked. To end this book on a hopeful note, it is important to consider that, whatever its vicissitudes, human factors will continue in one form or another, because a human factors discipline is a necessity for a technological society.

SUMMARY

Human factors is also influenced by nontechnical factors stemming from the human factors community itself, from government, industry, and academia. Funding is the one critical element that binds these four sectors together, because human factors research and development are driven by the interests and attitudes of research sponsors and system developers.

The industrial community is a potential source of research questions, but it also serves as a set of constraints on behavioral development. Attitudes of the engineering community toward human factors have a great effect on how successfully human factors is applied to system development.

Government is important because it supplies almost all funds for human factors research and application. Most behavioral research sought by government is mission-oriented. Department of Defense research is tied to the hardware development cycle, which is not completely compatible with human factors requirements. Much research is performed by research contractors who have little or no influence over the questions they study.

Academia has considerable influence over human factors because it trains specialists and sets research strategy and standards that persist in professional life. Although much of the training that specialists receive in the university is appropriate, much is not.

The worth or utility of human factors is a topic of significant interest to the discipline, because funding for research and application is highly dependent on worth-related attitudes of sponsors and developers. The difficulty of measuring the contribution of human factors to system development can be attributed to an inability to isolate the impact of the individual engineering discipline to specific system designs, the lack of a human performance data base associated with equipment design features, and design objectives that are phrased solely in physicalistic terms.

References

Note: References with AD numbers can be secured from the U.S. Department of Commerce, National Technical Information Service, 5285 Port Royal Road, Springfield, Virginia. 22161.

Ackerman, P.L. 1986. Skill acquisition, individual differences, and human abilities. *Proceedings, Human Factors Society Annual Meeting* (pp. 270–274).

Acton, W., W. Percz, and G. Reid. 1986. On the dimensionality of subjective workload. *Proceedings, Human Factors Society Annual Meeting* (pp. 76–80).

Adams, M.L., A. Barlow, and J. Hiddlestein. 1981. Obtaining ergonomics information about industrial injuries: A five-year analysis. *Applied Ergonomics* 12:71–81.

AGARD (NATO Advisory Group for Aerospace Research and Development). 1978a. Assessing pilot workload (Report AGARD-AG-233). Neuilly-sur-Seine, France.

———. 1978b. Methods to assess workload (Report AGARD-AG-216). Neuilly-sur-Seine, France.

Army Research Institute. 1977. Women content in units force development test (MAX-WAC). Alexandria, Va.: Army Research Institute. (AD A050 022)

Askren, W.B., and R.R. Newton. 1969. Review and analysis of personnel subsystem test and evaluation literature (Report AFHRL-TR-68-7). Wright-Patterson AFB, Ohio: Air Force Human Resources Lab. (AD 859 300)

Baker, C., D.R. Eike, T.B. Malone, and L. Peterson. 1988. Update of DOD HDBK-761, Human Engineering Guidelines for Management Information Systems. *Proceedings, Human Factors Society Annual Meeting* (pp. 335–339).

Baker, C.C., J.J. Johnson, M.T. Malone, and T.B. Malone. 1979. Human factors engineering for Navy weapon system acquisition. Alexandria, Va.: Essex Corp.

Banks, W.W., D.I. Gertman, and R.J. Petersen. 1982. Human engineering design considerations for cathode-ray-tube-generated displays (Report NUREG/CR-2496, EGG-2161). Idaho Falls: EG&G Idaho.

Barnes, R.M. 1980. *Motion and Time Study*. New York: Wiley.

Bavelas, A. 1950. Communication patterns in task-oriented groups. *J. Acoustic Society* 22:725–730.

Berliner, D.C., D. Angell, and J. Shearer. 1964. Behaviors, measures, and instruments for performance evaluation in simulated environments. *Proceedings, Symposium and Workshop on the Quantification of Human Performance,* Albuquerque, N.Mex.

Bernberg, R.E. 1972. Cost-effectiveness and crew system design (Pub. no. 11757). Woodland Hills, Calif.: Litton Systems.

Berson, B.L., and W.H. Crooks. 1976. Guide for obtaining and analyzing human performance data in a material development project (Technical Memorandum 29–76). Aberdeen Proving Ground, Md.: Human Engineering Lab.

Bertalanffy, L. von. 1968. *General System Theory: Foundations, Development, Application*. New York: Braziller.

Bittner, A.C., R.C. Carter, R.S. Kennedy, M.M. Harbeson, and M. Krause. 1986. Performance evaluation tests for environmental research (PETER): Evaluation of 114 measures. *Perceptual and Motor Skills* 63:683–708.

Bittner, A.C., W.W. Wierwille, R.E. Christ, P.M. Linton, and F.A. Glenn. 1987. Operator workload (OWL) program for Army systems: Overview and progress (unpublished paper). Willow Grove, Pa.: Analytics.

Blanchard, R.E. 1973. Requirements, concept, and specification for a Navy human performance data store (Report 102–2). Santa Monica, Calif.: Behaviormetrics.

Bloom, R.F., J.F. Oates, and J.W. Hamilton. 1985. An initial analytic process model for systems measurement: Extensions of the Systems Taxonomy Model (Research Note 85–19). Fort Benning, Ga.: Army Research Institute. (AD A160 473)

Boff, K.R., L. Kaufman, and J.P. Thomas (Eds.). 1986. *Handbook of Perception and Human Performance* (vols. 1 & 2). New York: Wiley-Interscience.

Boff, K.R., and J.E. Lincoln (Eds.). 1988. *Engineering Data Compendium: Human Perception and Performance*. Wright-Patterson AFB, Ohio: Aerospace Medical Research Laboratory.

Brinberg, D., and J.E. McGrath. 1982. A network of validity concepts within the research process. In D. Brinberg and L.H. Kidder (Eds.), *Forms of Validity Research* (pp. 5–21). San Francisco: Jossey-Bass

Brinberg, D., and J.E. McGrath. 1985. *Validity and the Research Process*. Beverly Hills, Calif.: Sage Publications.

Brune, R.L., and M. Weinstein. 1980. Procedure evaluation checklist for maintenance, test, and calibration procedures. (Report NUREG/CR-1369 and SAND80-7064). Washington, D.C.: Nuclear Regulatory Commission.

Campbell, D.T., and D.W. Fiske. 1959. Convergent and discriminant validation by the multitrait-multimethod matrix. *Psychological Bulletin* 56:81–105.

Campbell, J.P. 1986. Labs, field, and straw issues. In E.A. Locke (Ed.), *Generalizing from Laboratory to Field Settings* (pp. 269–279). Lexington, Mass.: Lexington Books.

Chapanis, A. 1970. Relevance of physiological and psychological criteria to man-machine systems: The present state of the art. *Ergonomics* 13:337–346.

———. 1986. A psychology for our technological society. *Human Factors Society Bulletin* 29:1–4.

Chapanis, A., W.R. Garner, and C.T. Morgan. 1949. *Applied Experimental Psychology: Human Factors in Engineering Design*. New York: Wiley.

Checkland, P.B. 1981a. Rethinking a systems approach. *J. Applied Systems Analysis* 8:3–14.

———. 1981b. *Systems Thinking, Systems Practice*. New York: Wiley.

Chiles, W.D., and E.A. Alluisi. 1979. On the specification of operator or occupational workload with performance-measurement methods. *Human Factors* 21:515–528.

Chiles, W.D., E.A. Alluisi, and O.S. Adams. 1968. Work schedules and performance during confinement. *Human Factors* 10:143–195.

Christal, P.E. 1968. Selecting a harem—and other applications of the policy capturing model. *J. Experimental Education* 36:35–41.

Christensen, J.M. 1962. The evolution of the systems approach in human factors engineering. *Human Factors* 5:7–16.

Coburn, R. 1973. Human engineering guide to ship system development: Responsibilities, procedures, and methods for carrying out human engineering programs (Report NELC-TD 278). San Diego: Navy Electronics Laboratory Center.

Comer, M.K., D.A. Seaver, W.G. Stillwell, and C.D. Geddy. 1984. Generating human reliability estimates using expert judgment (vol. 1, main report) (Report NUREG/CR-3688/1 of 2, SAND84-7115, RX). Washington, D.C.: Nuclear Regulatory Commission.

Committee on Human Factors, National Research Council. 1983. *Research Needs for Human Factors*. Washington, D.C.: National Academy Press.

Connelly, E.M., F.J. Bourne, D.G. Loental, and P.A. Knoop. 1974. Computer-aided techniques for providing operator performance measures (Report AFHRL-TR-74-87). McLean, Va.: Quest Research Corp. (AD A014 330)

Connelly, E.M., and N.A. Sloan. 1976. Manned system design using operator measures and criteria (Report OTR-62-76-1). Vienna, Va.: Omnemii. (AD A032 687)

Conrad, R., and A.J. Hull. 1968. The preferred layout for numerical data-entry keysets. *Ergonomics* 11:165–173.

Cook, T.D., and D.J. Campbell. 1979. *Quasi-Experimentation: Design and Analysis Issues for Field Settings*. Chicago: Rand McNally.

Council, G.S. 1986. Early consideration of human factors in weapon system design. *Proceedings, Human Factors Society Annual Meeting* (pp. 1290–1293).

Davis, L.E., and A. Cherns. 1975. *The Quality of Working Life*. New York: Free Press.

DeGreene, K.B. 1974. Models of man in systems in retrospect and prospect. *Ergonomics* 17:437–446.

Department of Defense. 1979. Human engineering requirements for military systems (MIL-H-46855B). Washington, D.C.: Department of Defense.

————. 1981. Human engineering design criteria for military systems, equipment, and facilities (MIL-STD 1472C). Washington, D.C.: Department of Defense.

Deputy Chief of Naval Operations (Manpower, Personnel, and Training, OP-01B7). 1986. Master plan, manpower, personnel and training research, development, and studies. Defense Department Report. Washington, D.C.

Edwards, J.M., R.F. Bloom, J.F. Oates, S. Sipitowski, P.A. Brainin, R.J. Eckenrode, and P.C. Zeidler. 1985a. An annotated bibliography of the manned systems measurement literature (Research Note 85-18). Fort Benning, Ga.: Army Research Institute. (AD A160 333)

Edwards, J.M., R.F. Bloom, and P.A. Brainin. 1985b. System development and evaluation technology: State of the art of manned system measurement (Research Note 85–20). Fort Benning, Ga.: Army Research Institute. (AD A160 418)

Eekhout, J.M., and W.B. Rouse. 1981. Human errors in detection, diagnosis, and compensation for failures in the engine control room of a supertanker. *IEEE Transactions in Systems, Man, and Cybernetics*, SMC-11:813–816.

Eggleston, R.G. 1987. The changing nature of the human-machine design problem:

Implications for system design and development. In W.B. Rouse and K.R. Boff (Eds.), *System Design: Behavioral Perspectives on Designers, Tools, and Organizations* (pp. 113–125). Amsterdam: North Holland.

Elton, R.M. 1986. MANPRINT (Manpower and personnel integration). *Proceedings, Human Factors Society Annual Meeting* (pp. 905–907).

Erickson, R.A. 1978. Line criteria in target acquisition with television. *Human Factors* 20:573–588.

————. 1983. The human operator and system effectiveness (NWC Technical Memorandum 5060). China Lake, Calif.: Naval Weapons Center.

————. 1986. Measures of effectiveness in systems analysis and human factors (Report NWC TR-6740). China Lake, Calif.: Naval Weapons Center.

Ericsson, K.A. and H.A. Simon. 1980. Verbal reports as data. *Psychological Review* 87:215–251.

Finley, D.L., and F.A. Muckler. 1976. Human factors research and the development of a manned systems application science: The system sampling problem and a solution. Northridge, Calif.: Manned System Sciences.

Finley, D.L., F.A. Muckler, C.A. Gainer, and R.W. Obermayer. 1975. An analysis and evaluation methodology for command and control. Northridge, Calif.: Manned System Sciences. (AD A023 871)

Finley, D.L., R.W. Obermayer, C.M. Bertone, D. Meister, and F.A. Muckler. 1970. Human performance prediction in man-machine systems, Vol. 1: A technical review. (Report CR-1614). Washington, D.C.: National Aeronautics and Space Administration.

Fitts, P.M., et al. (Eds.). 1951. Human engineering for an effective air transportation and traffic control system. Washington, D.C.: National Research Council.

Fleishman, E.A., and M.K. Quaintance. 1984. *Taxonomies of Human Performance: The Description of Human Tasks*. Orlando, Fla.: Academic Press.

Francas, M., D. Goodman, and J. Dickinson. 1985. A reliability study of the task walkthrough in the computer communications industry. *Human Factors* 27:601–605.

Gagne, R.M. 1965. *The Conditions of Learning*. New York: Holt, Rinehart, and Winston.

Gartner, W.B., T.A. Hussman, W.P. Shanahan, H.E. Price, R.L. Hackman, and A.R. Askenasy. 1958. An experimental evaluation of the application of human engineering principles to mine test set design (Report PRA 58-2). Arlington, Va.: Psychological Research Associates.

Geer, C.W. 1976. Analyst's guide for the analysis section of MIL-H-46855 (Report D180 19476-1). Seattle: Boeing Aerospace Co.

————. 1981. Human engineering procedures guide (Report AFAMRL-TR-81-35). Wright-Patterson AFB, Ohio: Aerospace Medical Research Labs. (AD A108 643)

General Accounting Office. 1977. Human resources research and development efforts can be better managed (Report FPC7 77-43). Washington, D.C.:General Accounting Office.

————. 1981. Effectiveness of U.S. forces can be increased through improved system design (Report PSAD-81-17). Washington, D.C.:General Accounting Office.

Gilbreth, F.B. 1911. *Motion Study*. New York: Van Nostrand.

Goclowski, J.C., W.D. Askren, G.F. King, and P.G. Ronco. 1978. Integration and application of human resources technologies in weapon system design: Processes for the coordinated application of five human resource technologies (Report AFHRL-TR-78-6 [II]). Wright-Patterson AFB, Ohio: Air Force Human Resources Lab.

Goodstein, L.P, H.B. Andersen, and S.E. Olsen (Eds.). 1988. *Tasks, Errors, and Mental Models: A Festschrift to Celebrate the 60th Birthday of Professor Jens Rasmussen.* London: Taylor & Francis.

Greenwald, A.G., A.R. Pratkanis, M.R. Leippe, and M.H. Baumgardner. 1986. Under what conditions does theory obstruct research programming?*Psychological Review* 93: 216–229.

Grings, W.W. 1953. Shipboard observation of electronics personnel: A description of the research (Technical Report No. 1). Los Angeles: University of Southern California Department of Psychology.

Harris, D.H., and F.B. Chaney. 1969. *Human Factors in Quality Assurance.* New York: Wiley.

Havron, M.D. 1961. Evaluation of combat systems: Establishment of criteria and their use in selection of key system factors (Report HSR-RR-61/3-SM). Arlington, Va.: Human Sciences Research. (AD 257 608)

Hendrick, H.W. 1987. Macroergonomics: A concept whose time has come. *Human Factors Society Bulletin* 30:1–3.

Henneman, R.L., and W.B. Rouse. 1986. On measuring the complexity of monitoring and controlling large-scale systems. *IEEE Transactions in Systems, Man, and Cybernetics,* SMC-16:193–207

Hennessy, R.T., and M.E. McCauley. 1986. Proposal and justification to establish a Department of Defense Crew Systems Ergonomics Information Analysis Center (CSERIAC) (Report AAMRL-TR-86-002). Wright-Patterson AFB, Ohio: Aerospace Medical Research Laboratory.

Hill, S.G., B.D. Plamondon, W.W. Wierwille, R.J. Lysaght, A.O. Dick, and A.C. Bittner. 1987. Analytic techniques for the assessment of operator workload. *Proceedings, Human Factors Society Annual Meeting* (pp. 368–372).

Hillner, K. 1985. *Psychological Reality.* Amsterdam: North-Holland.

Hollnagel, E. 1983. What we do not know about man-machine systems. *International J. Man-Machine Studies* 18:135–143.

Hollnagel, E., and D.D. Woods. 1983. Cognitive systems engineering: New wine in new bottles. *International J. Man-Machine Studies* 18:583–600.

Holshouser, E.G. 1977. Guide to human factors engineering general purpose test planning (GPTP) (Airtask A3400000054C/7W0542-001) (Technical Publication TP-77-14). Point Mugu, Calif.: Pacific Missile Test Center.

Howard, G.S. 1985. The role of values in the science of psychology. *American Psychologist* 40:255–265.

Howell, W.C., H.A. Colle, B.H. Kantowitz, and E.L. Wiener. 1987. Guidelines for education and training in engineering psychology. *American Psychologist* 42:602–604.

Johannsen, G. 1979. Workload and workload measurement. In N. Moray (Ed.), *Mental Workload: Its Theory and Measurement* (pp. 3–11). New York: Plenum Press.

Johnson, E.M., and J.D. Baker. 1974. Field testing: The delicate compromise. *Human Factors* 16:203–214.

Keenan, J.J., T.C. Parker, and H.P. Lenzycki. 1965. Concepts and practices in the assessment of human performance in Air Force systems (Report AMRL-TR-65-168). Wright-Patterson AFB, Ohio: Aerospace Medical Research Labs.

Kidd, J.S. 1959. Summary of research methods, operator characteristics, and system design specifications based on the study of a simulated radar air traffic control system (Technical Report 59-236). Wright-Patterson AFB, Ohio: Wright Air Development Center.

Kiesler, S.B. 1977. Research funding for psychology. *American Psychologist* 32:22–32.

Kimble, G.A. 1984. Psychology's two cultures. *American Psychologist* 40:255–265.

King, G.F., and W.B. Askren. 1980. Human resources, logistics, and cost factors in weapon system development: Methodology and data requirements (Report AFHRL-TR-80-29). Wright-Patterson AFB, Ohio: Air Force Human Resources Lab.

Klein, G.A., and C.P. Brezovic. 1987. Human performance data needed for training device decisions (Report AAMRL-TR-87-01). Yellow Springs, Ohio: Klein Associates.

Knauper, A., and W.B. Rouse. 1985. A rule-based model of human problem-solving behavior in dynamic environments. *IEEE Transactions in Systems, Man, and Cybernetics*, SMC-15:708–719.

Knowles, W.B., W.T. Burger, M.B. Mitchell, D.T. Hanifan, and T.W. Wulfeck. 1969. Models, measures, and judgments in system design. *Human Factors* 11:577–590.

Koffka, K. 1935. *Principles of Gestalt Psychology*. New York: Harcourt Brace.

Krasner, L., and A.C. Houts. 1984. A study of the "value" systems of behavioral scientists. *American Psychologist* 39:840–849.

Kreilkamp, K. 1971. Hindsight and the real world of science policy. *Science Studies* 1:43–66.

Kuhn, T.S. 1970. *The Structure of Scientific Revolutions*. Chicago: University of Chicago Press.

Lane, N.E. 1986. Issues in performance measurement for military aviation with applications to air combat maneuvering (Report NTSC TR-86-008). Orlando, Fla.: Naval Training Systems Center.

———. 1987. Evaluating the cost-effectiveness of human factors engineering (Draft paper P-XXXX). Washington, D.C.: Institute for Defense Analyses.

Levy, G.W. (Ed.). 1968. Symposium on applied models of man-machine systems performance. Columbus, Ohio: North American Aviation Co. (AD 697 939)

Lintz, L.M., W.B. Askren, and W.J. Lott. 1971. System design trade studies: The engineering process and use of human resources data (Report AFHRL-TR-71-24). Wright-Patterson AFB, Ohio: Air Force Human Resources Lab. (AD 732 201)

Locke, E.A. 1986. Generalizing from laboratory to field: Ecological validity or abstraction of essential elements? In E.A. Locke (Ed.), *Generalizing from Laboratory to Field Settings* (pp.1–9). Lexington, Mass.: Lexington Books.

Mackie, R.R., and P.R. Christensen. 1967. Translation and application of psychological research (Report 716-1). Goleta, Calif.: Human Factors Research.

Malone, T.B. 1986. The centered high-mounted brake light: A human factors success story. *Human Factors Society Bulletin* 29:1–3.

Markel, G.A. 1965. Toward a general methodology for systems evaluation. State College, Pa.: HRB Singer. (AD 519 373)

Mattessich, R. 1982. The systems approach: Its variety of aspects. *J. American Society for Information Science* 33:383–394.

McGrath, J.E., and D. Brinberg. 1984. Alternative paths for research: Another view of the basic vs. applied distinction. In S. Oskamp (Ed.), *Applied Social Psychology Annual*. Beverly Hills, Calif.: Sage Publications.

McGrath, J.E., P.G. Nordlie, and W.S. Vaughan. 1959. A systematic framework for comparison of system research methods (Report HRS-TN-59/7-SM). Arlington, Va.: Human Sciences Research. (AD 229 923)

McKendry, J.M., and P.C. Harrison. 1964. Assessing human factors requirements in the test and evaluation stage of system development (Report ND 64–68, vols. 1 & 2) State College, Pa.: HRB Singer. (AD 603 303, 603 304)

Meister, D. 1971. *Human Factors Theory and Practice*. New York: Wiley.

————. 1976. *Behavioral Foundations of System Development*. New York: Wiley.

————. 1977. Implications of the system concept for human factors research methodology. *Proceedings, Human Factors Society Annual Meeting* (pp. 453–456).

————. 1978a. A theoretical structure for personnel subsystem measurement. *Proceedings, Human Factors Society Annual Meeting* (pp. 458–461).

————. 1978b. A systematic approach to human factors measurement. San Diego: Navy Personnel Research and Development Center. (AD A132 423)

————. 1979. The influence of government on human factors research and development. *Proceedings, Human Factors Society Annual Meeting* (pp. 5–13).

————. 1980. The concept of macro-basic research in human factors. *Proceedings, Human Factors Society Annual Meeting* (pp. 458–461).

————. 1981. *Behavioral Research and Government Policy: Civilian and Military R&D*. Elmwood, N.J.: Pergamon Press.

————. 1982. The role of human factors in system development. *Applied Ergonomics* 13(2):119–124.

————. 1984. Human engineering data base for design and selection of cathode ray tube and other display systems (Report NPRDC TR-84–51). San Diego: Navy Personnel Research and Development Center.

————. 1985a. The two worlds of human factors. In R.E. Eberts and C.G. Eberts (Eds.), *Trends in Ergonomics/Human Factors, II* (pp. 3–13). Amsterdam: North Holland.

————. 1985b. *Behavioral Analysis and Measurement Methods*. New York: Wiley.

————. 1986. *Human Factors Testing and Evaluation*. Amsterdam: Elsevier.

————. 1987. Behavioral test and evaluation of expert systems. In G. Salvendy (Ed.), *Cognitive Engineering in the Design of Human-Computer Interaction and Expert Systems* (pp. 539–549). Amsterdam: Elsevier.

————. 1988. Operational reality and human factors measurement. *Proceedings, Human Factors Society Annual Meeting* (pp. 1169–1173).

Meister, D., and D.E. Farr. 1966. The methodology of control panel design (Report AMRL TR 66–28). Wright-Patterson AFB, Ohio: Aerospace Medical Research Labs.

————. 1967. The utilization of human factors information by designers. *Human Factors* 9:71–87.

Meister, D., and R.G. Mills. 1971. Development of a human performance reliability data system. *Annals of Reliability and Maintainability—1971*, pp. 425–439.

Meister, D., and G.F. Rabideau. 1965. *Human Factors Evaluation in System Development*. New York: Wiley.

Meister, D., and D.J. Sullivan. 1967. A further study of the use of human factors information by designers. Canoga Park, Calif.: Bunker-Ramo Corp.

Meister, D., D.J. Sullivan, and W.B. Askren. 1968. The impact of manpower requirements and personnel resources data on system design (Report AFHRL-TR 68-44). Wright-Patterson AFB, Ohio: Air Force Human Resources Lab. (AD 678 864)

Meister, D., D.J. Sullivan, D.L. Finley, and W.B. Askren. 1969a. The effect of amount and timing of human resources data on subsystem design (Report AFHRL TR-69-22). Wright-Patterson AFB, Ohio: Air Force Human Resources Lab. (AD 699 577)

———. 1969b. The design engineer's concept of the relationship between system design characteristics and technician skill level (Report AFHRL TR-69-23). Wright-Patterson AFB, Ohio: Air Force Human Resources Lab. (AD 699 578)

Melkus, L.A., and R.J. Jorres. 1988. Guidelines for the use of a prototype in user interface design. *Proceedings, Human Factors Society Annual Meeting* (pp. 370–374).

Miller, R.B. 1953. A method for man-machine task analysis (Report 53-137). Wright-Patterson AFB, Ohio: Wright Air Development Center.

Mirabella, A., and G.R. Wheaton. 1974. Effect of task index variations in transfer of training criteria (Report NAVTRAEQUIPCEN 72-C-0126-1). Orlando, Fla.: Naval Training Equipment Center. (AD 773 947/7GA)

Montmollin, J.D., and L. Bainbridge. 1985. Ergonomics or human factors? *Human Factors Society Bulletin* 28:1–3.

Moray, N. (Ed.). 1979. *Mental Workload: Its Theory and Measurement*. New York: Plenum Press.

Munger, S.J., R.W. Smith, and D. Payne. 1962. An index of electronic equipment operability: Data Store (Report AIR-C43-1/62-RP[1]). Pittsburgh: American Institute for Research.

Nelson, A., E.J. Schmitz, and D. Promisel. 1984. Impact of personnel quality on STINGER weapon system performance (Report TR-640). Alexandria, Va.: Army Research Institute.

Pahl, G., and W. Beitz. 1984. *Engineering Design*. New York: Springer-Verlag.

Parks, D.L. 1979. Current workload methods and emerging challenges. In N. Moray (Ed.), *Mental Workload: Its Theory and Measurement* (pp.387–416). New York: Plenum Press.

Parks, D.L., and W.E. Springer. 1975. Human factors engineering analytic process definition and criterion development for CAFES (Report D180-18750-1). Seattle: Boeing Aerospace Co. (AD A040 478)

Parsons, H.M. 1972. *Man-Machine System Experiments*. Baltimore: Johns Hopkins University Press.

Payne, D., and J.W. Altman. 1962. An index of electronic equipment operability: Report of development (Report AIR-C-43-1/62 FR). Pittsburgh: American Institute for Research.

Penn, D. 1988. User interface design tools. *Proceedings, Human Factors Society Annual Meeting* (pp. 25–29).

Perrow, C. 1983. The organizational context of human factors engineering. *Administrative Science Quarterly* 28:521–541.

Pew, R.W., C.E. Feeher, S. Baron, and D.C. Miller. 1977. Critical review and analysis of performance models applicable to man-machine systems evaluation (Report AFOSR-TR-77-0520). Cambridge, Mass.: Bolt, Beranek, Newman. (AD A038 597)

Potempa, K.W., L.M. Lintz, and R.S. Luckew. 1975. Impact of avionic design characteristics on technical training requirements and job performance. *Human Factors* 17:13–24.

Potter, N.E., K.D. Korkan, and D.L. Dieterly. 1975. A procedure for quantification of technological changes in human resources (Report AFHRL-TR-75-33). Wright-Patterson AFB, Ohio: Air Force Human Resources Lab. (AD A014 335)

Price, H.E. 1985. The allocation of functions in systems. *Human Factors* 27:33–45.

Price, H.E., M. Fiorello, J.C. Lowry, M.G. Smith, and J.S. Kidd. 1980a. The contributions of human factors in military systems development: Methodological considerations (Report TR-476). Alexandria, Va.: Army Research Institute.

———. 1980b. Department of Defense and service requirements for human factors R&D in the military system acquisition process (Report ARI RN-80-23). Alexandria, Va.: Army Research Institute.

Pritsker, A.A.B., D.B. Wortman, C.S. Seum, G.P. Chubb, and D.J. Seifert. 1974. SAINT, Vol. 1: Systems Analysis of Integrated Networks of Tasks (AMRL-TR-73-26). Wright-Patterson AFB, Ohio: Aerospace Medical Research Labs.

Promisel, D.M., C.R. Hartel, J.D. Kaplan, A. Marcus, and J.A. Whittenburg. 1985. Reverse engineering: Human factors, manpower, personnel, and training in the weapon system acquisition process (Report TR-659). Alexandria, Va.: Army Research Insitute.

Rau, J.G. 1974. *Measures of Effectiveness Handbook*. Irvine, Calif.: Ultrasystems. (AD A021 461)

Rasmussen, J., K. Duncan, and J. Leplat. 1987. *New Technology and Human Error* Chichester, Eng.: Wiley.

Reid, G. 1985. Current status of the development of the subjective workload assessment technique. *Proceedings, Human Factors Society Annual Meeting* (pp. 220–223).

Rogers, J.G., and R. Armstrong. 1977. Use of human engineering standards in design. *Human Factors* 19:15–23.

Rogers, J.G., and C.D. Pegden. 1977. Formatting and organization of a human engineering standard. *Human Factors* 19:55–61.

Rolfe, J.M., and S.J.E. Lindsay. 1973. Flight deck environment and pilot workload: Biological measures of workload. *Applied Ergonomics* 4:199–206.

Rouse, W.B. 1978. A model of human decision making in a fault diagnosis task. *IEEE Transactions in Systems, Man, and Cybernetics*, SMC-8:357–361.

———. 1985. On the value of information in system design: A framework for understanding and aiding designers. *Information Processing and Management* 22:217–228.

———. 1986. Decision support systems. Presentation at Seventeenth Meeting of the Department of Defense Human Factors Engineering Technical Advisory Group, Monterey, Calif.

———. 1987. Much ado about data. *Human Factors Society Bulletin* 30:1–3.

Rouse, W.B., and K.R. Boff. 1987. Designer tools and environments: state of knowledge, unresolved issues, and potential directions. In W.B. Rouse and K.R. Boff (Eds.), *System Design Behavioral Perspectives on Designers, Tools, and Organizations* (pp. 43–63). Amsterdam: North Holland.

Rouse, W.B., and S. Rouse. 1979. Measures of complexity of a fault diagnosis task. *IEEE Transactions in Systems, Man, and Cybernetics*, SMC-9:720–727.

Salvendy, G. (Ed.). 1987. *Handbook of Human Factors*. New York: Wiley-Interscience.

Sanders, M. 1985. Human factors graduate education: An update. *Human Factors Society Bulletin* 26:1–3.

Sawyer, C.F., M. Fiorello, J.S. Kidd, and H.E. Price. 1981. Measuring and enhancing the contributions of human factors in military system development: Case studies of the application of impact assessment methodologies (Technical Report 519). Alexandria, Va.: Army Research Insitute.

Scarr, S. 1985. Constructing psychology: Making facts and fables for our time. *American Psychologist* 40:499–512.

Schneiderman, B. 1987. *Designing the User Interface: Strategies for Effective Human Computer Interaction*. Reading, Mass.: Addison-Wesley.

Schwartz, M.A. 1981. Austere manning in the guided missile frigate (FFG-7 class): Lessons learned (Report NPRDC TR 81-10). San Diego: Navy Personnel Research and Development Center.

Schwartz, M.A., and R.A. Sniffen. 1980. Final report on the shipboard facilities maintenance demonstration program, Vol. 1: Test and evaluation results, conclusions, and recommendations (Report DTNSRDC-80/035). Annapolis, Md.: David W. Taylor Naval Ship Research and Development Center. (AD B050 969L)

Seaver, D.A., and W.G. Stillwell. 1983. Procedures for using expert judgment to estimate human error probabilities in nuclear power plant operations (Report NUREG/CR-2743, SAND82-7054, AN, RX). Falls Church, Va.: Decision Science Consortium.

Selye, H. 1973. Stress in aerospace medicine. *Aerospace Medicine* 44:190–193.

Shackel, B. 1985. Ergonomics information technology in Europe: A review. *Behavior and Information Technology* 4:263–287.

Shaffer, M.T., J.B. Shafer, and G.B. Kutche. 1986. Empirical workload and communications analysis of Scout helicopter exercises. *Proceedings, Human Factors Society Annual Meeting* (pp. 628–632).

Siegel, A.I., and M.A. Fischl. 1971. Dimensions of visual information displays. *J. Applied Psychology* 55:470–476.

Siegel, A.I., W. Miehle, and P.J. Federman. 1964. The DEI technique for evaluating systems from the information transfer point of view. *Human Factors* 6:279–286.

Siegel, A.I., and J.J. Wolf. 1969. *Man-Machine Simulation Models: Psychosocial and Performance Interaction*. New York: Wiley.

Siegel, A.I., W.R. Leahy, and J.J. Wolf. 1978. Human performance tradeoff curves for use in the design of Navy systems. Wayne, Pa.: Applied Psychological Services. (AD A053 332)

Simon, C.W. 1977. New research paradigm for applied experimental psychology: A systems approach (Technical Report CWS-04-77). Westlake Village, Calif.: Canyon Research Corp.

Singleton, W.T., J.G. Fox, and D. Whitfield (Eds.). 1971. *Measurement of Man at*

Work, An Appraisal of Physiological and Psychological Criteria in Man-Machine Systems. London: Taylor and Francis.

Smith, K.U. 1987. Origins of human factors science. *Human Factors Society Bulletin* 30:1–3.

Smith, S.L., and J.M. Mosier. 1986. Guidelines for designing user interface software (Report ESD-TR-86-278). Hanscom AFB, Mass.: Electronic Systems Division, Air Force Systems Command.

Smode, A.F., A. Gruber, and J.G. Ely. 1962. The measurement of advanced flight vehicle proficiency in synthetic ground environments (Report MRL-TDR-62-2). Wright-Patterson AFB, Ohio: Behavioral Sciences Lab. (AD 273 449)

Sniffen, R.A., J.J. Puckett, and P.M. Edmondo. 1979. The integrated bridge system (IBS) project: Final report (Report PAS 79–3). Annapolis, Md.: David W. Taylor Naval Ship Research and Development Center.

Snyder, M.T., J.P. Kincaid, and K.W. Potempa (Eds.). 1969. Proceedings of the human factors testing conference, October 1–2, 1968 (Report AFHRL-TR 69-6). Wright-Patterson AFB, Ohio: Air Force Human Resources Lab. (AD A866 485)

Stinson, W.J. 1979. Evaluation of LVA full-scale hydrodynamic vehicle motion effects on personnel performance (Report NRPDC TR-79-16). San Diego, Calif.: Navy Personnel Research and Development Center.

Streufert, S., and R.W. Swezey. 1986. *Complexity, Managers, and Organizations*. Orlando, Fla.: Academic Press.

Strieb, M.K., and R.J. Wherry, Jr. 1979. An introduction to the Human Operator Simulator (Technical Report 1400.02D). Willow Grove, Pa.: Analytics.

Swain, A.D. 1967. Some limitations in using the simple multiplicative model in behavior quantification. In W.B. Askren (Ed.), Symposium on reliability of human performance in work (Report AMRL-TR-67-88) (pp. 17–31). Wright-Patterson AFB, Ohio: Aerospace Medical Research Labs.

Swain, A.D., and H.E. Guttmann. 1983. Handbook of human reliability analysis with emphasis on nuclear power plant applications (Report NUREG/CR-1278, SAND80-0200, RX, AN). Washington, D.C.: Nuclear Regulatory Commission.

Taylor, F.W. 1911. *The Principles of Scientific Management*. New York: Harper.

Thackray, R.T., J.P. Bailey, and R.M. Touchstone. 1979. The effect of increased monitoring load on vigilance performance using a simulated radar display. *Ergonomics* 22:529–539.

Topmiller, D.A., J.S. Eckel, and E.D. Kozinsky. 1982. Human reliability databank for nuclear power plant operation, Vol. 1: Review of existing human error reliability databanks (Report NUREG/CR-2744/1 of 2, SAND82 7057/1 of 2). Dayton, Ohio: General Physics Corp. (NUREG 2744-VI)

Van Cott, H.P., and R.G. Kinkade (Eds.). 1972. *Human Engineering Guide to Equipment Design* (rev. ed.). Washington, D.C.: U.S. Government Printing Office.

Van Gigch, J.P. 1974. *Applied General System Theory*. New York: Harper and Row.

Vreuls, D., and R.W. Obermayer. 1985. Human-system performance measurement in training simulators. *Human Factors* 27:241–250.

Vreuls, D., R.W. Obermayer, I. Goldstein, and J.W. Lauber. 1973. Measurement of trainee performance in a captive rotary wing device (Report NAVTRAEQUIPCEN 71-C-0194-1). Orlando, Fla.: Naval Training Equipment Center.

Whalen, G.V. and W.B. Askren. 1974. Impact of design trade studies on system human resources (Report AFHRL TR-74-89). Wright-Patterson AFB, Ohio: Air Force Human Resources Lab. (AD A009 639)

Wherry, Jr., R.J. 1986. Theoretical development for identifying underlying internal processes, Vol. 3: Random sampling of domain variances, a new experimental methodology (NAMRL Special Report 86-3, NADC Report 86105-60 [vol. 3]). Pensacola, Fla.: Naval Aerospace Medical Research Laboratory; Warminster, Pa.: Naval Development Center.

White, T.H. 1973. *Making of the President: Nineteen Seventy-two.* New York: Atheneum.

Whitfield, D., R.G. Ball, and J.M. Bird. 1983. Some comparisons of on-display and off-display touch input devices for interaction with computer-generated displays. *Ergonomics* 26:1033–1053.

Wickens, C.D. 1981. Processing resources in attention, dual task performance, and workload assessment (Technical Report EPL-81-3/ONR-81-3). Champaign: University of Illinois. (AD A102 719)

Wiener, J.S. 1982. The measurement of human workload. *Ergonomics* 25:953–965.

Williges, B.H., and R.C. Williges. 1984. Dialogue design considerations for interactive computer systems, chapter 5. In F.A. Muckler (Ed.), *Human Factors Review, 1984* (pp.167–208). Santa Monica, Calif.: Human Factors Society.

Wilson, D.A. 1967. Application of automatic data processing techniques to task analysis diagramming (Report SRM 68–8). San Diego: Navy Personnel Research Activity.

Woodson, W.E. 1981. *Human Factors Design Handbook.* New York: McGraw Hill.

Woodson, W.E., and D. W. Conover. 1964. *Human Engineering Guide for Equipment Designers.* Berkeley and Los Angeles: University of California Press.

Wortman, D.G., S.D. Duket, D.J. Seifert, R.L. Hann, and G.P. Chubb. 1977. Simulation using SAINT: A user-oriented instruction manual (Report AMRL-TR-77-61). Wright-Patterson AFB, Ohio: Aerospace Medical Research Labs.

Yarnold, K., and R.C. Channell. 1952. Systems research with special reference to human engineering (Report SPECDEVCEN 641-2-13). Port Washington, N.Y.: Navy Special Devices Center.

Yeh, Y-Y., and C.D. Wickens. 1988. Dissociation of performance and subjective measures of workload. *Human Factors* 30:111–120.

Zwahlen, G.T., and N. Kothari. 1986. Effects of positive and negative image polarity VDT screens. *Proceedings, Human Factors Society Annual Meeting* (pp. 170–174).

Index

Conceptual Aspects of Human Factors

Designed by Ann Walston

Composed by The Composing Room of Michigan, Inc.
in Times Roman

Printed by Thomson-Shore, Inc.
on 50-lb. Glatfelter Offset
and bound in Holliston Roxite